Projective Identification in the Clinical Setting

The concept of projective identification, first introduced by Melanie Klein in 1946, has been widely studied by psychoanalysts of different persuasions. However, these explorations have neglected to show what Kleinians actually do with the projective identification phenomenon in their daily casework.

Projective Identification in the Clinical Setting presents a detailed study of Kleinian literature, setting a background of understanding for the day-to-day analytic atmosphere in which projective identification takes place. Extensive clinical material illustrates issues clearly identified for clinical practice, including:

- the ways projective identification occurs within various psychological constellations;
- the role of the analyst in countertransference experiences;
- work with difficult patients who experience life within a paranoid or psychotic framework;
- the path of projective identification and pathological greed.

This comprehensive account of Kleinian literature on projective identification and wealth of clinical material provide a powerful and clear account of clinical practice around projective identification that all practitioners, psychoanalytic psychotherapists and trainees will benefit from reading.

Robert Waska has worked in the field of psychology for the last twenty-five years. Certified as a psychoanalyst and psychoanalytic psychotherapist from the Institute of Psychoanalytic Studies, Dr Waska maintains a full-time private practice in San Francisco and Marin County.

Projective Identification in the Clinical Setting

The Kleinian Interpretation

Robert Waska

Brunner-Routledge
Taylor & Francis Group
HOVE AND NEW YORK

First published 2004 by Brunner-Routledge
27 Church Road, Hove, East Sussex BN3 2FA

Simultaneously published in the USA and Canada
by Brunner-Routledge
29 West 35th Street, New York NY 10001

Brunner-Routledge is an imprint of the Taylor & Francis Group

Copyright © 2004 Robert Waska

Typeset in Times by Mayhew Typesetting, Rhayader, Powys
Printed and bound in Great Britain by TJ International, Padstow, Cornwall
Cover illustration by Kay Simon
Cover design by Hybert Design

This publication has been produced with paper manufactured to strict
environmental standards and with pulp derived from sustainable forests.

British Library Cataloguing in Publication Data
A catalogue record for this book is available from the British Library

Library of Congress Cataloging-in-Publication Data
Waska, Robert T.
    Projective identification in the clinical setting : the Kleinian
interpretation / Robert Waska.
        p. cm.
Includes bibliographical references and index.
    ISBN 1-58391-953-8 (hbk : alk. paper)
1. Projective identification. 2. Klein, Melanie. I. Title.

    RC455.4.P76W375 2004
    616.89'17—dc21

                                                    2003012024

ISBN 1-58391-953-8 (hbk)

Contents

Acknowledgments

I gratefully wish to acknowledge the generosity of the *Journal of Psychotherapy Practice and Research*, the *Journal of the American Academy of Psychoanalysis*, the *Journal of Contemporary Psychotherapy*, and the *Bulletin of the Menninger Clinic* for permission to reprint material found in Chapters 4, 5, 6, 7, 9, and 11.

Also, I want to express my thanks to my wonderful wife, Elizabeth, for providing emotional guidance and support as I worked on this project.

Finally, I am grateful to all my patients. In working with them I am constantly enriched and pushed to learn more about the human experience.

Introduction

There have been hundreds of articles and many books written by Kleinian analysts on the theoretical and technical aspects of projective identification (PI). These writings usually explore the concept of PI and cover the author's theoretical views of this mental mechanism. In other words, the question of "what is PI" has been deliberated many times over in the literature. I will not duplicate these efforts.

Instead, I am interested in what happens in the clinical situation, between patient and Kleinian analyst, regarding PI and the Kleinian interpretive stance. In other words, how exactly do Kleinians interpret projective identification? Rather than looking at what Kleinians propose would be theoretically helpful to interpret, I am focusing on what they actually say in the session to the patient to interpret the projective identification process. To better do this, I will summarize and comment on the overall direction Kleinians take in interpreting PI. After this review of the literature, I will take up my own approach, as a Kleinian analyst, to exploring and interpreting PI. I will do this by sharing extensive case studies in which PI played a central role.

Some Kleinian authors express specific ideas about the intrapsychic meaning or motivation of PI, but they do not necessarily take that up in their clinical interventions. There are many articles in which the author makes general, 'all-purpose' recommendations about what to interpret or in which the author states something to the effect of "I interpreted some of her phantasies about me, the internal objects she was trying to deal with, and the ways she was projecting them into me." Unfortunately, quite a few articles are presented in this vague manner, which makes it hard to see what is actually done in the clinical setting. Instead, I am looking at verbatim accounts of exactly what analysts said to the patient to interpret current PI dynamics occurring within the analytic situation.

Later, I will demonstrate with my own clinical material exactly what I say to patients who rely on this important psychological method of coping and relating.

In Chapters 1 and 2 I start out by presenting a detailed study of the literature, noting exactly what Kleinian analysts say and do in the PI moment. While these literature reviews are lengthy and categorical, they serve to set a background of understanding for the day-to-day analytic atmosphere in which PI takes place. One realizes from this detailed study that actual clinical evidence of Kleinian work with PI analysis is sparse.

Chapter 1 looks at the more usual methods Kleinians utilize when encountering the PI process. These approaches are organized into the main categories that emerge in the literature.

Chapter 2 examines the same data, but looks at the more atypical ways some Kleinians choose. There are far fewer examples, but they provide a glance at more novel or unusual ways of working with patients who rely on PI dynamics.

After Chapters 1 and 2 set up a history of what has been reported in the field, Chapter 3 provides a synthesis of these findings. Links are provided between the various approaches so one can better see how these methods really work in the real world. In doing so, one notices quite an overlap in these different technical methods.

Chapter 4 begins the more clinical side of the book. Here, I explain the ways PI occurs within various psychological constellations. Depending on the intrapsychic make-up of the patient, he or she will experience and use PI in very different ways.

Building on Chapter 4, Chapter 5 takes up the varying internal perspectives and shows several potential outcomes in the PI process. Depending on the patient's inner view of the self and the object, their interpersonal and internal participation in PI will cast the transference in a certain light. The Kleinian method is demonstrated in the case material.

In Chapter 6, the role of the analyst is taken into account. The process of PI brings out particular countertransference experiences. As the recipient of the patient's projections of love, hate, and other aspects of personality and phantasy, the analyst must find ways to process the material and interpret it productively. Part of this chapter looks at how the analyst can fall into acting out these PI cycles before and during the struggle to understand them therapeutically.

Chapter 7 examines work with difficult patients who experience life within a paranoid or psychotic framework. These types of patients often necessitate a modified or flexible method of analytic work. The topic of self-disclosure is discussed in light of these often atypical transference–countertransference situations. Case material shows how I, as a Kleinian, work at these clinical crossroads.

Symbolism, loss and the PI process are explored in Chapter 8. Loss and symbolism are seen very differently through the intrapsychic lens of the paranoid-schizoid position. One extensive case report is used to show the moment-to-moment effect PI has on symbolism and loss, as well as the nature of transference within states of primitive loss. Matters of analytic technique are illustrated using a Kleinian framework.

Chapter 9 comes back to the matter of countertransference as it is colored by PI. Again, case material provides a window into the analyst's struggle within PI-induced phantasies and feelings. Integration, detoxification, and translation of raw PI-related feelings become problematic when pathological PI is recurrent in the analytic relationship.

Greed is a noteworthy element in the treatment of many hard-to-reach patients. In particular, PI and greed can combine to form destructive cycles that immobilize the patient's inner world and their analytic experience. Chapter 10 uses clinical material to explore the path of PI and pathological greed as it distorts the transference. Again, the importance of analytic technique is made clear and my Kleinian style is compared to the usual and unusual Kleinian responses to PI.

Finally, Chapter 11 provides more moment-to-moment case reporting to further build the case for how to analyze PI within a Kleinian strategy. Like previous chapters, the different aspects and manifestations of PI are examined, along with approaches that fit best with the patient's current internal experience. The question of how a Kleinian method might look, in the immediate clinical PI situation, is again addressed in a very clear and illustrative manner.

Melanie Klein's view of projective identification

Melanie Klein presents the term "projective identification" (PI) for the first time in her 1946 paper, "Notes on Some Schizoid Mechanisms." It is the first introduction of the term, and a summing up of her thinking about it at the time. She explains:

> In hallucinatory gratification, two interrelated processes take place: the omnipotent conjuring up of the ideal object and situation, and the equally omnipotent annihilation of the bad persecutory object and the painful situation. These processes are based on splitting both the object and the ego . . . In so far as the mother comes to contain the bad parts of the self, she is not felt to be a separate individual but is felt to be the bad self.
> Much of the hatred against parts of the self is now directed toward the mother. This leads to a particular form of aggressive object-relation. I suggest of these processes the term 'projective identification'. When projection is mainly derived from the infant's impulse to harm or to control the mother, he feels her to be a persecutor . . .
> It is, however, not only the bad parts of the self which are expelled and projected, but also good parts of the self. Excrements then have the significance of gifts; and parts of the ego which, together with excrements, are expelled and projected into the other person, represent the good, i.e. loving parts of the self. The identification based on this type of projection again vitally influences object-relations. The projection of good feelings and good parts of the self into the mother is essential for the infant's ability to develop good object-relations and to integrate his ego. However, if this projective process is carried out excessively, good parts of the personality are felt to be lost, and in this way the mother becomes the ego-ideal; this process too results in weakening and impoverishing the ego. Very soon such processes extend to other people, and the result may be an over-strong dependence on these external representatives of one's own good parts . . .
> The processes of splitting off parts of the self and projecting them into objects are thus of vital importance for normal development as well as for abnormal object-relations.
> (Klein 1946: 7–9)

Melanie Klein was explaining the details of the unconscious, dynamic, self–object phantasy of splitting off intolerable aspects of the self and depositing them into another object. Hatred, anxiety, or love are externalized for protective, defensive, or aggressive reasons and then managed with certain defenses before reinternalizing them. PI is part of normal, healthy psychological development as well as part of pathological, destructive maneuvers. Therefore, PI can produce chronic cycles of internal anxiety and chaos or a sense of soothing, safety, and support.

Repeatedly situating aspects of the self into the object results in ego depletion and a weakened sense of identity. For this reason, one goal of the analytic process is to restore the integrity of the ego.

Klein (1957) thought that envious forms of PI led to the phantasy of a forced entry into another person in order to destroy their best qualities.

Also, Klein (1952a) wrote:

> it seems that the processes underlying projective identification operate already in the earliest relation to the breast . . . Accordingly, projective identification would start simultaneously with the greedy oral-sadistic introjection of the breast. This hypothesis is in keeping with the view often expressed by the writer that introjection and projection interact from the beginning of life.
>
> (Klein 1952a: 69)

This link between greedy introjection and PI becomes very important in working with certain patients. Later, in Chapter 10, I will address this matter in greater detail. When greed and PI stand together as the core transference profile, the analyst must consistently interpret this greed and its effect upon the analytic relationship.

Klein (1955) explored the persecutory anxieties and splitting mechanisms that lead to many PI phantasies. In 1957, she elaborated on these thoughts:

> When things go wrong, excessive projective identification, by which split-off parts of the self are projected into the object, leads to a strong confusion between the self and the object, which also comes to stand for the self. Bound up with this is

a weakening of the ego and a grave disturbance in object relations.

(Klein 1957: 192)

This excessive PI process shatters the internal self- and object-representations into many bits and pieces, leading to borderline and psychotic distortions. One psychological fatality of this dynamic is the ability to symbolize. In Chapter 8 I will go into detail about this, as it presents a real technical problem for the analyst. Interpretations need to be directed at the destructive PI process and the imagined dangers of allowing symbolism to breathe life into the self–object bond.

The Kleinian view of interpretation

Hanna Segal (1975) states:

> [Melanie Klein's] interpretive technique (with children) was based, as with the adult, predominantly on the transference, and by transference I do not mean here-and-now interpretations, but suitable links being made between the here-and-now, the child's inner world of phantasies, and its links with external reality, present and past. Klein used no educational methods, gave no instructions, nor reassurances.
>
> (Segal 1975: 2)

From her work with children, Klein had discovered that anxiety was important to focus on from the very beginning of a treatment. Therefore, her interpretations were aimed at the patient's anxiety, usually about the analytic relationship. Klein found that these types of interpretations reduced anxiety. She also felt that the negative transference had to be addressed from the start for an analysis to be effective. Once this occurred, there was more room for the patient's love toward the analyst to become known (Hinshelwood 1991).

Melanie Klein was strongly influenced by Freud and tried to keep her theories close to Freud's core methodology (Klein 1926; Schafer 1994; Bion *et al.* 1961). Indeed, Kleinians are, as was Klein herself, extending Freudian thought rather than offering a paradigm shift (Stein 1990; Segal 1974).

Clearly, Klein followed Freud's basic ideas in formulating inter-pretations. However, she made particular emphases and certain new extensions. She felt interpretations should focus on the trans-ference nearly exclusively. This was to be done in the here-and-now as well as in genetic reconstruction. Phantasy has a primary influ-ence upon the transference. Therefore, interpretation of phantasy material was vital. To Klein, interpretations were to aim at the principal anxiety the patient was experiencing. So, in place of the focus on analysis of defense, characteristic of Freud and his followers, Klein emphasized analysis of both defense and the core, unconscious anxieties. While this at times meant deeper and faster interpretations, usually it meant complete and complex interpreta-tions. The patient's total internal experience was sought out and then explained to him. The patient's affect, phantasies, and total relationship to the analyst were considered pathways to making the most useful interpretation at the most useful moment.

Kleinians have subsequently minimized some aspects of Klein's interpretive approach and expanded other aspects.

The contemporary Kleinian approach is grounded in Melanie Klein's original theory and technique, yet has grown to be different in some ways and expanded in others. Spillius (1988) writes:

> Most of the basic features of Kleinian technique, as Segal notes, are closely derived from Freud: rigorous maintenance of the psychoanalytic setting so as to keep the transference as pure and uncontaminated as possible; an expectation of sessions five times a week; emphasis on the transference as the central focus of analyst–patient interaction; a belief that the transference situation is active from the very beginning of the analysis; an attitude of active receptivity rather than passivity and silence; interpretation of anxiety and defense together rather than either on its own; emphasis on interpretation, especially the trans-ference interpretation, as the agent of therapeutic change.
>
> (Spillius 1988: 5–6)

Certain themes have emerged in modern Kleinian thinking. Spillius (1988) has noted the decrease in the Kleinians' use of part-object language and the increase in more balanced exploration of aggression. She also points to the increased focus on PI as critical to understanding the transference and how countertransference can be used in this respect. The past and the present are given equal value in terms of seeing a continuity in the patient's phantasy life and their internal world. Schafer (1997) adds to this by stating:

> [Current Kleinians are] rather measured in the speed and quantity of their interpretations, as well as oriented toward gathering immediate evidence on which to base each aspect of their interventions. They favor "showing" over "telling" what's what.
>
> (Schafer 1997: 5)

Finally, Hinshelwood (1991) summarizes some ideas about current Kleinian approaches:

> Kleinian technique today emphasizes (i) the immediate here-and-now situation, (ii) the total of all aspects of the setting, (iii) the importance of understanding the content of the anxiety, (iv) the consequence of interpreting the anxiety rather than the defenses only (so-called deep interpretation) . . . in the last two decades, based on the understanding of projective identification and of acting in the transference, (technique) has focused instead on the way these processes in the analytic setting defend against the patient's experience of dependency and envy in the here-and-now.
>
> (Hinshelwood 1991: 23)

Here, Hinshelwood is noting how great an impact the analysis of PI has had on clinical technique. The entire understanding of the transference has been widened and enriched, leading to a greater ability on the analyst's part to make interpretations that truly reach the patient at the place where they need help the most.

Chapter 1

The Kleinian approach to projective identification

The more usual interpretive stance

When closely examining the literature for examples of what Kleinian analysts actually do and say to analyze and interpret PI, there are certain patterns that emerge. There are several approaches that seem more common and a few that are atypical or are used less frequently. Countertransference issues, precision of the interpretation, the here-and-now quality of interpretations, affect and phantasy, transformation of meaning, containment, and showing/explaining are the principal concepts that most Kleinians utilize when interpreting PI.

Countertransference

Countertransference is a common theme taken up by Kleinians in theoretical and clinical investigations of PI. It is considered an important element of correct technique. There are frequent examples in the literature of verbatim interpretations that incorporate countertransference as a tool in interpreting PI. I will start by looking at a more general description of a Kleinian's work with PI through utilization of countertransference.

Leon Grinberg (1962: 437) thinks the analyst normally reacts to PI by "properly interpreting the material brought up by the patient and by showing him that the violence of the mechanism has in no way shocked him." He writes of an experience in which one patient's resistance to feeling guilt was placed in the analyst through PI. This caused the analyst to over-identify with the resistance and to develop the symptom of drowsiness. After understanding this phenomenon, Grinberg then "interpreted the whole situation and made him conscious of his resistance, which I had been able to perceive through my own sensations" (ibid.: 439). Grinberg uses his countertransference to inform his thoughts and then makes an interpretation of that information. Grinberg's more general description is better expanded by Eulalia Torras De Bea (1989), who writes:

> a patient speaks to us and his story awakens emotions, conjures up images and fantasies in us, evoking also those other fantasies, memories and feelings relationed to the patient himself, to our work or lives in general. We find ourselves with emotions and images of every kind, comforting or disturbing, the conjunction of which we refer to as countertransference . . . it is this wealth of fantasies, emotions, and associations awakened in us by our patient which permit us, so long as we can tolerate it, to 'grasp' him. The reorganization of this internal experience in the matrix of former experiences, relating and articulating with them, starts the process of making sense and suggesting new meaning. We take them, actively observe the processes and 'think about them' without disrupting them; we connect them with words and consciousness. In this way knowledge is created and through verbalization we convey this new meaning to the patient. The end result, when successful, is the transformation of defensive projective identification into communicative projective identification.
>
> (Torras De Bea 1989: 266)

I think the difficult part of dealing with countertransference and PI has to do with letting ourselves acknowledge the flood of feelings and phantasies that emerge and then to tolerate them long enough to begin transforming them back into verbal comments to the patient. Part of dealing with defensive PI maneuvers is to not become defensive ourselves. Invariably we do, but this is hopefully temporary and a part of the working-through process in the countertransference.

Kernberg (1987), in discussing countertransference and PI, describes one session where he started to feel confused, awkward, and ready to give up. This was in response to a patient who disguised her condescending attitude with friendliness. Only toward the end of the hour did the analyst begin to notice how he had become one more devaluated man in her life. Based on his countertransference, Kernberg started to sort out the intrapsychic and interpersonal impact the patient was having on him. The same type of dynamic continued into the next hour and Kernberg began to understand the meaning of the PI. Based on his understanding, he told the patient her vision of him as a slow, unattractive loser was her "image of herself when she felt criticized and attacked by her mother, particularly when mother did not agree with her selection of men" (1987: 107). Kernberg told her that her attitude in treatment was the superiority and devaluation she had painfully felt from her mother. He also said she was scared of destroying him and then being left all alone. She was trying to leave treatment to escape this despair. The patient felt understood, and acknowledged her feelings that Kernberg had interpreted.

In the same paper, Kernberg discusses another case in which he felt physically threatened by an angry patient. Feeling he was about to be assaulted after a steady escalation of hostility throughout the hour, Kernberg "broke from technical neutrality" and told the patient he was too intimidated to be able to help him therapeutically. This disclosure seemed to steady the patient and allow Kernberg time to collect his thoughts. Kernberg writes:

> I then said that a fundamental aspect of the relationship with his father had just taken place, namely, the enactment of the relationship between his sadistic father and himself, in which I had taken on the role of the frightened, paralyzed child and he the role of his father under conditions of rage.
>
> (Kernberg 1987: 813)

After this and other interpretations of the patient's PI, the patient became curious about his recent behavior with friends and acquaintances.

This material shows how Kernberg technically approaches PI. He puts words to his countertransference, he points out the specific intrapsychic roles that are played out interpersonally, and he interprets the motives and affects behind them. It also appears that he emphasized the use of genetic reconstruction, as opposed to more here-and-now focus. This may be why the patient associated to his external relationships rather than to become more curious about his connection with the analyst.

In 1983, O'Shaughnessy wrote about her countertransference experience with a patient, Mr E:

> Not during, but after, his sessions I was invaded for hours by feelings relating to Mr. E of anxiety, confusion, guilt and need;

since these occurred only after his sessions, as regards immediacy of interpretation and effective containment, I was rendered impotent. Mr. E split off and projected his impotent, confused and anxious self into me, while he himself was identified with sadistic superego persecutors . . . even though my talk at times was so stimulating and exciting to Mr. E as to be useless analytically, I continued to put into words his feelings of excitedly invading me and knowing me, and my equally excitedly trying to penetrate him with interpretations. I talked about the code 'signs', etc. Gradually, Mr. E felt safer with me, was less wild, and concrete representations of various bits of his psychic state began to appear in his sessions. His excitement began to decline, ushering in a new phase . . . it was a phase in which words became paramount.

(O'Shaughnessy 1983: 285)

Here, O'Shaughnessy makes use not only of her countertransference feelings but also of their sequence and timing. She notes that she was unable to think clearly or potently for a while. Therefore, she notes the probable function of the PI mechanism. She notes the importance of transforming the affect and phantasies embedded in PI into words for the patient.

The efficacy of this is in Mr E feeling safer and slowly shifting his phantasies and affect into words. Shifting the countertransference into verbal communication is the essence of the PI interpretation.

Segal (1977) comments on her dealings with PI, in the context of countertransference, in the second hour of a new analysis. During the first hour the patient had talked about being a disappointment to her parents. In the second hour, the patient felt very depressed and discussed how terrible and in pain she felt. Segal writes:

I wondered if I had done something wrong in the previous session. I felt helpless and terribly eager to understand her . . . I slowly came to realize that I now felt that I was a disappointment to both her and to myself. I was in the position of a helpless and rather bewildered child, weighed down by projections coming from a depressed mother, and it was an interpretation emphasizing that aspect which produced a change in the situation.

(Segal 1977: 34)

So, Segal listened to her own internal state to gradually understand how the patient was using PI. Without any type of self-
disclosure, she then interpreted how the patient had communicated
the nature of her experience with her mother to the analyst. This
level of understanding eased the patient's suffering.

I would add that the patient did not need to suffer at that point,
as the projected suffering was the communication. The patient's
symptom of suffering was in the service of letting the analyst know
more about her internal identity and inner conflicts.

I think this form of PI, an effort to communicate, is easier for
the analyst to tolerate, sort out, and gradually interpret. When PI
is more an effort to evacuate toxic phantasies and force the analyst
to be the permanent receptacle for them, it is much more difficult
to tolerate, understand, and make therapeutic use of the countertransference.

Precision

Some Kleinians feel it important to be quite precise in what they
say to the patient when interpreting PI. They feel it important to
avoid general or vague interpretations.

O'Shaughnessy (1983) wrote of her work with a Mr B:

> As I tried to work, I felt almost as if Mr. B was physically
> pushing into me: I felt watched in my head, uncomfortable,
> restricted in what I could say – only obvious familiar inter-
> pretations seemed to exist as possibilities. These experiences
> were my reception of Mr. B's primitive communications and
> defenses, the interaction between patient and analyst concep-
> tualized and explained by Klein and Bion in terms of projective
> identification. I tried to put these experiences into words to
> Mr. B. I spoke about his need to get into my mind, his feeling
> of being located there, his maneuvering of me to give him
> familiar interpretations, and his relief at interpretations he
> knew would come.
>
> (O'Shaughnessy 1983: 282)

O'Shaughnessy makes specific use of her countertransference
feelings. She is informed by her countertransference and then proceeds to make concise interpretations based on the information it
gives her. She does not remain silent and she does not make broad

or generalized interpretations about the PI process. She makes precise, moment-to-moment PI interpretations based on counter-transference.

I think this is particularly important when dealing with more disturbed patients. More fully integrated, neurotic patients can usually find understanding and direction through more general or broad interpretations. They can find reassurance and insight in them and then feel free to expand them to find more specific feelings and thoughts to explore, thus generating a healthy cycle of insight and growth. More disturbed patients can hear a generalized interpretation as a confirmation of their distortions of reality and feel even more persecuted. They can feel abandoned or attacked by the lack of specificity. So, more detailed and precise interpretations of PI, as understood through the countertransference, are much more helpful and healing to the regressed patient who is already lost in the generalization of their fragmented mind.

Betty Joseph (1993) describes the need for the analyst's PI interpretations to be focused on the moment-to-moment nature of the transference in a precise manner, to avoid a mutual acting out. She writes:

> we shall only succeed if our interpretations are *immediate* and direct. Except very near a reasonably successful termination, if I find myself giving an interpretation based on events other than those occurring at the moment during the session, I usually assume that I am not in proper contact with the part of the patient that needs to be understood, or that I am talking more to myself than to the patient.
>
> (Joseph 1993: 87; italics in original)

While these directives show the proximity of her PI interpretations, Joseph also has technical guides as to what to focus on closely. She writes:

> the guide in the transference, as to where the most important anxiety is, lies in an awareness that, in some part of oneself, one can feel an area in the patient's communication that one wishes not to attend to – internally in terms of the effect on oneself, externally in terms of what and how one might interpret.
>
> (Joseph 1993: 111)

The countertransference feeling of wanting to avoid a certain area of difficulty with the patient helps center the analyst on what the most current PI anxiety might be. Being precise about exactly what the PI anxiety could be is important to the effectiveness of the interpretive process. The "I don't want to talk about it" sensation is a guidepost to the analyst as to what the patient is careful to avoid.

Joseph describes her treatment of a young woman who impressed her in the first few weeks by talking a great deal and presenting a wealth of material, yet it all seemed somehow hollow. Joseph began to get the picture, through the transference, of a woman who tried to fit in with her objects as best as possible, but felt despair at the hope of ever being truly understood. Joseph writes:

> she had deeply unconscious despair about ever achieving anything of value and being understood, valued, or cared for. This I tried to convey to her, showing how she projected into me an internal phantasy mother who was felt not to understand, to be apparently incapable of contact; and how she built up a defensive system against recognizing her despair by fitting in, accepting, flattering, and adjusting to me or what she phantasied about me.
>
> (Joseph 1993: 118)

Joseph goes on to illustrate the difficulty of this type of PI situation. The woman could rarely accept such interpretations because her phantasies disallowed the taking in of such gifts and rejected the image of a giving or understanding object. Nevertheless, the analyst verbally conveyed the intrapsychic dynamic that was occurring in the PI mechanism that shaped the transference. Joseph was precise about the nature of the intrapsychic relationship this patient was projecting.

In investigating patients who are self-destructive, Joseph notices how PI plays a role. She writes:

> a type of [PI] in which despair is so effectively loaded into the analyst that he seems crushed by it and can see no way out. The analyst is then internalized in this form by the patient, who becomes caught up in this internal crushing and crushed situation, and paralysis and deep gratification ensue.
>
> (Joseph 1993: 133)

Again, Joseph is very careful, technically, in how to interpret PI. Precision guides her words. There are multiple affects and phantasies operating within the PI mechanism, therefore what is emphasized in the interpretation is a clinically vital decision. Joseph states:

> I believe it is technically extremely important to be clear as to whether the patient is telling us about and communicating to us real despair, depression, or fear and persecution, which he wants us to understand and to help him with, or whether he is communicating it in such a way as primarily to create a masochistic situation in which he can become caught up.
>
> (Joseph 1993: 133)

Joseph constantly searches for the deeper unconscious aspects of PI. She writes, "if we work only with the part that is verbalized, we do not really take into account the object relationships being acted out in the transference" (1993: 158). She notes that this lack of precision leads to inaccurate technique:

> interpretations and understanding remain on the level of the individual associations, as contrasted with the total situation and the way that the analyst and his words are used, we shall find that we are being drawn into a pseudo-mature or more neurotic organization and missing the more psychotic anxieties and defenses . . . being acted out in the transference.
>
> (Joseph 1993: 166)

So, Joseph is once again pointing out how overly generalized interpretations can mask the patient's real pathology and lead to a mutual acting out, a false sense of cure. This is an unconscious, global agreement between analyst and patient that progress is being made. Issues are only examined in safe, broad, and general ways. Both parties avoid any real or specific focus as a way to escape the mutual anxiety of the patient's fears and aggressive phantasies that are occurring through a PI process.

I would add that the analyst's broad or general interpretation might be helpful on occasion if the patient uses the broadness as a vehicle to associate and bring in more specific material. However, if the patient matches the broad interpretation with their own vague or general associations, then it becomes a collaboration in evasive pathology, a PI acting-out process.

Here and now

In examining accounts of Kleinian PI interpretations, there are analysts who feel that immediate, here-and-now interpretations best deal with PI. They emphasize the value of being direct and interpreting the moment-to-moment transference aspects of PI, as well as the immediate internal relationship the patient appeared to be dealing with. These analysts value genetic reconstruction as well, but find it helpful only occasionally.

Paula Heimann (1956) feels that if left alone, without interpretation, PI will simply foster greater pathology. She notes that while the patient may introject an idealized vision of the analyst that will then combat the bad internal objects, this is not the analytic goal. If the introjection of an idealized analyst goes unanalyzed, the treatment has merely promoted a greater degree of splitting. Finally, she feels that if interpretations are withheld, it pushes the treatment into more of an acting out of primitive object relations rather than a working through of those relations. Therefore, she is always exploring, interpreting, and analyzing the moment-to-moment, here-and-now unfolding of the PI.

Heimann explains that to make the interpretation, the analyst has to constantly ask herself or himself, "Why is the patient now doing what to whom?" While she is discussing various manifestations of PI, Heimann calls her interpretations "transference interpretation." This seems to be an outgrowth of the implicit notion that PI is at times the core of the transference relationship. She writes:

> it is the transference interpretation which fully re-instates the past in the present and makes it accessible to the patient's ego. The patient is not then looking back coolly and intellectually at what he once felt with his parents, but is experiencing his immediate feelings and their phantasy contents towards the analyst as the real and living equivalent of his past life with his original objects who have indeed been intra-psychically preserved.
>
> (Heimann 1956: 307)

Another way to clarify the relationship between the transference and PI mechanisms is to examine how the transference becomes known. It is often through the intrapsychic and interpersonal vehicle of PI that the exact nature of the patient's transference phantasies become clear and alive in the consulting office.

Herbert Rosenfeld (1958) discussed a patient who had projected a persecutory father into the analyst and then split it off onto a bank manager. These projections protected her from the guilt she felt at having castrated the analyst/father. The patient became anxious and insisted the analyst help her by convincing the bank manager she was trustworthy. Rosenfeld writes:

> I interpreted to her that at that moment she wanted to have a guarantee from me that I remained a friendly father to her, in order to keep me apart from the bank manager, who had become very threatening and frightening. I also showed her that she had suddenly become frightened because I had turned into the bank manager who represented that aspect of herself which had recently been finding out things about him which her father had never known . . . I showed her that the muddle which she had been making over her money matters represented a hidden attack on the analysis, since she would be unable to pay my fees . . . I showed her that the main resistance was against recognizing the intense guilt and anxiety about depriving and injuring me.
>
> (Rosenfeld 1958: 239)

Rosenfeld goes on to explain that his interpretations of the PI process helped the patient become less anxious and that she then was more in touch with her external realities and how to deal with them. By staying with the here-and-now, present manifestation of PI, he helped the patient work through her PI phantasies and start to deal more with reality.

I think it would not have been as productive for Rosenfeld to have concentrated on the patient's history and simply interpreted the one-to-one parallel between the patient's view of the parents and of the analyst. Nor would it have helped as much to make a general interpretation about the patient's fear of her own aggression. The here-and-now, in the room nature of his comment was what helped most.

Kernberg *et al.* (1989) described a PI situation in the initial hours of a new analysis. The patient provocatively wondered if she could make it to her appointments. Kernberg writes:

at this stage no effort should be made at an in-depth interpretation. The therapist addresses the patient's resistance to the contract by returning to the realistic reasons for the contract, not by interpretation. Interpretive work should be introduced only after the contract has been established.

(Kernberg *et al.* 1989: 36)

He clearly sets a limit on when and how the analyst should proceed in interpreting PI. This would be an example of not focusing on the here-and-now as a guideline to making PI interventions.

I would not agree with this stance, as it artificially divides the transference and PI dynamic from the external "realistic reasons for the contract." While it is helpful to address the external environment and to bring reality into the conversation to discuss why the patient can't get to her appointment, to not put them into the context of the transference and PI process via an interpretation seems to be a missed therapeutic opportunity.

While Kernberg believes in not interpreting PI in certain clinical situations, his clinical work and supervisory work can also demonstrate the importance of direct interpretation. One patient would attack the analyst for any comment she made but also attacked her for making no comments. As a result, the therapist became relatively passive. Kernberg writes:

this enraged the patient even more, and he threatened to dismiss the therapist. At this point, the therapist recalled the patient's moving descriptions, during the initial interviews, of fear of his own passivity as he entered into depressive states of mind. The therapist pointed out to the patient that he had cornered her into inaction by his repeated attacks whenever she spoke and thus induced in the therapist the very passivity that he hated in himself. Seeing the therapist as passive allowed the patient to disown this quality in himself. This comment, an interpretation of projective identification, led the patient to speak tearfully of his fear of passivity, and completely defused the request for a new therapist.

(Kernberg *et al.* 1989: 99)

Here, the analyst demonstrates how helpful, in the moment of transference connection, the here-and-now interpretation of PI is.

The here-and-now focus on the exact nature of the PI process not only prevented the threatened termination but allowed the patient to access his defended sadness, fear, and anxiety.

Affect and phantasy

Some Kleinians consider affect and the specific phantasy involved in PI as crucial elements to consider when formulating effective PI interpretations.

Herbert Rosenfeld (1952a) wrote of his work with psychotic patients who used PI as a way to grapple with severe paranoid-schizoid anxieties. Technically, he believes in interpreting the primary phantasy associated with the anxiety. He writes of his work with one patient:

> I told him that he was not only afraid of getting something bad inside him, but that he was also afraid of taking good things, the good orange juice and good interpretations, inside since he was afraid that these would make him feel guilty again. When I said this, a kind of shock went through his body; he gave a groan of understanding, and his facial expression changed. By the end of the hour he had emptied the glass of orange juice, the first food or drink he had taken for two days . . .
>
> (Rosenfeld 1952a: 119)

In describing his work with another patient, Rosenfeld (1954) states:

> I interpreted that she had put herself into me and that she felt that I was her and had to talk and think for her. I explained to her that this was the reason why she felt so shut in when she came to my house and why she had to escape from me. She was now looking much more comfortable and trusting, and said: 'you are the world's best person'. I interpreted that because she felt I was so good she wanted to be inside me and have my goodness. Following the interpretations . . . she was able to extricate herself out of me which lessened her confusion. She then became more aware of me as an external object and was able to talk . . .
>
> (Rosenfeld 1954: 137)

In both these cases, Rosenfeld directly addresses the primary phantasies within the here-and-now analytic situation. Part of his PI interpretation concerned the erasing of self/object differentiation. This fading of boundaries is typical of PI, especially when used excessively, in a defensive posture. This pathological overuse of PI is common with more disturbed patients and is often part of the death instinct's effort to destroy any distinction between self and object. When Rosenfeld interpreted this internal strategy, the patient could begin to discern what was separate from her ego and in the external world.

In 1990, Herbert Rosenfeld wrote of several clinical experiences with PI, again involving psychotic patients. Along with other material, a Mr A told him that he had been up all night worried that he might drown from water that could come flowing out of the sink. He had kept checking to see if the stoppers were in place. The analysis was about to be interrupted by the analyst's two-week trip. Rosenfeld writes:

> I interpreted to him that after he felt that he was making progress and feeling separate from me he was suddenly over-come with impatience and envy of me and other men who were able to move about and were active. I suggested that it was the envious part which drove him into the identification with myself and other men in order to take over their strength and potency, and in this way the omnipotent part of himself could make him believe that he could be mature and healthy instantly.
>
> (Rosenfeld 1990: 130)

The patient responded by saying he was bothered at having to listen to such ridiculous voices in his head pushing him to dominate others when he knew better.

Rosenfeld writes: "I interpreted to him that I thought that the threatening separation was stimulating his wish to be suddenly grown up and independent in order not to have to cope with the anxieties of being separate from me" (1990: 130). The patient went on to talk about how he felt drawn into his television without any power to stop himself. He said he could not get out of bed in the morning for the same reason. He said he felt like a parasite. Rosenfeld writes:

I pointed out that he felt angry with that part of himself which stimulated him to get inside external objects . . . and also into internal objects which were represented by his bed. I stressed that at first he felt he probably could control and possess these objects entirely when he got inside them, but very soon he felt enclosed and trapped and persecuted, which roused his wish to destroy the bed and the television screen which had turned into persecuting objects.

(Rosenfeld 1990: 131)

At the start of the next hour, this patient said he felt better. However, later in the hour he said he was very uneasy because he was evermore aware of a deep hatred he had for Jewish people. He said he felt they were only after money and he wanted to attack them and punish them. Rosenfeld writes:

I interpreted . . . [that] he now felt awful towards me because after yesterday's session he had got rid of the greedy parasitical exploiting part of his self but had pushed it into me. He felt now that I had become his greedy exploiting self and this made him feel intensely suspicious about me.

(Rosenfeld 1990: 132)

The patient said he was frightened that the analyst must now hate him, and felt that the only way out was to destroy himself and that dreadful part of himself. Rosenfeld says:

I interpreted his fear of my retaliation because when he saw me as a greedy, exploiting Jew he attacked and despised me, and feared that I would hate him because he believed I could not bear that he had pushed his own greedy self into me, not only as an attack but because he could not bear it himself and wanted to get rid of it. I suggested that it was when he felt that I could not accept his bad and hated self that he attacked himself so violently . . . He calmed down considerably after the interpretations.

(Rosenfeld 1990: 132)

Overall, Rosenfeld showed this patient the intimate details of how his PI phantasy made the analytic relationship unsafe, unpredictable, and unsatisfying. Rosenfeld's interpretations explicated the elements of loss, paranoia, and guilt. Also, his comments offered this patient an inherent clarification of reality. All these interpretive approaches to PI helped reduce the patient's psychotic tensions.

The material illustrates how Rosenfeld's PI interpretations focus beautifully on the details of the patient's unconscious phantasies and the affects that accompany them. Because he is so in tune with the patient's fears and hostilities, the interpretations have a secondary, non-explicated benefit of addressing the pathological splitting and loss of ego boundaries in this patient.

Mario Pacheco de A. Prado (1980) discusses work with a psychotic patient who hardly ever said no to anything in life, which made him easy to be with and pleasing to others. However, he felt overwhelmed by personal failures in life and disorganized to the point of not functioning in daily living. During the second week of psychoanalysis, the patient was talking about how he spent the weekend thinking of the analyst and the wonderful feeling of closeness he had with him. Then he talked of feeling overcome by laziness and exhaustion. He tried to call someone for support. While he failed to reach anyone, he felt better for a while but then succumbed to the exhaustion. The patient felt "As though I were full of cracks and I were leaking out of one, out of another, and when the time comes to do something, there is no more water!" (de A. Prado 1980: 161). The analyst made an interpretation of the PI, "you are spilling into me your aspects of mood, of will, and you feel emptied of yourself and as if what you did were ordered by me." The patient replied:

> why do you say it is you who gives me orders . . . isn't it myself? I telephoned a lot of people, I pinched myself to wake up and it was good, but I don't feel I am making a choice. I keep on calling, and whoever I find first is the one I invite. Sometimes I hope secretly not to get anyone and so I calm down. I carry out what I feel responsible for and so I can rest.
> (de A. Prado 1980: 161)

De A. Prado writes:

> he refers to the anxiety experienced at the weekend with an allusion to his feeling himself full of cracks by which his impulses, his interests, escape . . . although he is leaking like water from a container full of cracks, he tried to defend the

analyst from the feelings of hate he experienced when [the analyst was unavailable]. He inserted the 'good' analyst among those he sought to reach by phone . . . the analyst was indeed inaccessible . . . what resulted . . . was the distress, the frustration, and the threat of desperation . . . unable to contain those sentiments for him . . . The analyst interprets the projective identification in the telephone numbers and the girl, in the transference relation of that instant of the session, showing him his fear, of spilling out into the analyst, of being swallowed by the analyst and becoming his puppet, without options.

(de A. Prado 1980: 161)

The analyst directly interpreted the PI, translating the patient's phantasy into elements of desire, fear, and defense. This is a focus on the intrapsychic meaning of the PI mechanism, rather than a focus on the interpersonal. Therefore, it has both the timeless quality of the patient's phantasy and it matches with each component of the phantasy. De A. Prado also shows the patient what affect he is struggling with in regard to both paranoid-schizoid and depressive delusions.

I think this illustration of technique also shows one of the problems in the literature on PI. De A. Prado's description of his intervention is somewhat vague. While he does interpret the primary phantasy involved in the PI, one is left wondering what exactly did he say to the patient and how exactly did the patient respond. Since the reader isn't privy to the actual exchange, there is a question of how he got from A to B in his interpretation. This type of global reporting is common in the literature and makes it difficult for the reader to really examine, evaluate, and learn about the analyst's technical approach.

My aim is to first show the bulk of the literature that provides the clearest and most concise examples of verbatim interpretations in the PI clinical situation. Then I will show how I make interpretations of PI with my own patients in the clinical moment.

Paula Heimann (1956) believes the use of interpretations in the analysis of PI is vital to the treatment, along with proper use of the countertransference. She writes:

the therapeutic task of extending the patient's conscious knowledge about himself, about his unconscious impulses and defenses and anxiety and pain, makes it necessary to bring his unconscious phantasies to consciousness . . . When the analyst expresses these . . . in his interpretations, the patient's ego makes contact with them and so discovers something which is in reality its own, although he was unable to verbalize these phantasies or can remember only fragmentary flashes of such feelings or ideas flitting through his mind at some former time . . . words are of the greatest significance, because they remove the barriers between the different strata of the ego, they promote clear and critical thinking, and they are the vehicle of conscious, explicit communication between patient and analyst . . . necessary if analysis is to bring about the patient's fuller understanding of himself.

(Heimann 1956: 306)

Clearly, transformation of unconscious affect and phantasy is the goal that guides her PI interpretations.

Transformation of meaning

Providing new meaning to the patient's PI phantasies is a goal for some Kleinians. Through analysis and verbalization of the patient's unconscious phantasy, a new meaning is constructed for the patient to internalize.

Malin and Grotstein (1966) point out the importance of PI receptivity in the analyst. The ability to receive the projections and then modify them for the patient is crucial for a successful working-through process. The patient hopes that the analyst can handle their ejected psychic material without being destroyed. Sometimes this hope collapses into dread and the patient feels alone with an overwhelmed object.

The principal manner in which the patient feels the analyst has survived the ego's deposit of material is through the nature of the analyst's interpretation. Therefore, Malin and Grotstein emphasize the therapeutic value and the necessity for direct interpretation of PI. They write:

correct interpretations can be seen as an important way in which the patient can observe how his projections have been received and acknowledged by the analyst. If this does not take place the patient is left with futility, despair, and doubt . . .

(Malin and Grostein 1966: 29)

These authors state the importance of understanding what can appear to be a negative therapeutic reaction, especially with more disturbed patients. They describe the patient's need to preserve the analyst as a good object by maintaining distance from him. By not being close to the analyst, the patient prevents the projection of bad objects into the analyst and thus the risk of destroying him and their only hope for survival. However, the same patient may keep their distance if they feel they have already contaminated the analyst by projecting bad objects into him.

Malin and Grotstein provide a case study in which the patient felt the analyst was rigid, hard to please, and snotty. This was a projection of a father identification. At other times, the patient felt the analyst was insincere and martyr-like. This was a projection of a mother identification. Malin and Grotstein write:

> the projections were accepted by the analyst for their psychic validity, and then interpreted as his need to put bad parts of himself . . . into the analyst in order to rid his ego of these bad contents . . . Not only was he repeating with the analyst what he had experienced with his father and mother, but he was also taking possession, in fantasy, of the analyst from within to guarantee total possession of the object . . . Without this guarantee, as it were, there existed no relationship for him.
>
> (Malin and Grotstein 1966: 30)

The authors go on to describe how the patient needed to not only own the analyst to prevent the loss of the relationship but that he felt his love was bad and would be rejected as well. Therefore, he related to the object with his "bad" self in order to protect the object from the bad loving aspects of himself. Also, he was excited if he felt he hurt the object in this way. If the analyst was hurt, the patient felt he had an effect on another person, thus confirming his existence. This also gratified his intense envy of the analyst's strength.

Malin and Grotstein explain their technical approach and its results:

> consistent interpretations of all of these mechanisms wherever they occurred considerably lessened the negative transference, and the patient was subsequently able to recognize that he was warding off his deep feelings of dependency on the analyst. Changes occurred by virtue of analyzing the projections rather

than by the analyst's unconsciously or consciously responding as if they were objectively valid. In other words, it was a new experience for the patient which allowed him to integrate the previously projected parts, now reintegrated into the ego, so that a higher level of functioning could occur.

(Malin and Grostein 1966: 30)

One aspect of this approach is to show the patient a new take on an old belief. This is done by the analyst not acting out the PI phantasy with the patient and instead interpreting the patient's self–object conflicts. In this way, there is a new experience of self and object.

I think this is accurate and a vital part of analytic technique. At the same time, I think all analysts need to not idealize this transformative function and realize that it is very common to, at first, act out the PI, then understand it, and then interpret it for the patient. In that sense, we often become part of a living, here-and-now transformation of self and object within the intrapsychic and interpersonal world of the transference–countertransference.

In a rather extreme case example, David Rosenfeld (1992) shows his technical style with PI. He writes of a patient who burst into a staff meeting at the hospital. The patient told Rosenfeld that he hated him and was going to kill him because he resembled the patient's father. He said he would then kill everyone else in the room. Rosenfeld states:

I told him he wanted to kill a crazy part inside his head and a crazy father inside him, that he projected this and wanted to see it in me, instead of seeing it inside his head. He replied that he was going to kill all the social workers and psychologists. Then I told him that he scattered onto everyone what was going on in his head and that he wanted to get rid of that crazy Samuel by seeing him in me and then in the people there, but that what he wanted to see outside and kill was what was crazy in him . . . I insisted that he wanted to kill his own crazy part and we wanted to help him be cured by means of words, that there was no need to kill.

(Rosenfeld 1992: 20)

Rosenfeld was direct with the patient about what he felt was being projected and the motivations behind those actions. In doing so, he transformed the intrapsychic meaning of this patient's angry and scary phantasies.

Part of this direct interpretation and transformation was the converting of a dangerous projection back into an internalization of bad objects. With a patient as disturbed as this and wanting so desperately to get rid of the toxic internal objects, that sort of interpretation would need to be repeated many times over, from many different avenues. Such a patient would undoubtedly resist and reject the interpretation much of the time, with the analyst needing to follow up with more understanding and discussion.

In 1983, Herbert Rosenfeld mentions the importance of being careful in interpreting to overly anxious patients as they may take the interpretation in as yet another persecutory object. While he suggests using a minimum of verbal interventions in these types of situations, he still feels that direct interpretation of PI is essential to successful technique. He describes how in one form of PI, the patient believes he has forced himself omnipotently into the analyst, creating anxieties about loss of self. The patient then fears the analyst will control his mind and drive him mad. This pushes the patient to attack back and fight for his life. Rosenfeld writes:

> it is then, of course, essential to establish with the patient that he is afraid he has forced the mad parts of his self into the therapist and that he is now terrified that the analyst will retaliate and force the madness back into him and, as a punishment, entirely deprive him of his sanity.
>
> (Rosenfeld 1983: 263)

I find it fascinating that looking back on David Rosenfeld's case of the patient wanting to kill the staff, one would see the patient potentially taking Rosenfeld's interpretation in this persecutory manner.

Later in the paper, Herbert Rosenfeld discusses a patient who brought in a dream of a starving baby and a starving mother. After telling the dream, she realized she never knew whether she was devouring others or being devoured by others. She then felt intense pressure on her head and felt like bursting. Rosenfeld writes: "I interpreted that she felt that she wanted to project the starving, demanding mother into me to get some relief" (1983: 265). This illustrates his goal of putting the patient's phantasy into words and then describes to the patient the motivation and subsequent results of his phantasies. The desires, the anxieties, and the outcome of the PI phantasy are articulated to the patient. The analyst then waits to hear the next association. By showing the patient the details of their core unconscious beliefs, it provides room for them to generate new meaning, within the context of the transference. Transformation of the old PI process allows room for new, more integrated object relations.

Containment

Containment is an issue integral to Kleinian thinking about PI. Kleinians feel containment is part of the analytic struggle and should be included in the formulation of an interpretation.

While she advocates containment as a technical tool with PI, Torras De Bea (1989) points out the many ways this can be unsuccessful. If the analyst merely projects back the patient's material it makes for a mutual acting out of old, pathological object relations. This is similar to Rosenfeld's warning about interpretations with overly anxious patients. Torras De Bea notes how the initial experiences of PI may overwhelm the analyst, leading to an over-identification with the patient's bad objects or with the patient's own anxieties. If the analyst can manage to contain these painful states, each time may go better until the analyst is able to sort out what is occurring and gradually find a way to interpret it. She feels this helps the patient differentiate between his or her own internal objects and the actual reality of life. She states, "the best service an analyst can do for a patient is, I believe, to differentiate where the patient dissociates" (Torras De Bea 1989: 271). She goes on to say that this containing, sorting out, and interpreting of PI processes helps the patient to differentiate the good object from the bad, which produces meaning and reduces anxiety.

Therefore, Torras De Bea feels a careful mixture of counter-transference focus, containment, and interpretation best deals with the PI of specific phantasies, anxieties, and desires. She feels this sequence leads to a reduction of fear and an increase in awareness and ego function.

In 1978, Betty Joseph discussed a patient who used PI to get the analyst "to collude with denials of his anxieties and feelings and [to be used] as a receptacle for parts of his self which, if recognized, would cause extreme anxiety" (p. 225). The patient was a man who

used intellectualization to ward off his anxieties and was unconsciously scared of having a psychotic breakdown if he stopped
splitting off his emotional troubles. Denial and reason was used as
a shield against his fears. This created a bland, emotionless
atmosphere in the treatment. The patient said he felt good about
the treatment and didn't like to miss hours due to his work
schedule, but it all seemed untouched by real emotion. Joseph felt
that a goal of the analysis was to find the lost parts of the patient
and thus locate his primary anxiety.

The patient had to miss one hour in the week and said he
regretted it. He said this in his usual bland manner. At this point,
the patient presented a dream about going into the flat next door to
his to see what was happening. When he came back, the owner of
his flat and the one he visited was suspicious of him. The patient
knew that this was due to the owner's paranoia. This owner
reminded the patient of a "Mrs. Hours" that he knew. Joseph felt
that he projected his anxieties about being without his analyst for
an hour into Joseph as they were intolerable and triggered his
psychotic fears about women and his relations with them. Therefore, in projecting these unwanted states into the analyst, he saw
Joseph as suspicious, anxious, and worried about his missing hours.
Since Joseph felt it would be overwhelming to him to interpret this
projection into her, which he would probably use intellectualization
to ward off, she instead interpreted his phantasy of her as affected
by his anxieties. She commented on how he saw her as worried and
restless, concerned with his upcoming absence (Joseph 1978: 225).

Thus, Joseph's interpretation of the PI was a combination of
remaining a container for his discarded anxieties and a comment
about what he felt he was left with because of those projections.

Technically, this is an interesting point. Rather than interpret
something about the patient, which might be taken as an attack,
the analyst interprets how the object appears to the patient. This
provides a buffer of distance and safety for the patient while still
exploring the outcome of their PI efforts.

Kernberg (1989) points out that PI typically produces persecutory anxieties as a secondary by-product. He feels direct interpretation of this facilitates working through. While Kernberg
obviously sides with putting words to the patient's PI phantasies, he
does feel it is important to deal with temporary psychotic regressions with clarification and reality testing. At these turbulent times,
he advocates the analyst stop interpreting the PI and help focus

the patient in reality. This would mean the analyst serves a temporary containing function for the PI process, not by interpretation of internal anxiety but by means of cognitive confrontation and clarification.

Kernberg *et al.* (1989) emphasize the importance of the analyst "staying in role." By this Kernberg seems to mean that the analyst must contain the PI efforts by the patient until it is clear what is occurring in the analytic relationship. Otherwise, Kernberg sees the possibility of mutual acting out as rather high. He notes one demanding borderline patient who was furious about the analyst starting the hour five minutes late. The analyst noticed the urge to explain herself as a way to fend off the patient's attack. She realized that she was feeling unfairly treated just as the patient had felt unfairly treated by her father. By reflecting on her countertransference feelings silently,

> the therapist was able to elaborate the effects of the patient's projective identification first (her identifying herself with a guilt-inducing father and projecting her guilty self onto the therapist), and then form a concordant identification with the part of the patient that feared being attacked, and thus to understand the intensity of the patient's need to counterattack.
> (Kernberg *et al.* 1989: 83)

Again, I think the idea of keeping oneself steady in the face of powerful PI forces is useful. However, it is seldom an all-or-nothing process. The containing function of the analyst is often triggered by the analyst noticing their own lack of containing ability or the analyst's own wish for an object to contain the analyst's anxieties.

Malcolm (1980) discusses a clinical case of PI where stagnation permeates the analytic work. This was in part due to the patient's sadistic superego. At one point, the patient could reflect more openly and wondered if he were a pervert. His self-exploration triggered internal attacks and strong anxiety. He began to worry about how damaging and cruel he was to the analyst and felt the term "pervert" was insufficient to describe how bad he was. Malcolm writes:

> I sometimes also pointed out to him how much he wanted me to call him a pervert; the word would then acquire a moralistic meaning and he could feel me as accusing and punishing. In other words, through projective identification, I would be the punisher, and he thought that then he could avoid his own

anxieties. When I managed to get this across to him and he did
not feel me punitive, he experienced intense pain that drove him
into panic, which in turn prompted him to intensify the cruelty
. . . if he did not succeed in this, and my words had some impact
on him, he would also force himself to sleep in the session.

(Malcolm 1980: 561)

Malcolm is interpreting the patient's attempt to project the
persecutory superego attacks into the analyst as a way to escape
the internal punishment.

Malcolm describes how her countertransference was very difficult to bear with this case. She felt she had to do something before
she ran out of time. She thought she might have tried too hard in
the sessions to compensate for her anxiety. Once she realized how
the patient had successfully projected feeings of being broken and
beyond repair into her, she could make appropriate interventions.
Malcolm made less frequent interpretations and tried to contain
the patient's projections for a longer period. She felt the projections
were partly a test of whether she could endure the patient's anxious
attacks. Malcolm writes: "it required a careful balance, since if
waiting was perceived just 'a fraction too long', it also was proof
that my mind was out of action" (1980: 562).

So with this patient Malcolm felt the best way to analyze the PI
was to first contain it and understand it, giving the patient a
nonverbal message or interpretation about his effects on the
analyst. In addition, she carefully articulated his desire to make her
into a punitive superego figure so as to elevate his inner anxieties.

In addition, I think her case illustrates how PI situations can
often be very taxing and confusing for the analyst. The interpersonal and intrapsychic impact of PI can easily throw the analyst
off balance and lead to a feeling of helplessness. So, there is a need
for the analyst to not only function as a container for the patient's
projections but for the analyst's own conflicts as well. This self-
containing, self-soothing ability is something every analyst must
cultivate throughout their career.

Showing and explaining

A great number of Kleinians use interpretation to show the patient
exactly how his/her mind works. In making their interpretation,
they try to explain, in both an educative and analytic manner, how

the unconscious might be operating at that time within the transference. Frequently, this leads to more complex interpretations that
have a stronger quality to them. It creates more of a convincing
story that embraces many aspects of the PI dynamic and gives
room for so-called deeper interpretations.

Discussing how he would intervene in a particular case being
presented at a conference, Mason (1987) says he would have interpreted the patient's PI anxieties about intimidation, humiliation,
and envy. He writes:

> [I would have interpreted to the patient the following] the
> intimidation you feel comes from the part of you that hates
> being a little girl and expects you to be as big as and have as
> much as daddy. You feel you ought to have a penis like him
> and as much money as he has. 'Then,' it says, 'mommy
> wouldn't leave you!' The smallness of your penis and money
> also make you attack daddy's penis to make it bad and
> dangerous so that mommy hates it too. This causes men's sex
> today to frighten and disgust you because you still believe your
> little girl's view of it . . .
>
> (Mason 1987: 195)

Mason's interpretations are deep and complex. He really tells a
story with his interpretations in that he does not state one fact. He
shows the patient the complicated twists and turns of their
phantasy with the various characters and multiple layers of affect
and meaning. These are long explanations of the patient's unconscious phantasy process, involving patient and analyst.

Segal (1990) illustrates her technique with PI in discussing the
analysis of a man who used PI and splitting throughout the
treatment. She writes:

> one day, . . . he ended the session in a very adoring way typical
> of his idealizing, 'Doctor, when you look at me with your kind
> eyes I can feel you drawing the illness out of me and throwing
> it out of the window.' He started the next session by describing
> vividly how he felt attacked outside my house as soon as he left
> the consulting room: 'you can't imagine how it got into me,
> how it squeezed me, how it burned me.' ("It" being the usual
> way of describing his hypochondriacal symptoms.) He could
> not deny the interpretation that the same kind doctor who

drew the illness out of him seemed to have thrown it at him outside the window.

(Segal 1990: 176)

She used the context of the phantasy to illustrate to the patient how his mind operated. Getting inside the PI "story" is a particularly helpful way of showing the patient the nature of their internal conflict. Segal (1974) expands this idea by explaining how

> in interpreting projective identification one tries to interpret the details of the phantasy . . . One aims at making the patient aware of the motives of the projective phantasy, and its effects on the perception of the object and of the self. For example, one can show a patient how the projection of his own aggressive sexuality into the parental intercourse, gives rise both to the perception of his parents as cruel and sexually dangerous, and also to the perception of himself as devoid of aggression and sex . . . One has to interpret always in the context of the whole relationship, taking into account the patient's motives, anxieties and the aim of the projections.

(Segal 1974: 121)

Then, Segal illustrates these points with a clinical illustration:

> her silence was linked with projective identification, but as it proceeded, the meaning of it kept changing. At first I interpreted it primarily as a communication: I interpreted to her that she wanted to make me experience what it felt like to be cut off and unable to communicate. Later on, when she was on the threshold of the depressive position, I interpreted that she wanted to make me feel what it is like to have a lifeless internal object (herself on the couch) and to feel both guilty about it and helpless in bringing it to life. Later on, as the patient's distress and her need to project in order to communicate, had lessened a great deal, when she was silent the silence was much more aggressive. Now I could interpret the projection into me of feelings of failure and inadequacy, the motives being two-fold: she partly wanted to get rid of such feelings from within herself and partly wanted to project them into me out of revenge, spite and envy.

(Segal 1974: 121)

This beautifully illustrates Segal's careful examination of the patient's phantasy to determine what aspect of it is occurring within the vehicle of PI at that particular moment. It also demonstrates the sensitive way she shows, explains, and guides the patient to a fuller understanding of their unconscious struggle at that specific time.

Ruth Riesenberg Malcolm (1986) writes:

> the knowledge of projective identification is central to the understanding of the analytical material . . . The patient does not only express himself through words. He also uses actions, and sometimes words and actions. The analyst listens, observes and feels the patient's communications. He scrutinizes his own responses to the patient, trying to understand the effect the patient's behavior has on himself, and he understands this as a communication from the patient . . . It is this, comprehended in its totality, that is presented to the patient as an interpretation. This interpretation should be verbalized directly and concisely in terms of the present. We describe to the patient what is going on, and we explain why we think it is going on; we allow the relationship to evolve and we try to draw the patient into looking at the relationship.
>
> (Malcolm 1986: 434)

Malcolm describes a patient who routinely answered "yes" to most everything the analyst said. The "yes" had no particular connection to what was being discussed at the time. Malcolm's countertransference was of a mother reassuring a baby. At the same time, due to the disconnectedness of his "yes" statements, she also thought of a mother who was unable to truly minister to her baby. She pointed out her observations to the patient, who replied with another "yes." She mentioned that perhaps he was trying to reassure her and saw her as vulnerable. His "yes" changed to a moment of reflection. Malcolm then told him that perhaps there was an internal part of himself trying to speak to another part of himself that was unable or unwilling to respond but tried to soothe the other part. The patient muttered "mmmmm." Malcolm then suggested that he had split a part of himself into her and saw her as needing reassurance. She writes:

I ended by saying that his lodging a bit of himself in me was done both to get rid of the part of him that felt so unhappy and lonely and also to make me know how it feels when not listened to or understood properly. He looked relaxed . . . in my view, [the projective identification process was] used by him at that moment both as a defense and a communication.

(Malcolm 1986: 435)

So, Malcolm has something in mind about PI from a theoretical perspective. She believes this patient uses PI as both communication and defense. And she is able to weave this theory into the clinical moment and speak to the patient directly about both these ways of relating. This is an example of theory and clinical practice being truly joined; something quite rare.

In discussing another patient, Malcolm makes interpretations of the PI that took place in the patient's dream. She writes:

I spoke about the way he dealt with those painful feelings and with his menacing anger, by cutting them off and pushing them out of his mind and lodging them in me. And that, as a consequence of this lodging, his perception of me as someone like the woman with the girls in the dreams – powerful and menacing; and that on coming back from the weekend, he did not know if there was any friendliness left between us or if this would just be a hellish place.

(Malcolm 1986: 439)

Malcolm makes it clear that she sees PI as a central dynamic in the transference and in the total treatment situation. She makes direct interpretation of PI within the context of the present moment and the current relational anxiety between patient and analyst. She makes a point of explaining to the patient what she observes, how she understands the nature of the PI mechanism being used, and the intrapsychic consequences for the patient of using it.

Hanna Segal (1993b) states:

You [the analyst] must understand what they're projecting and show them how they are doing it and then gradually why they're doing it. Was it because the stress was too great or is it an envious attack? And then you gradually come to it.

(Segal 1993b: 19)

She is pointing out the analyst's role in explaining and showing through words the nature of the patient's PI. She focuses on telling the patient what, how, and why they are using PI. I would add that her use of the word "gradually" is useful for all analysts to note. Like most clinical situations, PI is complex and takes time to understand and then intervene with. The analyst is at her or his best when able to be patient with the PI dynamics going on in the transference and patient with her or his own ability gradually to make sense out of it for both parties.

Chapter 2

The Kleinian interpretation of projective identification

The atypical and less usual interpretive stance

In the previous chapter I outlined the types of Kleinian interpretation that show up most regularly. Those examples were the most common reports of what Kleinians actually say to their patients in an effort to analyze PI dynamics. Now, I turn to the less common interpretive stances found in the literature. A smaller group of Kleinian analysts make most of their interpretations around issues of silence, interpersonal factors, modeling, voicing, body language, dreams, and motivation.

Silence

Some Kleinians feel silence is an important part of the dynamic sequence in constructing PI interpretations.

G. De Racker (1961) describes a very difficult case where the patient needed to reject interpretations. The young girl came in with an angry face and was silent. The analyst tried to make an interpretation about the silence but the patient yelled at her to leave her alone. De Racker tried

> to interpret that she does not want to listen because she fears that I will force something very bad into her (through her ears). The patient tells her to be quiet again and the analyst attempts "to show her her phantasy of having herself forced her own 'bad' part (anger) into me, as the basis of her fear and rejection."
> (De Racker 1961: 53)

The analyst felt stuck. If she remained silent, the patient would feel she has controlled and tamed the bad object and made it, omnipotently, into a tamed good object.

This material shows how De Racker generally translates PI into words via an interpretation, but is also open to remaining silent and containing the material. In other words, she molds her technique with PI to the way the patient imagines they are relating to, controlling, or receiving the analyst.

Pasqual J. Pantone (1994) notes that there are three main methods of managing PI in the analytic situation. He outlines the first as direct verbal interpretations of the deeper anxieties within the transference, which include both genetic and here-and-now links to the patient's PI phantasies. This type of interpretation typically results from the patient's projection, a period of containment and translation within the analyst, and then a deliberate reformulation of the material back to the patient.

The second type of technical approach to PI is what Pantone terms "silent countertransferencial self-analyzing." This would include the regular mental formulation of the patient's material into a proposal, the interpretation. However, the analyst would make the intervention in silence to himself. This would be necessary with patients who for some reason would not be at that moment ready to accept the interpretation, with the analyst's uncertainty of the interpretation, with the possibility of the interpretation becoming a part of a mutual acting out, or with the possibility that the analyst would be regurgitating the patient's projection too quickly and maliciously.

I think another reason to be silent in relation to counter-transference and PI is when the analyst feels overwhelmed by emotion, be it positive or negative. To build a proposal or potential interpretation silently helps steady and calm the overwhelmed analyst until he or she can regain their analytic clarity. At that point it would be necessary to reconsider the validity of the initial silent proposal as it may have been founded on the analyst's own reactions and defenses to the overwhelming PI.

Finally, Pantone cites his third approach to PI as the "here-and-now process interpretation." The analyst includes his own experience in the interpretation, creating affectively toned statements about the current analytic dynamic between patient and analyst.

Pantone illustrates these three technical approaches to PI in a case example. The patient had a father who suffered from kidney problems, and the patient and his mother were in charge of caring for him. Pantone describes how his initial feelings of compassion turned into irritation. This was the result of the patient's subtle ingratiating and passive–aggressive style of relating. He was always trying to be helpful in an irritating manner. The patient picked up on it and a discussion followed, but the patient was unable to explore his deeper feelings toward the analyst. As the analyst began silently to investigate his countertransference, he saw that several dynamics were taking place. There was a PI of a helpless and angry, yet thankful father and a helpful, but upset, angry child. Additionally, the analyst slowly realized he played at least two roles. He was the angry caregiver with a false smile and he was an angry father who resented being infantilized by his sickness. The analyst noted his own phantasy of the patient as a television character who was known to be sickly sweet to everyone, except behind their back. He then shared this image with the patient and explained the affective nature of the analytic relationship that had developed. In other words, he used the image of the character as a vehicle to show the affective flavor of the PI dynamic and the transference that had emerged. These interactions led to a new atmosphere in the analysis that lent itself to more direct interpretations of the PI mechanisms. The patient and analyst were able to discuss the patient's fears of making the analyst ill with all his problems, much as the patient had feared overwhelming his sickly father.

Interestingly, Pantone told the patient that he had not only endured the PI but survived it as well. This seems like a use of reality as suggestion and the encouragement of a mutative experience with a new object. To tell the patient that he has survived the PI might act as a confirmation of the patient's phantasy of harming the analyst. In other words, his interpretation seems to take out the element of fiction. Instead of talking about how the patient imagined injuring the analyst and now is able to imagine an analyst who has survived such imagined dangers, Pantone may be making the patient feel he really is capable of destroying the analyst and was just lucky this time around.

Thomas Ogden (1982: 40) feels the clinical handling of PI should be designed "to make available to the patient in a slightly modified form that which was already his but had been formerly unusable for purposes of integration and psychological growth." Ogden feels that interpretation of PI is essential at certain periods in the analysis, but is not always the best method. He understands the containing function of the analyst to be far better for some patients, particularly more disturbed patients, at certain points in the treatment. He writes:

the perspective of projective identification neither requires nor excludes the use of verbal interpretation; the therapist attempts to find a way of talking with and being with the patient that will constitute a medium through which the therapist may accept unintegrable aspects of the patient's internal world and return them to the patient in a form that the patient can accept and learn from.

(Ogden 1982: 42)

Therefore, he would remain silent during periods of difficulty with certain patients, living with the projections and analyzing them silently, until the time seemed right to verbalize the material as an interpretation.

Regarding technique, Ogden (1982: 50) writes: "once one has begun to formulate an interpretation in terms of projective identification, it is often useful to refrain from interpreting or intervening until one has lived with the evoked feelings for some time."

Overall, Ogden seems to favor a lengthy containment of the patient's projections, a steady self-analysis, and then an interpretation of the analyst's observations in some cases. At each stage, he feels that the interpersonal aspects of the patient are vital to explore, understand, and ultimately incorporate into the interpretation.

Interpersonal

In the literature, many Kleinians bring up the importance of the interpersonal aspects of PI and how it brings the mental mechanism to life in the analytic situation. However, only a few Kleinians have shown, through explicit case material, their belief in using the interpersonal dimensions of PI directly in their interpretations.

Otto Kernberg was trained in South America and his training was Kleinian based. Later, he trained in North America at a more ego-psychology oriented institution. Therefore he is difficult to evaluate regarding his contributions to Kleinian thought. While he has often criticized Kleinian approaches to psychoanalysis, his theoretical and clinical formulations certainly contain many Kleinian influences.

Regarding the analysis of PI, Kernberg favors the use of interpretation and tends to spell out the particular interpersonal and intrapsychic roles the patient is assigning to themselves and to the analyst. One patient tried to make him change scheduled hours and otherwise controlled the relationship, but then felt hurt and ignored by the analyst. Kernberg (1988) writes:

> I was gradually able to point out to the patient how, during the sessions, she was identifying with a controlling and sadistic person who had to demand of me total obedience, while, at the end of the sessions, she experienced me as a sadistic and controlling object who was treating her as worthless.
>
> (Kernberg 1988: 492)

Kernberg states that the patient was then able to understand this as an aspect of her relationship with her mother, combined with role reversals. Kernberg feels that such intrapsychic object relations, played out in the interpersonal realm of PI, are usually defensive and hide another more anxiety-provoking object relation. So, with this same patient, he later stated, "I then suggested that she seemed to want a relationship with me that was like one of a loved and preferred infant only child of a totally dedicated mother" (1988: 493).

In 1987, Kernberg clearly delineates his view of technique with PI. He writes:

> the analyst must diagnose in himself the characteristics of the self- or object-representation projected onto him, so that he can interpret to the patient, first, the nature of this projected representation, second, the motives for the patient's intolerance of that internal experience, and third, the nature of the relation between that projected representation and the one enacted by the patient in the transference at that point.
>
> (Kernberg 1987: 815)

It is within the interpersonal enactment of these self- and object-representations that Kernberg often interprets the PI process.

Spillius has written extensively on the concept of PI. In 1983 she provided material to show her clinical work with the type of PI that is primarily used for communication. Spillius notes the subtle interpersonal way the PI affected the analytic relationship. She writes:

> some years ago I had a woman patient much troubled by perfectionism. She attacked me mercilessly for being imperfect, but in a subtle way that always made me feel I wanted to do

better and that it was my fault I was doing so badly. Eventually she managed to get some insight into the process when I interpreted that she was trying to make me want to be perfect and then to feel discouraged and despairing, just as she expected herself to be perfect and was constantly disappointing herself. Once that made sense, we could link it with her father's exaggerated expectations of her and her constant feeling of failing to live up to his hopes.

(Spillius 1983: 322)

Spillius illustrated her interpretive work with PI in 1992 with more clinical vignettes. With "Mr. A," Spillius states,

I was using the idea of projective identification rather as I think Klein might have done. I thought my patient's perception of me was distorted by his unconscious phantasy of projecting aspects of himself and his internal objects into me. This involved in particular his inability to enjoy anything for its own sake.

(Spillius 1992: 64)

The patient had made some strides in his analysis and had accomplished a major project at work. But he then began to feel much worse. He said he was not creative or of any value and began to blame the analysis for all his misery. In the next hour, he had a phantasy of developing a wonderful research project that would gain him fame. Spillius writes: "I said he was telling me this plan in a way designed to lure me into making some sort of punitive interpretation about his omnipotence . . . and the work we had done to make it possible" (1992: 64). The patient proceeded to ignore the analyst in the grandiose manner he had felt in his phantasy about the project.

In the next hour, this patient reported a dream about going to his home country for a vacation. On the way he saw an accident but no one was hurt. Once home, he heard about his friend Mario getting married and felt left out since he was uninvited. The patient told the analyst he felt worthless and thought poorly of his friend Mario. Spillius writes:

I said I thought Mario represented that part of himself that had been incapable of any sort of relationship with me, but that in recent months this Mario aspect of himself had come into contact with me more and more . . . It was even producing "children" in the form of his research. I suggested that the non-Mario part of himself felt terribly left out of the growing alliance between Mario and me and it had been trying to re-assert its control over both of us.

(Spillius 1992: 65)

The patient responded that Mario's mother was very nice on the surface but wanted her son to be married and successful only for her sake.

Spillius reflects on her technical approach with this patient:

I was using the idea of projective identification in this session rather in the way Klein defines it. My patient was projecting into me his own incapacity to enjoy his success so that I, like Mario's mother, was perceived as wanting to help him for my own sake, not his.

(Spillius 1992: 65)

Looking back on the hour at a later time, Spillius felt she missed the connection in the dream about the collision and the "collision" between her interpretation in the previous session and the patient's experience of it. She thought the patient must have felt partly persecuted by her and tried to retaliate by devaluing her. Indeed, she noticed how she had been pushed to fight back at that point but had used reaction formation to avoid attacking him. Instead, she was more formal and careful than she usually was. Here we see Spillius making important use of the countertransference. She states:

to realize that his getting me to *feel* despised was just as important a projection, and perhaps even more useful for understanding his experience, than knowing about his projection of his inability to enjoy his and my success.

(Spillius 1992: 66; italics in original)

Spillius is clearly involved with this patient's intrapsychic PI dynamics. She is also aware, through countertransference, of how he interpersonally lures her and how she became stiff and formal in response to the patient's projections.

It is interesting to note how Spillius mentions that she is using the concept of PI much in the way Klein thought about it. I think Melanie Klein saw PI as an almost exclusively internal process. She certainly made mention of the effects of the environment on the psychic structure and how there is a reciprocal balance in how the external world always influences and shapes the internal world and vice versa. However, she did not write about the interpersonal aspects of PI. Therefore, it is Spillius who is rightly extending and enriching Klein's concept by including the interpersonal components that are almost always present.

Ogden (1982) illustrates the concept of using countertransference to understand the patient's PI and he emphasizes the interpersonal aspects of PI that trigger the countertransference. In Ogden's example, the patient did not let the analyst have room to ever say much and frequently told him he was incompetent and weak. Gradually, the analyst found himself thinking he was not a strong man or a decent therapist. The analyst began reflecting on his own feelings of weakness in relation to his own father. Only after several months of self-examination did the analyst realize that the patient was evoking in the analyst the same weak son/ strong father dynamic from which the patient was suffering. This realization by the analyst brought significant emotional relief to the analyst. This cleared the way for the analyst to begin looking at how to use his knowledge to help the patient deal with his own struggles with his internalized father/son relations. Ogden emphasizes the importance of the patient's interpersonal actions that provide the motion to PI. In fact, Ogden feels that without the interpersonal aspects of PI it is better termed "simple projection."

I agree with Ogden that the interpersonal dynamics of PI provide the vehicle for the realization of the intrapsychic relating that makes up the patient's phantasies and conflicts. Without it, the analyst has a very difficult task accessing the patient's phantasy life, as even free association includes interpersonal connections. Also, Ogden confirms my comments about it taking a while for the analyst to understand the particular PI situation. For Ogden, it literally took "several months."

Ruth Cycon (1994) writes on the importance of the counter-transference in the technical handling of PI. She also makes direct interpretations about how the patient seems to need to relate to the analyst interpersonally. She writes:

the concept of projective identification can be helpful in understanding the situation when the analyst feels forced to play a particular role or to react in a particular manner, or when certain feelings are stirred up. A long process of working through these countertransference feelings and reactions within oneself is often necessary for the analyst to grasp the complete transference situation and to follow changes within the course of a session.

(Cycon 1994: 450)

She is accenting the constant interplay of interpersonal and intrapsychic.

In discussing patients who appear unreachable in analysis, Betty Joseph (1993) notes that they project their curiosity and interest into the analyst. By remaining silent and distant, the patient manages to make the analyst tense and pressured to make interpretations. Typically, this interpersonal and internal situation results in a superficial and pressured atmosphere in the hour. Joseph writes:

if one examines the experience one can often find that the patient appears to have *projected the active, interested, or concerned part of the self into the analyst, who is then supposed to act out, feeling the pressure, the need to be active and the desire to get something achieved.* Technically I think that the first step is for the analyst to be aware of the projective identification taking place and to be willing to carry it long enough to experience the missing part of the patient. *Then it may become possible to interpret without a sense of pressure, about the process being acted out, rather than about the content of whatever may have been under discussion before.*

(Joseph 1993: 82; italics in original)

Joseph is stressing the importance of interpreting the process going on between patient and analyst, rather than the acting out of it. Holding on to the countertransference experience for a while may be necessary, until the analyst can sort out what the patient is encouraging. In this way, the PI countertransference atmosphere provides clues to the analyst as to what may be going on, beyond the superficial content that is being addressed in the moment.

Modeling

It is rare to find a Kleinian who tried to model behavior for the
patient in their interpretive efforts. However, this is an element of
the PI interpretive stance for Kernberg. This may be yet another
way that, while clearly maintaining strong Kleinian ties, he feels
free to move in other directions.

Kernberg is unique in advocating a modeling of behavior for
patients who use excessive PI and splitting. He feels that these
patients are so used to seeing the world in a black or white fashion
in which they have to win or lose, he models a flexibility within
giving his interpretations. Kernberg writes of one example:

> 'it could be that your reported difficulty getting here was a
> result of your fear that I would be angry with you, or it might
> be that something else was so much on your mind that you
> were preoccupied. I'm not sure, at this point, which is correct,
> and perhaps we can come to understand why you did this'. . . .
> The therapist also indicates a willingness to change an inter-
> pretation based on the patient's subsequent input: 'as you're
> showing me, my original idea no longer seems right. It's more
> likely, given what you just said, that . . .'
>
> (Kernberg *et al.* 1989: 117)

Kernberg (in Kernberg *et al.* 1989) thinks that the rapid oscillation of self- and object-representations that occurs in PI leads to
an undermining of basic ego functions. He points out that appro-
priately timed interpretations of PI will prevent unwanted transference regressions and help the patient retain important ego
boundaries and reality standards. Therefore, he advocates prompt
interpretation of PI whenever ego functions and ego boundaries
appear to be eroding. Kernberg feels this situation occurs primarily
with borderline patients. He states:

> the therapist working with borderline patients, needs to inter-
> pret the primitive projective mechanisms, particularly projective
> identification, which contribute powerfully to the alternating
> projection of self- and object-images, and therefore, to blurring
> the boundary between what is 'inside' and 'outside' in the
> patient's experience of his interactions with the therapist.
>
> (Kernberg *et al.* 1989: 174)

Here, Kernberg is implicitly modeling the alternative to the patient's loss of boundaries. He is saying, "while you may feel we are one, in fact this is the result of x, y, and z. What is really occurring is a, b, and c. But, that may be too painful for you to bear." In interpreting the PI, he is offering a model for a healthy alternative approach. This message is implicit in many analytic approaches; however, Kernberg seems to use it much more openly to support the reality principle with regressed patients.

Voicing

Another area of PI that is very unusual in the literature, at least as represented by verbatim notes, is the analyst's literal voicing of the projective content. In other words, the analyst says, almost play-acting, the words he imagines the ego or object would speak within the particulars of the PI phantasy.

Danielle Quinodoz (1994) believes it technically important to help the patient rediscover their bond with the part of themselves they have projected into the analyst. The analyst becomes a spokesperson for the portion of the patient he has projected and protects it from the other aspects of the patient that wish to harm it. She does this by giving a voice for the part of the patient projected into him. However, Quinodoz feels that by projecting not only a part of herself into the analyst, but certain affects as well, the patient becomes merged with the analyst and is unable to take in or understand interpretations. The analyst then must show the patient that the split-off affects in fact belong to him.

In one clinical example, she responds to a patient who is extremely upset and hostile over the analyst's upcoming vacation. The patient complains that even if she were to wait for years, the analyst does nothing to help her. The analyst replies, "Mummy always wants me to go faster, but I can't go so fast; how painful it is not to be able to go at my own little-girl pace." Quinodoz says the patient immediately calmed down because she now saw herself in the analyst. She then follows up with an interpretation that locates the affect:

> It is as if you needed to put into me a part of yourself that was angry at being dispossessed of its own pace in life and sad at never being able to satisfy the demands of the mother you love. Perhaps, by accusing me of not getting a move on, it is as if

you were expressing yourself in the way you imagine your
mother would have done.

(Quinodoz 1994: 758)

The patient was then able to emerge from the con-fusion of self
and object and perceive not only herself more clearly but her own
parents as well. Therefore, Quinodoz first feeds back the literal
result of the patient's PI by speaking for the projected object or
aspect of self. Later, she interprets the sequence, the motives, and
the affects of the PI. This explanatory interpretation is what helps
the patient make an internal and external differentiation and allows
the ego to reorganize the internal world.

In another case example, Quinodoz discusses a patient who was
attending his third hour of analysis. As a boy, this patient had
suffered loneliness for his depressed mother. She killed herself
when he was a teenager. The analyst felt that because of the early
nature of the therapeutic process she would best serve the patient
by using his own feelings when interpreting PI. Rather than speaking for the projected parts of self or object, the analyst com-
municates his own countertransference to the patient. When the
patient mentioned that he had expected to forget the appointment,
the analyst replied, "Hearing you tell me that, I felt like a little boy
who is so sad because he does not know how to make his mother
feel that she really has a place in life" (1994: 759). Later in the
analysis, the analyst felt it best to interpret the PI process as a
spokesperson for the projected object. The patient was feeling
passive, sad, and put upon. The analyst interpreted, "Mummy is
complaining that she is so exhausted from life; how could I make
her interested in living? I am so sad that I don't know how to help
her find a zest for life."

As before, the analyst followed this PI interpretation up with a
more explanatory comment:

perhaps you needed to put a part of yourself into me, a part
with emotions which you could not put into words yourself, as
if you wanted me to feel your distress at your mother's complaints and put them into words in your place. Maybe, you
without realizing it, complained to me in the same way you
imagined your mother might have done.

(Quinodoz 1994: 759)

The patient then felt more alive and a part of the hour as the result of becoming differentiated from the object. Finally, this method of interpreting PI combines countertransference, here-and-now focus along with genetic reconstruction, and direct verbalization of the self and object phantasies. In reviewing the literature, the way the analyst play-acts the projection is unique to Quinodoz. However, I suspect that in actual clinical practice there are many other analysts who use this technique, in limited ways. For example, I was seeing a patient who grew up with an abusive mother and a very ineffectual father. As an adult, my patient felt trapped in his job and bullied by his boss. During one session when he was telling me many details about how his boss was being abusive, I said, "Where is my father? I wish he would come and save me from this and make it better." This voicing interpretation was based on my sense that he felt unable to stand up to his boss/mother and wanted help, but also that he wouldn't attempt to stand up and instead was waiting for father to intervene and rescue him. My patient was silent for many minutes. Then, he said, "I have never thought of it like that. I think you are absolutely right, but the horrible feeling I am left with in my life is that my father was never an ally. There was never a shred of possibility that he could intervene for me. I think I long for that and wish for that, but I am trapped with the feeling that he was never and will never be capable of standing up to my mother." His associations went on for quite some time and opened up new avenues for us to explore his rage at his father, his identification with his father, and his abandonment of his father as a good and supportive presence in my patient's mind. So, the voicing interpretation can sometimes be helpful in widening certain moments in the analytic process.

Body language

Klein originally used "body language" in her interpretations. Some Kleinians still do, including in their analysis of PI.

James Grotstein writes of a borderline patient who reported a dream prior to the analyst's summer vacation. In the dream, a prostitute put her tongue into his penis and into his bladder. The woman seemed like a witch. The patient woke up and was disgusted. He groaned and it reminded him of his mother's sounds of sexual pleasure he had overheard as a child. Grotstein writes:

I interpreted to him that his bladder was full of feelings from his stomach about a mommy-me who was going away for a holiday with her analytic husband and taking the breast from him. The patient said, "you're way off today, Grotstein!" I then interpreted to the patient that, indeed, my interpretation may have been "way off" or might have been "right on". His fear of accepting the interpretation has to do, I suggested, with a fear that his urine had turned a caretaking "toilet breast" mommy-me – who was trying to help him with his pain by taking it away – into a victim of his urinary attack and into a person who would then, as a witch, urinate right back into him.

(Grotstein 1986: 197)

This patient felt Grotstein was accurate and began associating to fears of intimacy and how he would recoil and distance himself from people out of fright. He said he was afraid that his neediness would harm the person he became close to. He also felt his neediness must have caused his wife's cancer. Grotstein writes, "I was able to talk to the patient about his experience of a long history of empathic failures in which he had gotten the idea that his own neediness, including his urinary needs, was bad and destructive" (1986: 198). The patient reported that his stomach pain ceased at that moment. Clearly, Grotstein utilizes the body language Klein used with children and adults. He is also careful to explain, in the context of body language, what exactly is occurring in the patient's phantasy and what the central anxiety may be about.

I suspect what makes this interpretation work so well is a strong attachment and sense of understanding already in place between patient and analyst, as well as Grotstein's careful explanation of the patient's core phantasies and central fears. Otherwise, it might be alienating or frightening to the patient.

Mason (1987) responded to a case presentation by offering what he might do if it were his case. He felt the patient was involved in PI mechanisms and was a paranoid character. Mason writes:

when Dr. Silverman, listening to her complaints about waiting, thinks she is associating to her impending bill, the two-day weekend, and the upcoming vacation, I would have spoken. (I interpret: you are angry at the oncoming weekend and holiday, which brings back the feelings of a small child being left out and rejected for someone else. The mommy-me doesn't clean up and relieve you, but makes you wait while she goes off with the big father. You almost didn't come here today so that I should have the painful left-out feelings instead of you.)

(Mason 1987: 192)

A bit later in the hour, Mason states he would have interpreted the patient's anxieties about men, penises, and what she is lacking. He writes:

[I interpret:] my weekend and holiday cause you to hate the father-me for going off with my wife-mother but also because I have all the big 'things' to do it with. These things are like father's penis, which enables him to get into and possess mommy, and his mind, which fills her with ideas and conversation like his penis filled her with excitement and babies. You also hate the child part of yourself that can't speak and that has only a little girl's genital, and call it dumb, stupid, and a 'nothing'.

(Mason 1987: 194)

While using some of the patient's vocabulary, Mason also freely uses body language and referencing to deeply unconscious phantasies. He interprets the oedipal conflict inherent in the PI, linking the external situation of change and loss with the patient's internal experience of oedipal competition and feelings of inferiority.

Again, my own clinical experiences are that these types of interpretations are only helpful if there is a history of this type of language being used, along with a solid background of understanding and trust. Otherwise, the patient, especially if borderline or psychotic, can easily take the interpretation and make it into a persecutory attack or a sudden derailment in therapeutic mutuality.

Dreams

Some Kleinians are able to notice, explore, and interpret the PI mechanisms within dreams. When the patient reports a dream, these Kleinians locate the particulars of the PI dynamic in the dream and show the patient certain aspects of it. Sidney Klein, Caper, and Meltzer all illustrate this approach. Naturally, their interpretations show other dynamics being analyzed at the same time.

Sydney Klein (1981) describes a patient who made extensive use of PI. The analysis had been lifeless and lacking in any spontaneous emotional response. The patient had no overt hostility and little immediacy of feelings in general. Klein says he consistently drew the patient's attention to this apparent retreat and a short time later the patient presented two dreams on a Monday hour. The first dream was of her, the patient, driving up a hill in a red car. She told the analyst that without him over the weekend, she felt like a small child who couldn't go forward. The patient then told the second dream. She was lying in a hospital bed with her mother and there were cockroaches in the room. The mother was angry with the nurse, but the patient was calm. The patient associated to an operation in her teens after which her mother had been angry with the nurse for the room being untidy. Klein writes:

> I interpreted that she was afraid that I was like her mother and could not tolerate anything dirty in her like a cockroach, but this was also because she was putting into me her own impatience and intolerance of anything which was not ideal. She agreed and said rather ruefully that she supposed she expects a land of milk and honey.
>
> (S. Klein 1981: 106)

The patient went on to say how she hated cockroaches and remembered killing one that frightened her girlfriend. Klein recalled that the patient had recently mentioned how this girlfriend had started analysis and was doing well in it. Klein thought the patient must be secretly jealous of this girlfriend who in the patient's phantasy was seeing Klein. Therefore, Klein says:

> I interpreted that she turned me into a dirty cockroach and killed me off because of the hatred and jealousy that she experienced toward me at the weekend as a pregnant mother containing her baby sister and father's penis instead of being the ideal mother and breast who was there just for her.
>
> (S. Klein 1981: 106)

The patient responded by saying she didn't understand and referred to her husband who often told her she was blind to the point being made. Then she said, "it's only like this when you talk about separation." Klein writes, "I said that she kept herself in a shell in order to avoid the painful feelings I had just described." Klein illustrates the value of interpreting PI not only within the here-and-now transference atmosphere but from the patient's dream material as well. He also is keen to use the patient's genetic associations for information about the current state of the transference. In this specific case example, Klein makes an interpretation that appears to include remarks about both the patient's paranoid-schizoid anxieties as well as her more oedipal and depressive worries. Finally, he also makes use of body language in his interpretation.

Caper (1997) illustrates his interpretative stance with PI dreams by discussing a patient who pushed him to become a part of the patient's own critical and devaluing feelings. The patient had told the analyst of a plan to get an insurance company to overpay him. The plan was based on an illogical bit of reasoning that was a product of the patient's grandiosity. Caper felt pulled to show the patient the inconsistencies of his reasoning and went on to debate reality with him. Rather than analyzing the patient's grandiose phantasy, Caper was pulled to act out a debate over who was wiser and more astute.

The next hour, the patient brought in a dream. In the dream, the patient was holding his erect penis on a couch and another man was dilating his own anus. The man told the patient to put his penis in his anus. When the man pulled his fingers out of his anus for the penetration, they were covered in feces. The patient told the man he was disgusted and would never have sex with him. Caper writes:

> I said that the dream seemed to represent his subjective experience of the previous session, in which he felt that I was motivated by a desire to cast doubt on what was really a potent and ingenious plan to remodel and improve his house and his personality. My words were not meaningful, but simply sounds indicating that I was dilating my anus in preparation for covering his erect penis – his potent plan – with shit (disguised as interpretations) while triumphing over him in the process . . . [in the last hour, he felt as though he had almost fallen] prey to what he regarded unconsciously as my impotent, homosexual, anal obsessions with nonexistent structural problems, which would undermine what he considered to be his manly, can-do attitude.
>
> (Caper 1997: 25)

Caper is able to interpret the PI process that was occurring in the dream as a reflection of the PI process that took place in the prior session. This is a useful way of linking pieces of an ongoing PI dynamic that was still unresolved. It also shows Caper's understanding of the interpersonal, acting out aspects of PI that went into the dynamic. He chooses to not interpret them, but rather focus on the nature of the PI phantasy they managed to act out together.

Meltzer (1990) discusses a patient whose relation to internal objects was shaped by anal character pathology, a "pseudo-maturity," and PI. The patient related a dream about a murderer among gravestones, wandering about. The patient told his friends to not worry and he went on to try to lead the murderer to the bottom of a hill where he might confess his crimes. The patient associated to feeling the back of his teeth with his tongue, and they felt old and cracked. He also thought of putting on slippers like his father used to. Meltzer writes:

> [I interpreted] that his teeth are represented by the gravestones and his tongue as the murderer among his victims. His device in the dream is to rid his mouth of these dangerous qualities and transform them into slippery fingers which can be led down to his bottom, where the victims can be identified in his feces. But this device his finger-in-his-bottom, becomes confused with father's penis-in-mother's-vagina, an important source of the Nazi-daddy-who-kills-mummy's-Jewish babies whom we know so well from earlier work.
>
> (Meltzer 1990: 108)

Several weeks later, the patient arrived late and tracked mud into the office. The patient said he had "rubbishy" dreams over the weekend and didn't want to burden the analyst with them. Meltzer interpreted, "this conscious wish to spare is contrasted by an unconscious wish to dirty the analyst inside and out with his feces, a bit of which has been acted out by tracking the dirt into the room" (1990: 109). Meltzer seems to feel it best to go directly to the patient's core anxiety by interpreting the PI involved in the unconscious phantasy. He uses body language and the language of the unconscious, in terms of part objects and the place of feces, urine, penises, and vaginas. The dream material is approached as containing PI data identical to PI processes that can occur during the actual hour.

Finally, Meltzer, while seeming to make theoretical jumps from what the patient says, in fact listens very closely to the patient's associations to their dreams and their moment-to-moment feelings. He constructs his interpretation on that association and proceeds to outline the exact nature of the PI phantasy he believes the patient is currently working within.

Motivation and goals

Some Kleinians directly bring the patient's unconscious motivation behind the PI endeavor into their interpretive stance. Along with other features, the analyst highlights the ego's goals or aims. Steiner, Cycon, and Joseph represent this group.

John Steiner (1993) has written on patients who have lost parts of themselves through excessive PI. This leaves them feeling overly concrete and unable to mourn any object-related losses. He discusses the treatment of such patients and how to reverse such pathological PI processes. Steiner presents material concerning a "Mrs B" and shows how he interprets several aspects of her PI process, including the unconscious motivation behind it and the exact nature of her PI phantasies. She spent much of her time complaining, asking the analyst to tell her what to do, and generally filling the hours with whining and misery. Steiner felt she probably could not think clearly because of how she filled the hours with these complaints. She had resented most people, especially her family, from a young age. At the same time, she felt her home life was so oppressive that she was unable to rebel or complain. When she went to college, she was able to become independent and confident for the first time. Steiner reflects that this new capacity to think for herself threatened the former mental equilibrium and she had a breakdown in her second year of school. Steiner writes:

> thinking was permitted if it did not challenge an existing order which preserved her status quo, she could not think for herself and she had to make it clear that it was unfair to expect her even to attempt this.
>
> (Steiner 1993: 57)

The patient arrived late one day and said she hadn't been able to get away from a friend who wanted to talk with her. The patient then presented a dream about going underground and having to choose between two paths. One path went to town and one to home. She had a garden sickle in her hand. Finally, she realized her inability to decide on what path to take made it useless to go to town. She was happy with this because she could go home and do some gardening on her overgrown garden. The sickle was a tool she had borrowed from a neighbor. She hated the sharp thing and felt guilty for borrowing it and never using it.

Steiner felt this patient was using PI within the dream as well as the transference. He writes:

> I interpreted that the choice in . . . her dream represented the conflict . . . between doing the painful analytic work and fleeing from it . . . I connected her lateness . . . with her reluctance to leave a comfortable situation and use her intelligence in the session where, as in her garden at home, there was a lot of work to be done.
>
> (Steiner 1993: 57)

The patient responded by feeling criticized at having more work to do, as if the analyst was calling her ill. She complained that she was being put down and told she had to work harder. Steiner writes:

> I suggested that part of her despair at the idea of work was connected with her fear of using her intelligence which she knew could be sharp and hurtful like the gardening sickle but was also necessary for useful work. I thought she was afraid to use her intelligence because she was afraid that it could be used to attack me more openly and that this would be dangerous. She preferred to leave the responsibility for thinking in me and to watch how I worked, pouncing on me when I did something wrong . . . Thinking for herself, having desires and taking responsibility for herself was forbidden and the capacity to carry out these activities was projected.
>
> (Steiner 1993: 57–58)

Steiner shows how he is able to gather the interpretation from strands of extra-transference material, dream material, and particular, repetitious phantasies the patient has. His PI interpretations pointed out to the patient not only the direct transference implications of her PI, but the general nature of her mind and how it defends itself. He showed her how the aim of her PI was to hide her sickle-like intelligence and to protect the analyst. In other words, in making his interpretations, he clearly takes into account the patient's depressive anxieties over harming the object and the use of PI to save the internal relationship to the object.

Cycon (1994) seems to put a focus on the importance of showing the patient their phantasy of influencing or possibly damaging the analyst in their PI efforts. The patient's depressive fears about their actions upon their internal objects are detailed in his interpretation. After a patient told Cycon of a dream, Cycon states:

> I tried to show the patient how I thought that my inter-pretation of her dream had made her worry about whether I was able to stand and understand the feelings she had caused me by telling me the dream, and telling it in the way she did. Perhaps she was afraid that I, feeling hurt and angry, had withdrawn in to a world of thoughts, which shut out her feelings. She seemed somewhat relieved by this interpretation. She cried and said that sometimes she was able to have good experiences with me. But she could not imagine ever letting me know that, because it would be unbearable for her if she detected any satisfaction in my voice or face.
>
> (Cycon 1994: 449)

Cycon showed her, through his interpretation, how she tried to protect the analyst. This interpretation led her to elaborate and add information about her envy of the analyst's satisfaction.

Betty Joseph feels that it is critical to try to evaluate whether the patient is primarily using PI to communicate a state of mind that they cannot verbalize or to primarily attack and control the analyst. This goal would then be articulated to the patient.

One patient was feeling very hopeless and felt weak and full of despair. He mentioned that he noticed the different changes in the analyst's voice and in other people's voices. Joseph writes:

> I showed [him] his great fear that I showed with my voice, rather than through my actual words, that I could not stand the extent of his hopelessness and his doubts about myself, about what we could achieve in the analysis, and, therefore, in his life, and that I would cheat and in some way try to

encourage. I queried whether he had perhaps felt that, in that session, my voice had changed in order to sound more encouraging and encouraged, rather than contain the despair he was expressing. By this part of the session, my patient had got into contact and said with some relief that, if I did do this kind of encouraging, the whole bottom would fall out of the analysis.

(Joseph 1993: 176)

Joseph explains:

I could understand [the nature of the patient's communication] primarily through my countertransference, through the way in which I was being pushed and pulled to feel and to react. We see here the concrete quality of projective identification structuring the countertransference.

(Joseph 1993: 176)

It appears that Joseph interpreted the PI as both a communication and an attack. She shows the patient how he may be trying to deposit his despair into her, but then becomes worried that she is overwhelmed by it. He then tries to rescue the analyst by projecting encouragement into her, feeling she is unable to cope with or contain his anxieties. Technically, Joseph sums up her approach to PI by stating,

I am suggesting that if we listen to our patients first of all from the angle of the object relationship that is alive at the moment, this will enable us to see better the nature of the patient's conflicts and his methods of maintaining his psychic balance.

(Joseph 1993: 208)

She tries to show the patient the full extent of his unconscious aims that are being carried out through PI efforts.

In discussing a patient, James Grotstein (1986) shows how his theoretical impressions color the type of interpretation he makes in regard to both aims and motivation of the PI mechanism. The patient had an omnipotent phantasy that his cigarette smoking might magically convert the analyst into a cigarette smoker. The analyst interpreted the patient's phantasy of poisoning the analyst and that seemed to alleviate some of the patient's fears of hurting the analyst. Most of Grotstein's interpretations concentrated on the patient's fear of failing to convert or influence the analyst (1986: 195). This is in line with Grotstein's belief that, especially with more disturbed patients, the leading anxiety concerns the failure to "get it right" and be able to make an impact on their object. When interpreting the goals of PI, his comments are shaped by specific theoretical ideas about intrapsychic goals.

Michael Feldman (1994) has noted the technical difficulties PI creates and how the analyst must struggle to find the best clinical stance with the PI process. He writes of one difficult patient:

> it has often proved both unsatisfactory and ineffective to focus on the contents of the patient's material, without recognizing the function her communications serve in the analytic inter-action. It became evident that there was no point in trying to engage her as if she could make use of certain mental functions when these had already been disowned and projected into me. Nor could she make use of interpretations when she experienced the interpretive process as threatening and intrusive.
>
> (Feldman 1994: 427)

Feldman is saying that PI can easily subsume certain ego functions, and therefore the observing or rational aspect of the patient is an intricate element of the PI mechanism. In addition, the analyst faces very difficult moments when the patient feels the analytic method is a dangerous foe of some sort. For his patient, Feldman says, "the very process of communication between two people was often confused with physical or sexual touching or intrusion" (1994: 434).

Feldman describes his intervention with this patient's PI. He writes:

> after the period of tense silence, I began to make explicit what I thought was taking place between us. I said she had brought something into the session, and once she had told me, she expected me to think about it, make connections, and attach meaning to what I had heard. I thought this meant I was almost completely responsible for something difficult and disturbing. If I then tried to talk about what she had told me, perhaps making links that might exist to the situation between us, in this analysis, I thought she was liable to react as if I were

trying to do something awful to her, to get rid of something she had left with me, pushing it back to her.

(Feldman 1994: 430)

Feldman's patient relaxed a bit after his interpretation and made associations to how she viewed herself and her thoughts. Feldman points out that this particular patient was rather difficult to approach technically, as she had phantasies about each interpretation that then prompted her to make different and more complex PI maneuvers. Her fearing the analyst was so anxious or angry with what she had projected into him that he would retaliate in some way often prompted this. To this, Feldman interpreted, "that she did indeed seem very preoccupied with who knew what and what one did with knowledge" (1994: 431). Therefore, he alerts us to the importance of what PI can do to the analytic relationship and what interpretations of that influenced relationship can do to the patient's phantasies. This is often the case in a clinical hour, that the analysis of one PI phantasy either unveils another or triggers another.

Cycon (1994) describes a patient who on the one hand idealized the analyst. The patient was then able to subsume those qualities as her own. Meanwhile, the analyst was felt to be weak and worthless. Cycon writes:

I told the patient that she wanted to show me in a very specific way what 'being understood' meant for her, namely, not feeling dependent on my agreement with an analysis. I also tried to show her that she had evidently left the question of whether an analysis could help her up to me.

(Cycon 1994: 443)

So, Cycon not only interprets the patient's actions, anchored in the PI process, but what the nature of the intrapsychic communication is.

Extra-transference

Most Kleinians emphasize the immediate transference situation in their interpretive focus. However, some include extra-transference interpretations in their work with PI. Segal and Grotstein are among these analysts.

While this type of PI interpretation is very limited in the literature, I suspect it is much more common in clinical practice. I think it is always the norm for analysts to emphasize their transference work in their write-ups as that is what is considered our bread and butter. However, I think there are probably many sessions or parts of sessions in which every analyst finds themselves trying to understand the patient through extra-transference means. The analytic goal remains the same, but the transference isn't always readily accessible. PI is often the clue or set of clues that brings us back to understanding the link between extra-transference issues and the transference proper.

Segal (1990) illustrates how PI is found in dreams and must be interpreted as any other PI dynamic would be. In doing so, she also makes an extra-transference PI interpretation. Segal writes:

> this patient made very extensive use of [PI]. She had been in analysis previously with Dr. Z, who later left her by emigrating from this country. For the first few days of the analysis with me, my patient could make no contact, feeling only acutely anxious, empty, and depersonalized. After some interpreting on my part, she told me of the following dream: 'Dr. Z was sitting in an armchair in a foreign-looking flat and her belly was enormous, as though she was pregnant with a monstrous baby.' I interpreted that the monstrous baby was herself, and that she had put herself into Dr. Z and traveled with her to the foreign-looking flat. After this interpretation the patient became less depersonalized and could establish contact with me.
>
> (Segal 1990: 138)

It appears that Segal administered to the patient's greatest level of anxiety, the lack of contact with the prior analyst and her desire to be inside of the former analyst. This separation anxiety created distance between the patient and the current analyst, which was rectified by the extra-transference interpretation which addressed that tension.

Grotstein (1994) analyzed a man who had been abused and molested by his mother. The father divorced the mother when the patient was seven. Upon starting treatment, he started to break up his relationship with his girlfriend and treated her cruelly. He felt she was clinging, possessive, and infantile. Grotstein writes:

I interpreted to the patient, first, that, having begun analysis, his apparently shameful infant-like, dependent feelings had surfaced and that he now felt helpless and endangered *vis-à-vis* me as a mother who was attempting to disarm him only to attack him when his guard was down (a happening that often occurred when he was little). He hated these vulnerable feelings so much that he projected them into his mother whom he later began to victimize and now projected them into his girlfriend, toward whom he felt contempt. She was now the translocation of the disgusting, devalued, and vulnerable little boy that he never wanted to be . . .

(Grotstein 1994: 744)

This clinical example shows how Grotstein's interpretation of PI links the patient's past experiences, external objects and situations in his life, and the transference with the analyst. The analyst combines his extra-transference remarks with other portions of the overall PI analysis.

Segal (1977) describes a patient who had a fear of restaurants. She had been invited out to lunch but was terrified. Segal writes:

I reminded the patient of her childhood fear of wetting her pants in the restaurant and connected it with the dream in which the child pees in the soup. I interpreted her terror of the restaurant as a result of her [PI], the restaurant standing for the feeding mother. She felt that she had thrown her urine and feces and parts of herself into all the people in the restaurant as well as into the food. She, therefore, became depersonalized, afraid of the people containing bad parts of herself, and of the food bunged-up with her excrement. Then she had to avoid the restaurant so as not to have to reintroject this mess.

(Segal 1977: 141)

Here we see Segal using more body language in her interpretations and making very deep comments about the nature of the patient's phantasies. She also brings in a genetic link, involving a childhood fear. Segal not only interpreted the patient's attack on her internal mother, but her fear of confronting and taking in that damaged and angry mother. This particular example is one in which Segal does not include herself. It is an extra-transference interpretation of PI. Interestingly, Segal mentions in a postscript to that case that she would now handle the case differently. She states that she now would place a much greater emphasis on "showing her what she was actually doing in the session in the moment-to-moment interaction between us. I would concentrate less on the detailed content of her phantasies and dreams" (1977: 144).

Loss and separation

Issues of separation, loss, and PI are under-represented in verbatim clinical reports of Kleinian interpretations.

Segal (1997) reminds us that some PI situations are only understandable after the fact. Segal's patient had lost her mother, when a child, to a car accident in which her father had been the driver. Segal writes:

> one day she gave me a rather frightening account of how recklessly she drove her motor bike. The next day, she missed the session without letting me know – which had never happened before. I was exceedingly anxious, and also guilty, wondering what I could have done to induce her to have an accident. The next day, she turned up, cool as a cucumber, and I was furious. I recognized, however, that she had inflicted on me an experience of her own, of waiting for her parents to return home, and being told of the accident. But that recognition came to me only after her return. In between, I had been dominated by her projections.
>
> (Segal 1997: 113)

Segal was grappling with the countertransference that PI usually generates. It is usually only later that the analyst can sort out what has happened. Segal experienced the patient's chronic sense of loss through a PI transmission which shaped Segal's countertransference. Only later could she bring it back to the patient in the form of an interpretation.

Grotstein (1986) feels that PI takes many forms, including the difficulties of separation and loss between internal objects. One patient began the hour by disparaging a plant in the analyst's office. The patient used to think of herself as a poor gardener but now she felt like she had a "green thumb." Then she added that while she was making progress in her life, her analysis felt flat. Grotstein writes:

I made the following interpretations: the weekend break caused you to feel that I had taken the good green breast with me for the weekend, leaving you with a barren and desolate backyard to cultivate. You then had a phantasy about entering into me, stealing my venture, possessing it for yourself, and identifying with it as the possessor of a 'green thumb' which had no connection to me, and therefore you owed me no gratitude. At the same time, I am now believed to be the container of your undesired barren self which cannot make things grow. We have exchanged roles.

(Grotstein 1986: 182)

The patient made associations in the direction of the interpretation, at first directly and then by displacement. Grotstein made an immediate interpretation of the PI processes and analyzed the deeper phantasy material. Also, he makes use of body language. He used all these elements to address the sense of loss, separation, and loneliness that the patient communicated through PI.

In 1992, Spillius explored PI in the clinical setting:

This session was dramatic and painful – no question of maintaining my usual analytic stance on this day. In phantasy the patient was projecting a painful internal situation into me and acting in such a way as to get me to experience it while she got rid of it.

(Spillius 1992: 66)

With high expectations of herself, this patient often felt inferior and inadequate. She eliminated these self-attacks by not aspiring to much and by feeling powerless. Separations were difficult for her and this hour was right before an unusually long break. After a long and tense silence, Spillius said she thought the patient was angry. Then, the patient began to complain about things which she said were all petty. Spillius tried to comment again but the patient escalated into paranoia. She felt the analyst was manipulating her and hurting her. This left Spillius feeling like a failure as an analyst; she writes:

But I managed one small thought, which was that she must be feeling inadequate too, and that my leaving had a lot to do with it. Then came a second thought, that she hates herself for being cruel even though she gets excited by it. It felt to me as if I was like a damaged animal making her feel guilty, and she wanted to stamp me out.

I said she couldn't bear for me to know how painfully attacking she is, how much she wants to hurt me, how cruel she feels; but she also can't stand it if I don't know, don't react. It means she is unimportant.

(Spillius 1992: 67)

Screaming at Spillius, the patient said she was totally uninterested in what had been said. Spillius cautiously interpreted:

what I said . . . was that I thought she felt I treated her cruelly, with complete scorn and indifference, as if she was boring and utterly uninteresting, and that was why I was leaving her. She felt that the only way she could really get this through to me was by making me suffer in the same way . . . I said she thought I was cruel for leaving her on her own so arbitrarily and that she therefore had a right to attack me in kind. But she also felt I was leaving her because she was so attacking.

(Spillius 1992: 67–68)

Spillius explains the PI dynamics that held sway in the hour:

My self-doubt was, I believe, very similar to her feelings of unlovableness when her parent had left her. It was also very similar to the picture she painted of her parents, who had cruelly left her but felt very guilty and self-critical about it. Failure, damage, and imperfection were rampant in both of us. Her answer was to get the worst of it into me and then attack and abandon me. She became the cruel me who was leaving her and the cruel parents who had left her, and I became the stupid, miserable child fit only for abandonment.

(Spillius 1992: 69)

In 1994, Elizabeth Bott Spillius stated, "the basic features of Kleinian technique are . . . interpretation of anxiety and defense together rather then either on its own" (p. 348). This technical strategy was used in the moment-to-moment analytic work of her previous 1992 case example. She addressed both the anxiety concerning loss and abandonment, as well as the patient's defenses against it.

I find loss and separation issues to be at the heart of many difficult analytic situations and I think loss plays a major part in our most difficult cases. Specifically, I (Waska 2002) think loss is at the root of many paranoid-schizoid patients' use of PI mechanisms and in their struggle with their internal objects. Perhaps because it is such a common, overarching theme that colors the transference in most analysts' cases, and because of the anxiety issues of loss bring up in both analyst and patient, it is all the more difficult for the analyst to notice and interpret.

Timing

Timing is an important element of basic technique. The verbatim examples of timing in PI interpretations are sparse. However, Malcolm and David Rosenfeld provide a few.

In 1987, Malcolm discussed a patient who felt very persecuted and hostile. He saw the analyst as useless and cruel. After the analyst contained some of his projected anxieties, he felt better. At that point, his method of relating shifted. Malcolm writes:

> by multiple projective identification, we both became split. There we were, he and I, talking animatedly and in a friendly way to each other, but the issues we talked about (that is, his feelings and problems) were spread among many other people. Through this behavior he felt he could control me, and feel safe and friendly toward me. But the relationship is sterile, and new anxieties come to the fore – about disintegration and collapse. This could only be modified by persistent work of mine, showing the patient, in the very moment he was doing it, what he was doing, and how he did it.
>
> (Malcolm 1987: 316)

Malcolm explains how she shows the patient the intrapsychic maneuvers he makes at that exact moment in the hour, within the context of the analytic relationship. She had to be exact with this patient about the PI as it occurred, following each layer as it unfolded.

David Rosenfeld outlines his clinical approach with PI:

> The patient makes the therapist experience intense and violent emotions, which he cannot express in words. This is the analyst's paramount task: to be able to tolerate such emotions for days, weeks, months, or years and to decode them and translate them into words, with the appropriate timing.
>
> (Rosenfeld 1992: 4)

Later, he writes:

> The analyst must help the patient to recover what he has got rid of (not only objects and emotions, but also ego functions which the patient has got rid of through projective identification).
>
> (Rosenfeld 1992: 5)

Containment, use of timing, and providing words for the projections are what Rosenfeld feels is most important. He writes:

> Through projective identification, the psychotic patient projects parts of his ego into the therapist. The ego parts that do not function in the patient have to be contained by the therapist, who must wait for the right time to interpret them and give the patient back the parts of his projected self.
>
> (Rosenfeld 1992: 12)

Later, he cautions against premature interpretation of projections as it will increase the patient's anxiety. Rosenfeld emphasizes the important role of correct technical handling of PI and the issue of timing when he says,

> if the patient finds out that there is somebody capable of containing or tolerating unbearable feelings, while before he thought there was no one capable of doing that, this may mean the beginning of a new conception of the bond and of human relations.
>
> (Rosenfeld 1992: 13)

In 1990, O'Shaughnessy wrote of a patient, "M," who was a liar and used PI as a way of being with his analyst. "M" feared destroying his objects with lies, yet he felt great gratification and excitement in lying. By lying, he forced the analyst to become hurt and controlled. He identified with that role of martyr and expected the analyst to be sadistic with him. O'Shaughnessy wrote:

> M was often lost in masochistic phantasies during his sessions and he avidly sought to hear interpretations as sadistic beatings. This was the reason why I did not interpret his hatred in the initial stages of the analysis. His fear of a murderous superego made him instantly twist away from my one or two attempts to speak about his hatred and misunderstanding what I had said as a concrete gratification of his masochism. I am not sure, though, that I was right to delay; not interpreting the hatred he was expressing with his lying made him fear I would not, or could not, recognize it, and increased also his conviction of my masochism.
>
> (O'Shaughnessy 1990: 192)

She is noting the need to verbalize the nature of the patient's PI, even when it temporarily may reinforce or repeat certain pathological phantasies. In fact, to not interpret the particulars of the PI can leave the patient to deal with overwhelming anxieties of, in this case, torturing the analyst and phantasies of bringing out her own masochism. The use of timing was crucial in the interpretation of this patient's PI.

Here, O'Shaughnessy is also noting a technical matter concerning the interpretation of PI. She, and several other Kleinians already quoted, see the danger of not interpreting PI as generally overriding the problems or repetitions of pathology that may occur when making the PI interpretation. In my clinical experience, to not interpret PI, one must have very specific reasoning that has to do with particular aspects of the patient's phantasies and their unique transference profile. Otherwise, it is usually best to find a way to show the patient, through interpretation, their PI expression of fear, love, hatred, and other affects, as well as the communicative function within the PI process.

Direction of anxieties and phantasies

Some Kleinians feel the interpretation of PI should take into account what direction the patient's anxiety or phantasy takes. In other words, whether the interpretation be directed at the patient's PI phantasy of the object or at the state of the patient's ego is a technical concern.

In 1995, Malcolm made several distinctions concerning the interpretation of PI. She felt that if the patient functions mostly within the paranoid-schizoid position (Klein 1946), they would make extensive use of PI mechanisms. Therefore, she says the interpretations should center on the patient's phantasies of what is inside the analyst. This is in contrast to patients in the depressive position (Klein 1935) whose phantasies are more about what they contain or are responsible for.

In her analysis of a patient suffering from more paranoid-schizoid anxieties, Malcolm writes:

> my interpretation was based on what I was thinking about, but I only drew my patient's attention to the points I have just mentioned. I spoke mainly about two things: her perception of me and her defenses. What I interpreted was that I had become (in the transference) a bad object, and how she felt and what she did to create this. I described the defenses she used against the resulting situation as well as the way she acted them out with her family. In considering where, it was I who was felt to be bad, containing her mixed feelings. The interpretation was orientated to the analyst because that was where the problem seemed to be . . .
>
> (Malcolm 1995: 451)

Again, Malcolm shows how she makes extensive use of the countertransference in interpreting PI. In addition, she is sensitive to the nature of the patient's anxiety that is being processed through PI and tries to locate her interpretation accordingly.

In some respects, using the concept of direction in making PI interpretations can be fairly easy with patients. The paranoid-schizoid patient is typically quite direct about how they feel persecuted by the object. So, the analyst is often shown via the transference and PI what the fears are about the object and what the dangerous elements are. It follows that the analyst can readily interpret the patient's defenses that emerge in their attempts to manage that unreliable or threatening object.

However, some cases are more complicated. Some patients, fluctuating between paranoid-schizoid and primitive depressive concerns, will focus on paranoid phantasies rather than expose their feelings of grief about the loss of the object or their terror of harming or destroying the object. In addition, their phantasies often include terror at the retaliation from that destroyed object (Waska 2003). So, the idea of direction in interpretation can become cloudy. Often, there are multiple directions.

Chapter 3

What the literature states about clinical technique

While hundreds of articles and dozens of books on the subject of PI have appeared in the last twenty years, most pertain to theory. This body of literature is dedicated to a theoretical exploration of the various intrapsychic and interpersonal meanings and motivations behind the PI process. Technique is rarely addressed. For the most part, there is a minimal amount of case material to illustrate the theory. Without many actual verbatim accounts, the reader is left to assume there is a one-to-one correlation between theory and technique. When an author discusses a particular type of PI in patients, one has to guess that the analyst would then attempt to analyze that manifestation of PI directly. I tried to avoid these assumptions by limiting my survey of the literature to Kleinians who specifically point out how they would technically intervene.

Most concepts or theories in psychoanalysis generate a great deal of literature, yet one is seldom privy to how the analyst uses the idea in day-to-day clinical practice. Therefore, whether the literature is discussing repression, splitting, isolation, depressive guilt, reparation, transference love, acting out, or any other common clinical situation, it is rare to find much said about actual interpretations to the patient. It seems that this trend has gradually shifted in the last twenty years to more case reports with line-by-line case material. One reason why ongoing supervision, workshops, and study groups are vital to an analyst's career is that actual analyst–patient dialogue is much more available for examination.

The majority of Kleinian analysts reporting PI interpretations are writing within the last twenty years. Again, this seems part of an overall shift in psychoanalysis where there are more published reports of what actually takes place in a clinical hour. In regards to the concept of PI, I think this shift also reflects a better technical understanding of the process and how to interpret it to the patient.

When a Kleinian makes a PI interpretation, it rarely is an exclusive focus on one piece of the patient's mental life. It is more of a multifaceted interpretation that highlights PI at the forefront of multiple areas of dynamic activity. In Chapters 1 and 2 I have artificially separated the literature on PI interpretations into various categories. However, most of these interpretations involve several different messages being conveyed at the same time. This is important because the PI interpretation that contains multiple translations of the patient's projections can be much more effective. The combination of therapeutic focus may be more helpful because of the densely packed, all-inclusive quality. It also lets the patient pick what area of the interpretation to pick up on, which is of diagnostic interest.

There is a possibility that some or many Kleinians interpret PI in ways that are quite different from the ones on which I am reporting. However, restricted to what is reported in the literature, certain patterns emerge.

In examining the available data closely, Kleinians take a very intimate, in the moment, PI interpretive stance with the patient and his intrapsychic life. It seems that in totality, the usual focus of PI interpretations could be said to simply be a detailed analysis of the transference. However, this is a transference emphasis that relies on specific techniques. The most frequent finding was Kleinians offering direct, verbal PI interpretations of the here-and-now intrapsychic transference relationship.

Kleinians emphasize PI interpretations designed to show the patient how their mind functions. This is a way of explaining to the patient what they are doing in the act of PI. While this has a certain educative impact, it seems more of a well-thought-out explanation of what the deeper anxieties are, why they are occurring, what the patient is doing with them via PI, and how that is influencing their relationship to the analyst. The fact that this method of interpretation includes a cognitive component seems to be a bonus to the treatment. While the analyst is addressing the patient's intrapsychic phantasies and their affective links, the nature of the interpretation provides support and augmentation to the ego.

Kleinians are interpreting PI in a way that not only reveals its intrapsychic origins but the current transference manifestations as well. In some examples, it has the look and feel of an intricate story that they are relaying, a multilayered story about the deepest aspects of the patient's ego and its link to the object. For some Kleinians, this story includes an interpersonal aspect of the therapeutic relationship that is being used as a vehicle for the PI.

Countertransference played a large role in determining how to interpret PI. Kleinians listen closely to their internal reactions before making clinical comments. They relate the usefulness of monitoring countertransference in understanding the different ego↔object relations the patient is dealing with in their PI process.

Kleinians use the idea of precision to guide their PI interpretations. By this, they mean being very specific in what they say to the patient as well as being very clear about exactly what aspect of PI to interpret.

Certain technical guidelines seem implicit and run through most Kleinian approaches to PI. Some of these analysts believe in the concept of giving new meaning to the patient's phantasies by the PI interpretation. This idea was also evident in many other reports but not as clearly spelled out. The analysts I have quoted showed how verbalization and analysis of PI provided new intrapsychic meaning to phantasies, and thus mobilized structural change.

Another area that appears in many Kleinian PI comments, but is only underscored by a minority, is containment. These Kleinians show how they verbally address the issue of containment and PI within their interpretations. While they differ on why to contain or on what was being contained, they all think the interpretive effort was to contain PI material.

Some of the analysts I reviewed provided verbatim data concerning the transformation of affect and phantasy. This somewhat overlaps the last category and is again implicit in many other analysts' work. However, the passage of affect and phantasy from one domain to another was more specific and seemed to be aimed at the in-the-moment shifting and resolution of particular self↔object affects and phantasies.

There were quite a few categories of less usual or atypical approaches to PI interpretation. Most of these involved only a few Kleinian analysts and did not represent a common method of speaking to the patient. In actual clinical practice, I feel many of these categories are probably entwined, in the background, with more usual ones at the forefront of the interpretive stance.

Some analysts think silence is important as a way of interpreting. It is not that they choose to not interpret, but they think it best to do so silently.

Some Kleinians make verbal interpretations of the interpersonal aspects of PI. While these are a minority, I suspect that many more do so. In fact, I see it as an excellent pathway into interpreting the intrapsychic meaning of PI. This is a complex and controversial area. Melanie Klein originally meant PI to be a term that described a purely internal dynamic. Some Kleinians feel the same, while others have included the interpersonal manifestation of PI in their definitions of it. In general, there seems to be a gradual shift in Kleinian thinking to include the interpersonal manifestations of intrapsychic dynamics. This shift influences technique. Some patients clearly use acting out and interpersonal relating to facilitate unconscious PI mechanisms. Other patients do not seem to rely on interpersonal dynamics very much at all. So, the reports in this category still leave many issues of technique and theory unresolved. In my case material, which I will be presenting, I try to bring some clarity to this matter.

Genetic reconstruction appears in the interpretations of some Kleinians. However, it is not often used by itself as an interpretation but as part of a larger exploration of the PI dynamic. Kernberg, Quinodoz, Grotstein, Segal, and Spillius all use genetic reconstruction in their PI interpretations. Yet they are so intertwined with other areas of interpretive focus that it is more helpful to examine their verbatim comments in other categories. In other words, complex and integrated PI interpretations must match the complexity of PI. Overall, genetic reconstruction is not used very often by Kleinians. When it is, it is done in this combined manner.

Only one analyst in the literature used PI interpretations to model to the patient. This seems to indicate that this is rarely used as a technical device. While modeling may be an accidental by-product of the PI interpretation, a transference distortion, or a countertransference acting out, Kleinians have not deliberately used it.

Voicing of the PI dynamics was also quite rare. Essentially, the analyst role plays the internal PI mechanism, giving a voice to the ego–object struggles. However, as I mentioned in Chapter 2, I think it can easily be used as part of a PI or transference interpretation. I found only one analyst in the literature to represent this approach to PI interpretation.

The use of body language in PI interpretations was probably used much more in earlier years, although no extensive data on verbatim comments is available. What is available to study are the body-language-oriented interpretations of five contemporary Kleinians. Overall, most analysts seem to have moved away from using these terms and concentrate more on the here-and-now transference elements of PI rather than phantasies involving body parts.

One Kleinian showed the patient the direction of his PI mechanism via a verbal interpretation. This analyst pointed out where the PI was located, highlighting it as either ego-centered or object-centered. This seems to be an important technical device in being specific and exploring exactly what the nature of the PI entails. Interestingly, only this one analyst exhibited this method of interpretation. Perhaps the technique is more widely used, but underrepresented in verbatim accounts.

Two analysts stressed timing in their interpretations. They felt it was crucial to show the patient how they were using PI at the exact moment it was occurring. This seems helpful in preventing an intellectualized treatment where both parties talk about something other than the transference and the affects occurring in the moment.

Separation, loss, and PI are issues not usually addressed in the literature, especially regarding what was actually said to the patient. Two Kleinians did report verbatim interpretations in which they addressed loss. Most of the literature not only lacks examples of loss, PI, and interpretive efforts, but addresses loss only from the depressive position. The experience of loss within the paranoid-schizoid position and the use of PI to cope with loss in that position are not well documented. I will be touching on this neglected area in later chapters.

Extra-transference was the focus of PI interpretations by two analysts. The sparseness of examples in this category seems to show the Kleinian efforts to stay with the current transference material in the room rather than bring in external issues. The two analysts that did use extra-transference PI comments did so within the context of other interpretive moves. In fact, the transference was focused on as well. This issue of the relationship between internal and external is something I have explored (Waska 2002) in a book about how loss, abandonment, and persecution come together in many patients' phantasies as the core psychological struggle.

A few Kleinians brought the goals and aims of PI into their interpretations. They tried to show the patient exactly what their motivations were and how they were trying to meet certain intra-psychic goals through the use of PI.

Finally, several analysts brought patient dreams into their PI interpretations. This is somewhat unique in the literature. Usually analysts see dreams as adding transference information, and the dreams are interpreted via the transference but without reference to PI. These several Kleinians felt dreams are just as much a vehicle for PI as any waking material. Therefore, they felt free to analyze the PI functions of the dream as well as the transference implications.

Chapter 4

Projective identification

Some clinical and diagnostic considerations[1]

The limitations of the analytic relationship are a product of the analysis of transference and the resistances. PI is a fundamental element of the transference and often is the primary resistance. Therefore it can become the chief limitation to the exploration and enhancement of the analytic relationship.

In this chapter I will focus on specific manifestations of PI found within the autistic-contiguous mode of functioning (Ogden 1989), the paranoid-schizoid position, and the depressive position. Then, I will examine specific clinical implications for the day-to-day, moment-to-moment interpretation and understanding of PI by patient and analyst as a method of cultivating the therapeutic relationship. The actual criteria for when, how, and why to analyze PI processes will be discussed with clinical examples. As discussed in the previous chapters, what really goes on between analyst and patient within PI situations, and what exactly is said to make an interpretation of PI, needs to be more explicit.

Throughout this chapter and the rest of the book, I will be using a great deal of clinical material with actual "he said and then I said" data. It will be obvious, rather quickly, that my psycho-analytic technique, my way of being with a patient, is a mixture of many of the Kleinian styles discussed in the previous chapters. In addition, I add my own personality and style to the mix. I don't think my overall approach is unique, but rather a Kleinian model that includes flexibility, patience, and an effort at meeting the patient where they happen to be at any given moment.

V. Tausk (1919) made an early contribution to the study of what was later to be know as PI:

the projection of one's body may, then, be traced back to the developmental stage in which one's body is the goal of object finding. This must be the time when the infant is discovering his body, part by part, as the outer world, and is still groping for his hands and feet as though they were foreign objects. At this time, everything that "happens" to him emanates from his own body; his psyche is the object of stimuli arising in his own body but acting upon it as if produced by outer objects. These disjecta membra are later on pieced together and systematized into a unified whole under the supervision of a psychic unity that receives all sensations of pleasure and pain from these separate parts. This process takes place by means of identification with one's own body.

(Tausk [1919] 1948: 72–73)

While the dynamics Tausk describes are undifferentiated states of primary narcissism, they in fact begin a very basic process of separation by differentiating the self[2] from the various body parts. The motivation of the PI mechanism is to bring an experience of ownership and organization to the psyche. In Kleinian terms, Tausk is speaking about a primitive level of self–object differentiation. PI is a force that aids in this natural, healthy development of the personality. Since Klein introduced and elaborated the concept of PI, it has been redefined by many authors. Hanna Segal (1974) stated:

in projective identification parts of the self and internal objects are split off and projected into the external object, which then becomes possessed by, controlled and identified with the projected parts. Projective identification has manifold aims: it may be directed toward the ideal object to avoid separation, or it may be directed toward the bad object to gain control of the source of danger. Various parts of the self may be projected, with various aims: bad parts of the self may be projected in order to get rid of them as well as to attack and destroy the object, good parts may be projected to avoid separation or to keep them safe from bad things inside or to improve the external object through a kind of primitive projective reparation.

(Segal 1974: 27–28)

Betty Joseph (1987) said:

> the infant, or adult who goes on using such mechanisms powerfully, can avoid any awareness of separateness, dependence, or admiration or its concomitant sense of loss, anger, envy, and so on. But it sets up persecutory anxieties, claustrophobia, panics, and the like . . .
>
> From the point of view of the individual who uses such mechanisms strongly, projective identification is a phantasy, and yet it can have a powerful effect on the recipient. . . . we can see, however, that the concept of projective identification is more object related and more concrete, and covers more aspects than the term projection . . .
>
> (Joseph 1987: 65–66)

Finally, Otto Kernberg (1987) said:

> clinical experience has led me to define projective identification as a primitive defense mechanism consisting of (a) projecting intolerable aspects of intrapsychic experience onto an object, (b) maintaining empathy with what is projected, (c) attempting to control the object as a continuation of the defensive efforts against the intolerable intrapsychic experience, and (d) unconsciously inducing in the object what is projected in the actual interaction with the object. . . . with patients having psychotic object relations, it may represent a last-ditch effort to differentiate self from object . . . [I]n patients with borderline personality organization . . . projective identification tends to weaken the differentiation between self and external objects.
>
> (Kernberg 1987: 94–96)

These are all descriptions of methods of organizing phantasies and affects within the world of internal objects.

On the one hand, PI can build internal mental representations, perceptual capacities, and somatic stability, all of which create an enhanced ability to relate to objects. Conversely, failure of this most basic of human communications leads to gross disruption of fundamental mental states and to consequent disintegration of various aspects of the mind.

There are different possible outcomes to PI. There can be a parallel sending, receiving, and giving back between both parties or there can be an inability to access the potential receiver, leading to autistic annihilation. There also can be the experience of the receiver not being able to process the message leading to the sender's phantasy of hurting or destroying the object. Finally, the object can be experienced as becoming outraged at being pushed to receive a message and subsequently attacking the sender in retaliation.

I will examine these four possible outcomes in great detail in the next chapter. In this chapter, I look at how patients experience these outcomes according to what psychological structure their ego views life from and how that diagnostic criteria shapes the outcome of PI. In other words, there is a cross-influence between how the ego experiences the object and how PI influences the nature of the ego's experience of the object. First, I will examine the depressive position, the paranoid-schizoid position, and the autistic-contiguous mode as psychic medium for the PI process. In the following chapter, I will explore the four typical ways PI tends to unfold between analyst and patient, between subject and object.

When PI is within the subjective experience of the depressive position, certain elements are present. Whole and integrated internal objects are felt to be distinct and separate from whole and non-fragmented self-representations. If the primary object-representations can accept a projective communication in a curious, receptive, and caring manner, then the understanding, organizing, and processing of the communication can take place in the object's unconscious. Once the communication is accepted, held, and processed it can then be returned to and introjected by the sender. PI in the depressive position is often a growth-directed, psychological flow involving whole objects and structure building, unconscious dialogues between subject and object. Oedipal guilt, attempts at reparation, and periods of competitive aggression are parts of this and naturally occur in the transference.

One patient would get drunk after coming home from her job as president of a large corporation. She had always felt her mother and others demanded she perform as a "good little girl" and achieve greatness for their sake. She came into one hour and said she felt like she was coming to see her priest. We discussed how she wished that I be an understanding father–priest and talk with her about how she had recently gotten drunk at her mother's birthday party and "ruined her mother's big day" out of anger and rebellion. She also worried I would be a punishing and critical mother–priest so she wanted to keep her alcoholic secrets from me as a way to rebel and protect herself. She felt guilty about this rebellion and then felt compelled to "confess" that to me as well. She projected the idealized, caring-father phantasy onto me as well as the feared critical, phallic mother parts. I, in turn, felt like "making her free associate to all her sins" as well as wanting to tell her "Don't worry my dear. All is forgiven." Discussing these ways of relating to me proved very helpful in illuminating these oedipal conflicts. The interpersonal aspect of PI shaped the transference and gave us a window into the internal object relations world. My countertransference helped me formulate my interpretation of the PI dynamic.

A collapse of healthy PI mechanisms can occur within the paranoid-schizoid position. The analyst/mother may be unable to fully understand or organize the patient's unconscious material once it has been received. This could be due to fundamental anxieties and unresolved conflicts in the analyst or because of the inability of the patient to send "usable" unconscious messages, due to various conflictual or constitutional states that hinder primary mental operations. A breakdown in the PI process follows and the patient senses that the receiver is unable to understand and/or withstand their intrapsychic anxieties. Without help, the patient begins to feel there is a void inside of them and around them at the time of greatest need.

Two methods of coping then tend to emerge. Following a reactive projection of primary and secondary aggression into the object, this lack of receiving is felt as a deliberate and sadistic neglect on the part of the object and there is subsequent rage at the object's lack of aid. This is a use of rage as a defense and as a binding mechanism against the terrors of being alone, the lack of "sense" in the world, the experience of fragmentation, and the horror of being without a container for the disorganized pieces of the self. One patient would become enraged at me and the teachers in his college classes for how we appeared to treat him as an ignorant chess piece in our grand design for narcissistic splendor. These were usually times when he felt confused and in need of help in understanding what was going on either internally or externally, but felt the object was unable to meet his needs.

In the second method of coping with a PI collapse of self and object, the patient begins to phantasize that the object has been poisoned by the communication, that self-expression is somehow able to destroy or damage the receiver. This is more of a schizoid phantasy then a paranoid experience. The net result is that the patient feels they have a core make-up that is dangerous or never understandable to the object. This leads to a global and unbearable fear that the self can destroy, repel, or confuse the object. One's needs, including the need to express feelings of either love or hate, are kept in hiding in an effort to try and save the object. The actual desire for the object's love begins to be deformed into a need to love the object back to health.

Children often crystallize these fears into an approach of always trying to be helpful and submissive to the object as a way of hoping to save the object from dangerous aspects of the self and, secondarily, to seduce the otherwise neglectful object to come back to their aid.

One patient would try preventive maneuvers in which she would say: "I want to tell you before we start that I might have a cold today. If you want me to leave in case I might be contagious just tell me. I might be kind of droopy today because of it. I want you to know so you don't think I am bored or something." She would also say: "I don't turn on your light in the waiting room until five minutes before the appointment time, that way you aren't interrupted and bugged by me but you still have enough time to get ready at your own pace." This same patient came in recently and told me about how she had been extremely cold in the waiting room. When I asked her what stopped her from closing the window that was open she said that she presumed the office was "climate controlled" and she was afraid that if she closed the window it could set off some kind of chain reaction leading to the "entire system blowing up." I was able to speak to her at that point about how her own needs seemed to lead quickly to the destruction of my world so she had to sacrifice her needs for the good of my needs.

These experiences are primarily schizoid dilemmas and schizoid perspectives of how the object is either unavailable or made diseased by the subject. When more paranoid phantasies invade the internal world, the PI process can be experienced as an exchange with an object who reacts with outrage to the presence of the subject. The patient can feel that while the object was able to read the message, the object is outraged, insulted, and furious at being given the message. This phantasy state includes the idea of enraged retaliation and revenge from the object for this violation.

To summarize, the experience in the paranoid position is that of being in danger from an angry or even murderous object or a dangerous environment made up of multiple malicious objects. These objects are not conceived of as fully separate and internally alive entities. In addition, they are not seen as capable of understanding, forgiveness, or compassion. They are more of an extension of a larger threatening "other" that is felt to be looming. This nonhuman quality is often both a defense against the terror of one's dearest attachment being felt as dangerous and a recapitulation of the original nonhuman relational environment experienced with the primary caretaker.

The last outcome of the PI situation occurs in the autistic-contiguous position. The sender is not met in potential space (Ogden 1990) but rather is left alone, trapped within the experience of projecting into empty space or at an impenetrable wall. If the analyst refuses or is unable to receive the communication, the patient can experience their self-expression as hitting a barrier and bouncing off into endless space. If the analyst is unavailable, the impulse, thought, and affect are all destined to be lost forever in a shapeless mental void. This is equivalent to the lack of potential space.

One of my patient's experience of his mother was of a rigid, narcissistic, feminist who resented having a son and felt that any sign of need from her baby was an impingement on her and a sign of both weakness and aggression from her baby. The patient's experience of these situations was that "every time I needed her, she shut this giant door to the castle, with a thud. I was left out in the cold, lost and wondering what happened. I will never try that again. I would be crazy to try again." We understood the "crazy" to be a reference to the internal state of black, unrelated, floating bleakness that he experienced as an infant when shut out from the castle/breast. He desperately tried to avoid these feelings in his adult life. Of course, in the transference he was in a constant struggle about exposing his emotions to me and was fearful of my rejection and a subsequent return of the "crazy." He dealt with those fears by not allowing me access to his internal world. As a consequence, I felt on the outside of his castle desperately banging on the door, feeling shut out, alone, and "crazy." This would be the concordant (Racker 1968) portion of the PI process in which I experience his desperation at the hands of the bad object.

Patients who exist within a more isolated autistic-contiguous state tend to have no or minimal internal objects to receive their expression and therefore there is a lost and fragmented quality to most of their intrapsychic experiences that can then be felt in the analytic hour. With one psychotic patient, there were multiple occasions where I would reference a topic we had recently discussed and he would give me a particular type of stare which would launch me into a state of anxiety in which my thought was, "Oh my god, we never talked about that before. I must have just made it up in my head. I must be going insane!" In the countertransference, I was experiencing the patient's lifelong experience of his thoughts and feelings never being acknowledged by his mother, leaving him floating in a disorganized state of nothingness. He remembered on one occasion asking her why she and his father were always fighting and yelling, and his mother replied: "I think I am going to use the green flower pattern for the new drapes." He suddenly felt lost and catapulted into meaninglessness. On occasion he worried I would start talking about "the drapes," abandoning him to a state of nothingness. When he walked each day to grade-school and later to high-school, he would take the Bible with him and read the passages out loud because he "knew that God was listening and paying attention," fulfilling the function he hoped his mother would attend to.

Patients who have experienced these types of terrors for most of their lives find ways of adapting and quasi-organizing or binding themselves within that place. One patient said, "When I feel like I don't exist any more, I go to the mirror and look at a part of me like my leg and remember how a man told me I have nice legs and then my legs are all right. Then I look at my face and try and remember another man who said I have a pretty face and then that part of my body is OK again. I do that until I can salvage most of me back." This a method of using PI and introjective identification to cope with autistic-contiguous experiences. This patient would often demand that I tell her what to do in a manner that both made me feel compelled to fix her immediately and made me feel irritated and dismissive. I was able to explore with her the projection into me of both her angry and narcissistic parts and her anxiousness and worried elements of herself. She attempted to project her narcissistic father parts into me so that I would tell her if she mattered or not and whether she existed or not. By putting these parts of herself into me, she had at least a fifty-fifty chance of receiving my life-saving validations rather than the usual guarantee of no validation from herself.

I will now highlight the interaction between PI, the therapeutic relationship, and the psychoanalytic endeavor. While I first outlined specific modes of psychological functioning as they pertain to PI, I will now describe technical criteria regarding the analysis of PI.

PI is a helpful tool in understanding the patient. It is a bridge to sensitivity and compassion for both the patient and the analyst. Many times during my early training I would feel desperate, needy, and worried that a particular patient might leave me or "dump me." This often led to acting out on my part in the form of being extra nice or supportive, which I only later came to understand as the concordant portion of a PI process, in which the patient projected their scared and needy parts into me and began to relate to me as though they were the abandoning and persecutory object. Other patients would fill me with irritation and the hope that they would quickly terminate, leading to strong feelings of shame, guilt, and self-doubt about my capacity as an analyst. Only later did I have the knowledge about PI to help me understand that I was indeed being filled internally with the patient's rageful and rejecting objects, thus leaving me with a complementary (Racker 1968) countertransference experience.

While interpretation is the ultimate goal when analyzing PI, understanding the intrapsychic and interpersonal matrix it takes place in can initially be a journey in information collecting. There are frequent times in the course of an analytic hour that I become aware of certain parts of the patient being projected into me, but then decide to not comment on it until later. There may be more immediate issues that take precedence, there may be a sense of not yet being fully aware of what the projections are, or there may be factors about the patient's history that indicate other courses of action. The best clinical decision then becomes that of collecting data rather then commenting on that data.

A patient I saw for three months in analysis before he moved to Europe had not paid his bill by the time the last week arrived. This was a man who constantly railed against how life was so "unfair," how others "had what he wanted," and how he would like to be the sole owner of "the power" in all relationships instead of what he felt to be a chronic stealing of and assault on his self-worth. While he had presented himself by all accounts as someone to be trusted, had no history of gross acting out, and had asked if he could pay at the end of the treatment, I started to feel fearful that he would leave town and never pay me. I started to feel quite helpless and saw myself as victimized by a person who would use me and then throw me away, as a way of wreaking vengeance for various injustices. I felt I would be punished "as an example" to others that "beware, don't cross Mr X's path."

What was useful to the analytic relationship was for me to use these countertransference feelings as a way to understand how he was desperately projecting the castrated and manipulated infant parts of himself into me in hopes that I might be able to manage that anxiety. There was not sufficient interpersonal material nor cause for me to interpret this regarding the unpaid bill. He did pay as agreed. I had been able, however, to interpret the same PI dynamics in regard to many other interpersonal situations in our relationship. In the instance of the bill, it was primarily helpful simply to collect information as a way to further my understanding of the ongoing aspects of the analytic relationship.

In fact, this case was an example of my use of containment as part of my analytic intervention. I did my best to contain the PI, while I used my countertransference phantasies and feelings to understand the nature of my patient's PI. In addition, I used the interpersonal aspects of PI as part of my interpretation, or at least in facilitating the interpretation.

At certain times, an emphasis on the analysis of PI as a defense serves the analytic relationship best. While there are always particular anxieties and desires present, the interpretation of defensive maneuvers is at times technically primary. The examination of one's countertransference is usually the vehicle from which to gauge what direction to take and where to place the interpretive emphasis.

The regular meeting hour with one rather paranoid woman had been changed through mutual agreement to a different day and a different time of day. She came in at the first new hour and told me that I had made her come at a strange time as a "mean and deliberate way of making 'us' all crazy." While there had been times in the treatment when I felt she was truly experiencing me as a murderous "gas-lighter," this time she did not seem to be fully committed to her accusations. In fact, I felt invited to play with her through what seemed to be a dramatic and colorful teasing. In other words, I felt a tenderness from her toward me via these paranoid ramblings. For all these reasons, I felt she was using a persecutory defense to ward off the tender and playful desire to be with me. I told her I felt she wanted to be close to me and have me love her but was very afraid of this so she pretended that I hated her instead. She immediately broke into tears and began to tell me that she wanted to be near me and have me take care of her but was very scared that she was hopeless and unreachable.

Another patient had been in treatment for seven years without ever discussing any feelings about our relationship or ever referencing it. She had been chronically served up by her mother to her father as a confidant, emotional nurse, and at times a sexual companion. She had felt trapped and helpless to change that situation until I saw her at age twenty. She then was able to mobilize some of her feelings about the relationship and make some changes.

Remarkably, we recently began to explore her deep feelings of attachment and love for me that she kept hidden far away out of terror that she would instantly lose me and suffer "unspeakable annihilation." In one particular session she seemed very anxious and on edge. I noticed that she looked like she was about to be the victim of some kind of terrible situation. She commented that she might be feeling nervous about "getting to the point," but when I asked what she meant, she said she had no idea but that was what had come to her mind. By that time, I had the phantasy that she was in a dentist's office waiting to be called in for a drilling. It occurred to me that I was the dentist. I shared this idea with her and told her that I thought she was worried about being responsible for her positive feelings about me and to save herself she had projected those pressuring father–dentist parts of herself into me. She said, "How did you know that? – that is exactly it, I feel really afraid to be talking about those kinds of feelings and I am worried that I will 'have' to, like I don't have a choice." She had used PI as a defense against the overwhelming feelings of pressure and judgment. She had attempted to put those parts of herself into me and therefore the interpretation needed to address the defensive function of the process.

I interpreted the defensive aspects of the PI process, based on my own countertransference phantasy. Rather than simply tell my patient the dynamic matrix she imagined, I told her both the actual phantasy and the dynamic essence of that phantasy. I interpreted the vision she held of how the self and the object actually related in her phantasy.

The affects and phantasies that are stirred in the analyst by the PI situation are helpful in determining how to give voice to the intrapsychic and interpersonal exchange. The analytic relationship is only limited as far as the limits of interpretation regarding transference and resistances. Understanding and working through of PI exchanges in that relationship serve to allow the natural unfolding of that relationship. This in turn provides greater opportunity for the interpretation of the transference.

Determining what our "sum countertransference" is, including all affects and thoughts within our phantasy states, gives us a clue to various emotional states that the patient is feeling overwhelmed by and trying to cope with by projecting into us. Affect states are woven into phantasy states, making the analyst's own analysis of internal phantasies an ongoing necessity.

One patient would routinely become extremely vague with me, using only half sentences and trailing off words in a way that left me not able to quite hear the message in any coherent manner. When I commented about this, she said, "I can't decide what to say, there are so many images and options spinning in my mind that I start to judge them and try and figure out what would be the best one and then I get anxious and really fed up with myself so I give up and stop."

Based on a phantasy of mine of interrogating her until she finally told me what she was talking about, in full and audible sentences, I was able to talk with her about how she seemed to try and project severe superego parts into me, as a way of escaping self-punishment. This phantasy of mine was linked to an affect of irritation, anger, and judgment. As with all PI mechanisms, the intra-psychic always links with the interpersonal. I indeed acted out my phantasy by heckling her with volumes of questions about her vague communications. During these times she would tell me she felt judged and picked on. By exploring this type of process, we together began to understand more about how she felt constantly badgered and scrutinized by men, sexually and emotionally. She would project her own self-hatred and obsessive scrutiny into men and then invite them in subtle ways to attack her. It was my affect-laden phantasy of "wanting to grill her" that gave me the indication that some type of PI process was occurring. These mutual explorations led to her remembering aspects of her relationship with her father in which he would chronically interrogate her and demand that she produce ideas and conversations for his enjoyment. She also remembered that these moments were usually a part of a seductive and teasing type of exchange between them, much in the way they were between us.

In this example, I found my way to the interpretation as the result of a mutual acting out of the patient's phantasy. Rather than a hindrance, the acting out was an inevitable therapeutic situation that provided valuable information about the PI process occurring at that moment in our relationship. Also, I invited my patient to explore the PI process with me, making the interpretation of PI much more of a collaborative effort. I believe this helps in the working through and integrative process of psychoanalytic treatment.

Another patient called me two days before our regular scheduled appointment to tell me she felt very depressed and wanted to come in earlier. I told her I had no openings but I would let her know if one came available, and then I asked her what was troubling her. She said I was the only one who has ever shown her any caring, and then she began to sob. While this seemed very sincere and heartfelt, I realized my own affect and phantasy state to be quite different. I felt ambivalent and started to worry that she was becoming like a greedy creature stirred from sleep. I felt like she was about to assault me with relentlessly greedy parts of herself and I wanted to run for cover. Had I gone along with her manifest compliment of me, I might have made some type of comment in that direction. Based on my phantasy and affect state, I instead remained silent. She stopped crying after a bit and said, "Why don't you have enough time to see me. You are too busy seeing everyone else. I want to see you right now. I will spread terrible rumors about you until no one wants to see you and then I will have all the time I want with you." I said, "I don't imagine that time would be very pleasant for me, it would be difficult to see you under those circumstances." She laughed and said, "Yes, I know exactly what you mean. Thank you for calling me back, I will see you on Wednesday." My interpretation helped her see what her aggressive hunger did to her objects and how that in turn affected her. Again, my affect and phantasy served as the principal guide in knowing how to proceed with the PI process that had begun to limit our relationship.

The long-term analytic relationship provides the patient and the analyst with a detailed portrait of the patient's phantasy world and its internal objects. If the relationship is examined through the history of the transference, the history of the PI processes, and the history of how the patient has been able to use interpretations regarding these mechanisms, then what were at first "trial interpretations" and "therapeutic fishing expeditions" slowly become a more predictable and identifiable composite of how to intervene in the patient's internal world. The history of the analytic relationship therefore becomes increasingly profitable when determining how to conduct the analysis.

PI is a mixture of both interpersonal and intrapsychic phenomena that are forever linked, yet often are temporarily separate in moments throughout the analytic hour. Each patient seems to respond optimally to the interpretation of one or the other of these two portions of the dialectic.

One patient treated me quite rudely and insulted my office, my manner of dress, my technique, my choice of words when speaking, and so forth. It appeared she was involved in a very strong PI method of relating to me. When I would attempt to comment on the interpersonal aspects of this process, her reaction was extremely negative. In fact, a negative therapeutic reaction began to develop. It wasn't until I made interpretations regarding intrapsychic elements behind the interpersonal that she began to respond and relate very differently. The analytic relationship was no longer limited nor stagnated.

On the other hand, another quite disturbed patient would immediately and dramatically fall asleep upon hearing any intrapsychic-related interpretations regarding PI material. She would become fragmented and not be able to find her way to my office for days, finding herself at distant locations some 50 miles away. She felt I was against her in many ways and deliberately set out to make her life a living hell. Only when I began to interpret the interpersonal aspects of PI did she seem to be able to not only take them in, but actively respond and explore that phenomenon. Then, she became more interpersonally integrated and functioned better externally.

I have delineated some of the criteria for the exploration and interpretation of PI in the analytic relationship. While they have been separated for the purposes of exploration, much of the time they operate in combination during the analytic hour. The elements of understanding, history, affect, phantasy, countertransference, defense, and the dialectic between the interpersonal and the intrapsychic are always present in various weights at various times. They all influence the course of how to best analyze the PI situation. The interpretation of these dynamics is often what defines the presence or absence of limitations upon the analytic relationship.

Case study

A patient I have seen for several years, Miss X, had been adopted at birth and, in her words, "sold for $100 and some fucking paperwork." At age three her adoptive mother developed cancer and gradually declined through the struggles of chemotherapy and being wheelchair bound until she died when my patient was six years old. Six months later, her father, a distant and coldly logical man, remarried a woman who was extremely critical and rejecting of Miss X. When my patient was eight or nine, her stepmother left the marriage and never returned. Miss X has one sister, also an adopted child, who has been institutionalized for a chronic psychosis. Miss X has been able to find employment and very recently attend college despite the auditory hallucinations and persecutory anxieties she often suffers. Her loss of three different mothers and other factors in her early life has left her unable to be close to others. Our relationship has been the first close bond she has been able to tolerate in her thirty years of life.

For the first two years of treatment, she adopted a callous "gun moll" attitude, constantly telling me how much she didn't care about me and how she was about to terminate the "useless" therapy. The third year proved to be a time where she was able to work through this defensive posture and start to allow herself to feel attached to me. This progress resulted in frequent depressive periods and temporary regressions to marked disassociative states.

She came into one recent session and told me that she had a scheduling change at work which meant that she could no longer make it to that regular hour. She said she hoped I didn't mind and, if "it was OK," would I put her on a waiting list or at least consider her to fill in if anyone called in to cancel. I felt moved by this extreme politeness and thought about the fearful anxiety that she seemed to be showing via the interpersonal aspect of her relating to me. As she kept talking in this meek and almost pleading manner, I began to have the complementary affective countertransference phantasy of being in the grandiose position of possibly granting or denying the poor peasant girl a new appointment time with the mere wave of my hand.

Miss X mentioned she wanted to be careful to not pressure me. I interpreted that she had projected the hostile and rejecting mother parts of herself into me and then feared I might easily dismiss her and find her troublesome. I interpreted that this process defended her from the greedy parts of herself and her own desires to have all of me for herself. She then told me that she would have dropped the hour "anyway," as she would have signed up for school if her job hadn't required her presence. I commented that she was resorting to her old "gun moll" method of relating to avoid the deep wishes to be close to me and depend on me, as she was terrified that by pressuring me she might drive me away or cause me to die slowly of some horrible disease. In fact, she had to save me from being the dying victim of her poisonous love by elevating me to the status of powerful king. The interpersonal politeness was matched by the intrapsychic projections into me of these unwanted and terrifying phantasies. She then said she was almost always worried about "where she stood" with me and others and preferred to ignore it altogether as it made her very anxious and "foggy and strange." This opened up the discussion to her fears of and wishes about depending on me.

My affect and phantasy state were the complementary portions of a countertransference process, which allowed me to have a more sympathetic understanding of her internal world. By using my affective state and the accompanying phantasy, I was able to construct an idea of what my patient was projecting and what the PI motives might be. All this was further facilitated by my knowledge regarding the transference history that had gradually unfolded as our relationship grew over the years.

I showed my patient what her unconscious goals were and interpreted what she was projecting, how that made her feel, and how that changed her object. In doing so, I was also able to interpret the paranoid and depressive anxieties she defended against.

Due to all these factors, the analytic relationship was capable of continuing to be the vehicle of change and growth. In short, the limits of the analytic relationship were eased by the ongoing analysis of the PI process.

Chapter 5

Intrapsychic outcome in projective identification[1]

Since Klein's introduction of the concept, much has been formulated from the dynamic of PI (Bion 1959; Rosenfeld 1983; Ogden 1979; Kernberg 1965; Malin and Grotstein 1966; Spillius 1983; Segal 1974).

Ogden (1979: 362) has stated, "projective identification evolves in the context of the infant's early attempt to perceive, organize, and manage his internal and external experience and to communicate with his environment." I would add that the infant's primary method of communication is PI and the infant uses this tool to find ways of meeting his inherent struggles toward homeostasis. It operates as a rich method of relating, designed to maintain the general cohesion of the organism.

Hanna Segal (1974: 27–28) thinks of PI as a process in which there are "manifest aims." I would like to add the concept of outcome to her thoughts about manifest aims. In the psychoanalytic literature, outcome in the PI process has been discussed in reference to obtaining distance from unwanted aspects of the self (Ogden 1979), a confused state of fusion with the analyst/mother (Rosenfeld 1983), a new sense of control over perceived danger (Segal 1974), a reuniting of "links" between subject and object (Bion 1959), a curative self–object experience (Adler 1988), a containing function (Bion 1959; Hamilton 1990), and other complex and diverse dynamics occurring both intrapsychically and interpersonally.

The infant's state of need, whether at a level of intense anxiety or simple nutritional urges, is communicated via PI. This complements Rosenfeld's (1983) distinction between the defensive use of PI and its usefulness as a basic communicative tool. The infant is attempting a communication of core drive states and object-related concerns. It is both an intrapsychic maneuver and an interpersonal contact (Ogden 1982).

Spoken language is unavailable to the infant, so along with physical activities such as gesturing, excreting, and mouthing, an unconscious pre-wired language is put to use. While development brings additional internal and interpersonal coping mechanisms, PI continues to be a primary communication effort throughout the life-cycle. Maturity fosters other methods of relating and thereby creates a rich, less fragile flavor to the PI strategy. Nevertheless, PI remains at the forefront of all normal and pathological relational efforts.

I feel the distinctions that have been drawn (Sandler 1986; Kernberg 1987) between projection and PI are not usually helpful in the context of object relations theory or clinical practice. Malin and Grotstein (1966: 26) clarify this debate by stating, "all intra-psychic and inter-personal relations are transacted on the basis of object relationships, rather than on the basis of instinctual drives alone. The object is the irreducible vehicle in human interaction." Therefore, a projection is always intended for an object and when it finds none, there is a particular intrapsychic trauma. I will expand on this point shortly, with case material.

In the previous chapter I briefly outlined four possible outcomes from the infant's PI efforts. These potential outcomes are duplicated in the analytic situation. Now I will expand these four avenues with clinical material. These four potential outcomes are constantly overlapping and entwining, rarely appearing as specific or individually expressed as I will present them.

When the analyst notes within him/herself a particular response to a patient, it is useful to consider it as a historical repetition in the transference of a PI matrix originally located within early experiences of infant/mother interaction. With the course of time and the elaboration of phantasy, this repetition is of course not a blueprint but rather an outgrowth of the original internal mother/infant bond. The four outcomes I am demonstrating with case material are, no doubt, always cross-influencing each other. However, a certain particular emphasis in one area or another undoubtedly creates specific structural configurations.

The first psychological dynamic between ego and object I want to discuss is the optimum and hoped-for outcome. If the object can accept the ego's PI in a curious, receptive, and caring manner, then the understanding, organizing, and processing of that communication takes place in the object's unconscious. This is not to say that the receiver won't be ambivalent or uneasy. A certain degree of ambivalence allows for a heightened effort at understanding and an increased ability to discriminate the components of the message. Once the communication is accepted, held, and processed, it can be returned to and introjected by the sender.

The richness of the PI communication is lessened by trying to describe it in scientific terms or even with spoken language, as it is such a warmly human interaction. This is not to negate the potentially destructive and aggressive motivations that often drive the use of PI. Klein (1946) made clear that this dynamic included the projection of both good and bad aspects of the self. However, as Hamilton (1986: 496) has pointed out, "literature concerning projective identification has excessively focused on the projection of unwanted aspects of the self without giving adequate consideration to projective identification involving good qualities."

A scene that may help illustrate the essence of the first potential outcome of PI, and an example of what Hamilton feels has been neglected, is that of two friends in an increasingly trustful relationship. Based on this growing trust, built by mutual exchange over time, one man decides to risk a deepening of the friendship through symbolic action. He shows the friend a prized possession: an autographed baseball. The man senses how important this possession and the unspoken message are even though he is not knowledgeable about sports. When his friend carefully hands him the baseball/communication, he respectfully takes it into his palm. The intimate and polite moment the man spends holding the ball, looking at it, and then gazing to his friend with the powerful look of "Yes, this is a very special treasure!" are all elements of an unconscious intrapsychic communication process between two people within an interpersonal field. If the whole sequence were timed, it would have probably taken three or four minutes. If later questioned, the one man might say, "I don't know much about baseball but I know it's important to Joe so I looked at the ball." His conscious reflection barely begins to address the unconscious private moment that passed between them. I choose to use an example that seems to have a superficial quality to contrast the more vital latent elements that are always present.

The intensity and emotionality of PI are often hidden in the most "corny" or mundane moments of relating. It is not solely reserved for serious and outwardly intimate settings. On the other hand, poetry, songs, and sexual union are certainly examples of more manifestly intimate vehicles in which these truly universal elements also reside. Film, sports, and art have been able to present the parallel, nonverbal, dialectic reverie of PI in various forms: the Madonna and child, the "eyes that meet across the crowded room," and the union of pair-skating are some of many examples.

As mentioned, examples of PI in the psychology literature usually employ pathology and the processing of negative projections. However, PI is a universal, lifespan communication operating in health as well as in mental illness. Certainly, psychopathology can be generated through the vehicle of PI. However, PI is often an unburdened growth-enhancing psychological flow involving whole objects and structure-building unconscious dialogues between subject and object.

Now, if the baseball example were an analytic one, we would also have the dimension of interpretation. Psychoanalysis is unique in that we consider it paramount to use interpretation to give form, language, and meaning to unconscious manifestations of the human condition. As analysts we might comment on how the baseball is the symbol of an important hope of sharing and intimacy, indicating growing trust and attachment. Perhaps we would point out a connection between the interaction and the transference. Many possibilities exist. In any case, we would consciously speak from our lips what has already been unconsciously spoken from the mind. PI is a shared reverie. Both participants must be closely attuned to each other. The sender must be capable of expressing their message and the receiver must be able to contain (Bion 1959) and transform the message. Grotstein (1986) has described this idea as taking in the projection, creating an environment of containment, and gradually offering some sort of thoughtful action in the form of an interpretation. One way of picturing this is the idea of a constitutional "fit" between infant and mother. Both mother and infant are hopefully able to adapt to each other, internally and interpersonally, in ways that allow for a successful mutuality. This relational harmony is a profound human exchange that is extremely difficult to put into words. The concept of PI is the closest we have been able to come in pondering it consciously.

The second possible outcome of PI occurs when the sender is not met in potential space but is instead left alone and trapped within the experience of projecting into empty space or at an impenetrable wall. I am discussing all these ideas using the mother/analyst as the one who receives the communication in either a helpful or unhelpful manner. However, it is hopefully clear that PI is a dialectic in which either party can fail to participate for any variety of reasons. If the mother/analyst refuses or is unable to receive the communication, the child/patient can experience their self-expression or need as being blocked and falling into endless space. Once the projection is "spoken" by the mind, it is metaphorically released and sent outwards toward the object and cannot be taken back in or retrieved until it has been received, processed, and returned by the object. In this way, PI is the ultimate risk.

These patients' internal objects don't or won't receive their communication and therefore they feel lost and fragmented. One such patient said, without any prior introduction, "Now I certainly had my doubts about it, but I went ahead and followed through anyway." He did not say anything more and in fact calmly proceeded to the next topic. What was missing was the main body of the communication. Listening to this part-message, I began to feel eerily out of touch, hoping for some sign to organize myself around. Another patient told me he always felt like his hour with me was the first hour because he didn't ever remember anything that we talked about. He said, "Nothing sticks. I barely remember being here last time let alone what we talked about."

Over time, the revealing and emptying of the ego into a dark, cold, and formless void produces a psycho-biological failure of the mental processes. This is a starving of the most basic needs of the organism, far more crucial than food or water. Learning disabilities, failure to thrive infants, and various psychotic states are some of the psychological fallout. Ogden's term "autistic-contiguous mode" is helpful as it describes both an autistic encapsulation that occurs at this point and a non-organized, endless, falling, and leaking of the ego into a non-containing and non-receptive non-object. One patient said, "How can you possibly ask me to open myself up to you. It is so unbearably painful to reveal myself and then to have it drift into space and be left all alone forever. I can't do it. I would rather die." Another patient felt his body and mind literally got "sucked off the planet" when he considered the nature of his relationship to others. He said, "I always feel like gravity is really weak and I am hardly grounded onto the floor. At any moment I might go flying off into space." Patients who have experienced these types of terrors for most of their lives find ways of adapting and quasi-organizing or binding themselves within that place of horror. One such man told me he always wears clothes that are two sizes too small so he can feel the tightness of the cloth on his skin and "that way I know my skin won't fly off of the bones, it's held on by the tight clothing."

On the one hand, successful PI, as a communication, creates an internal structure building process which includes internal mental representations, perceptual capacities, somatic stability, and the ability to attach and to trust. On the other hand, failure of this most basic of human communications leads to gross disruption of fundamental needs states and to dis-integration of basic ego functions.

The third possible outcome of PI is a situation where the analyst may be unable to fully understand or organize the patient's unconscious material once it has been received. This could be due to fundamental anxieties and unresolved conflicts in the analyst or because of the inability of the patient to send "usable" unconscious messages. This might be due to multiple factors, including constitutional impairments or conflictual states that hinder primary mental operations. A breakdown in the PI process follows and the patient senses that the receiver is unable to understand and/or cope with their intrapsychic anxieties. Without help, the patient begins to feel there is a void inside of them and around them at the time of greatest need.

At this point the infant or patient may also phantasize that the object is poisoned by the communication, that self-expression or need is somehow able to destroy or damage the receiver. As I outlined in the previous chapter, the ego begins to feel dangerous to the object. One's need, love, or hate annihilate and enrage the object. Therefore, all feelings and thoughts need to be hidden or censored in an effort to try and save the object. The desire for love is mutated into loving the object back to health. Fairbairn (1952) has advanced these matters in his papers regarding the "schizoid" character and "endo-psychic structure."

One example of this type of outcome in PI is a young man who tells me over and over how depressed he feels about "draining" me of my vitality and depressing me with his "droning and pitiful" life. He says, "I am more then willing to sacrifice myself to you in whatever way I can to try and pay for how much you must be put out from having to sit with me." Rather than a feeling of guilt, he is fueled by a chronic sense of desperation and panic, feeling that he is slowly extinguishing the source of his own survival. My experience with him is often that of being confused and not really in-tune with him. I frequently find myself making interpretations that sound like they might fit someone who was somewhat like him, yet they clearly don't fit him. I end up feeling as though we are two people from foreign countries who have a small but insufficient mutual understanding of a third language. We have understood this as the result of his frenzy to provide me with what he phantasizes I want and need. This is his desperate atonement for draining me and hurting me. He is so busy trying to be somebody for me that I am never sure who he actually is, so I am unclear about our relationship. We seem to just miss each other in these moments and he will then frequently come to my aid and try to repair my confusion by either saying I was extremely accurate or spoon-feeding me more data to get me up to speed.

While this desire to protect or heal the object can be thought of as in some manner an attempt at primitive reparation for perceived damage to the object, the paranoid-schizoid character exists without neurotic, oedipal-based guilt. There is no real experience of a whole "subject" or whole "object" because of the globalized, non-separate, concrete world they exist within. Things "just happen" and "things" just "come and go." Rather than an attempt at reparation, I believe it is a desperate hope for a restoration of the subjective world. It is a desire for homeostasis of the organism, not for interpersonal harmony. If the object cannot be maintained and preserved, then the ego's life-line is severed, bringing on annihilation and the experience of eternal abandonment.

The fourth potential outcome of the PI process can occur in the interpersonal and/or intrapsychic situation of, in phantasy, the subject's communication received by an internal object who reacts with outrage. The subject can feel that while the object was able to read the message, the object is outraged, insulted, and furious at being given the message. "How dare you" is the imagined response of the object to the needs and psychic outreach of the child or patient. This phantasy includes the idea of enraged retaliation and revenge from the object for this violation. Within the paranoid-schizoid position, this also means a world without forgiveness or compassion. Therefore, the threat of attack or revenge feels even more dangerous and deadly.

One way to understand this is to explore a fear of mine that when the reader sees my prior baseball example they might feel it is a "sexist" example and then not want to read any more. So far, this is a phantasy involving two whole persons, the feeling of guilt or worry, and the fear of punishment. If I felt that my very existence was in danger due to the total withdrawal and attack of all readers, I would be having an experience more closely in the context of the paranoid-schizoid position. This would be a subjective experience of being in danger from an enraged monster or a dangerous environment, with the object not conceived of as fully separate or whole. This particular example is of a strictly intrapsychic phantasy of an aspect of my ego projecting into an internal representation of the reader. There is no actual external object. PI is at times a solely intrapsychic phenomenon and at other times comes to include interpersonal components that create additional complexity.

My stance is that PI is fundamentally an internal situation between different aspects of the mind. With the affective triggering of close personal relationships, such as is fostered in analysis, these intrapsychic phantasies are externalized or acted out. They are then either repeated and further entrenched or analyzed and recast as new self- and object-representations which are internalized as new psychic structure. One important clinical question would be why some patients favor almost exclusive intrapsychic manifestations of PI and others seem to favor an interpersonal acting out of those phantasies. I feel the deciding factor is the quantity of archaic mother/infant phantasy interactions that were shaped by sado-masochistic, controlling, or predatory dynamics. These economic factors either drive the patient to keep their internal world autistically hidden or to share it, interpersonally, through primary communicative means such as PI.

Another example of a more paranoid PI process in the fourth category was with a patient who was very provocative with me, in the sense of presenting herself as entitled and sadistically self-serving. My initial reaction was "How dare you treat me like this!" For a period of time, I would lash back in an equally sadistic manner at her misuse of me. At that point, I had failed to process her bitter, angry, and provocative communication adequately and failed to organize it into the desperate neediness and fear of neglect that it actually was. Later in the treatment I found a way to do this by examining my countertransference and then returning the modified material via interpretations. I spoke to her about her sense of helplessness and fear of dependency. Initially I was merely reacting to her efforts at linking with me by conducting violent assaults upon her mind. We were finally able to discuss how we had temporarily recreated the original dynamics that she grew up in, which included retaliation on the part of her psychotic mother for any expressions of thought or feelings from her children. This patient witnessed the father physically and sexually assaulting the mother for any direct expression of her own needs. The father finally killed himself, which we understood as the ultimate attack on himself for having his own needs for closeness and connection.

Another patient described her childhood memories with her father: "He would beat us and spank us until we were crying and out of control and then he would yell and threaten us with more beatings if we didn't stop crying and calm down. Everything just seemed to always be a threat and I slowly just felt I should put up with the world because otherwise everything flew apart and hurt me, so now I am really quiet." This patient is always wondering why "everyone seems to want to take advantage" of her and "why the world is always changing." I often feel, as the result of PI interactions with her, that I am swept up in the stampede of countless masses that threaten her. I usually feel things to be a blur at that point in the session and have the distinctive urge to lash out at this larger entity that seems to be taking me or us for a ride. This would be a concordant countertransference experience where I am in touch with how she feels oppressed and cornered. At that moment, my feeling is that "together, we will fight them off."

At other times, I have felt a wish to personally destroy her as a way finally to rid myself of what feels to be a torturous chipping away of my psyche. This feeling often overtakes me during periods in which this patient persistently echoes my comments. I will make a statement of some sort and she will immediately repeat back word for word what I have just said with a few token words of her own attached to the end of mine, seemingly thrown in for good measure if I am lucky. At these times, I feel particularly tortured and teased. I have a complementary countertransference experience in that I feel like the object that will do her wrong. So, my momentary feeling is, "I want to make your life hell, just like you have made mine so unbearable." This seeking of revenge makes me into the attacking object that she always feels oppressed by. I have understood all of these experiences to be a rather distinctive invitation into her internal world, via PI. These countertransference struggles have proved immensely helpful in the analysis and have offered both of us a vehicle from which we have gained a far deeper understanding of her personality and its historical development.

I have focused on four possible outcomes of PI mechanisms. These are a parallel sending, receiving, and giving back between both parties, an inability to access the potential receiver, the experience of the receiver not being able to process the message leading to the sender's phantasy experience of hurting or destroying the object, and finally the experience of the object becoming outraged and subsequently attacking the sender. These are states that come about in a dialectical process within both interpersonal and intrapsychic forums. The analyst can become aware of his or her participation in this basic form of communication through countertransference feelings and thoughts. Noticing the specific form the patient's phantasy takes and reflecting on the concordant or complementary position one is being invited into may give some information that assists in making an interpretation and organizing these otherwise raw mental states. The patient can then take them back in, leading to ego modification. Without sufficient countertransference awareness on the part of the analyst, as so frequently occurs in difficult cases, the patient's phantasies often are acted out within the therapeutic relationship. Thus, traumatic internal relations from early mother/infant situations are merely repeated. While there are perhaps infinite possible outcomes of the PI dynamic, I think these four intrapsychic and interpersonal possibilities are the main PI transference situations that clinicians encounter.

Chapter 6

Projective identification, countertransference, and the struggle for understanding over acting out[1]

PI is a form of adaptation, communication, defense, and creative expression that permeates the core of many psychotherapeutic treatments. A gradual mutual understanding by both patient and analyst of its multiple meaning within the therapeutic relationship and its place in the patient's unconscious functioning is crucial to the working-through process.

One aspect of PI is that it serves as the internal vehicle for the unconscious phantasies of loving and hateful feelings that are evacuated into the internal and external object. As outlined in Chapters 4 and 5, this evacuation can lead to either the phantasy of reinternalizing an injured object, causing depression and fear, or a reinternalizing of a now hostile and dangerous object, causing persecutory anxieties. Some patients fluctuate between both phantasies and other patients are functioning within a constant mix of both phantasy states.

Also, PI represents a very primitive means of communication that can lead to countertransference distress in the analyst and subsequent pathological interactions between patient and analyst.

Countertransference feelings, thoughts, and unconscious phantasies can be quite intense in response to PI experiences. Pick (1985) writes:

> To suggest that we are not affected by the destructiveness of the patient or by the patient's painful efforts to reach us would represent not neutrality but falseness or imperviousness. It is the issue of how the analyst allows himself to have the experience, digest it, formulate it, and communicate it as an interpretation that I address.

> (Pick 1985: 164)

In other words, countertransference is the result of the patient's PI dynamics and the totality of the therapeutic relationship. It exists. The question is not what to do if countertransference is present in a treatment, but what form it takes and how to use it effectively. By my case material so far, it should be clear to the reader how important the understanding of countertransference is to the formulation of PI interpretations.

Analyst and patient constantly struggle to make meaning and sense out of what takes place in the therapeutic bond. However, both parties are constantly tempted to act out these meanings rather than verbalize or mentalize them. There is a mutual resistance to feeling and working with the strong phantasy material in the room. Freud ([1915] 1959) wrote about how some patients remember nothing of their internal conflicts, but express them through action. Their behavior becomes a vehicle for the conflicts they would otherwise painfully have to face. Therefore action feels safer, or at least feels temporary relieving. It can be an excitement, a stimulation, an escape, or a revenge. Nevertheless, it remains as an unintegrated and split-off portion of the mind's urges and mobilized phantasies. PI can be an acting-out process of discharging internal pollutants into the object, followed by a denial of any connection or familiarity to such debris in the first place. While this may sound like simple projection, the ego is still responding to the phantasy of some type of object and some type of relationship to that object. In this case, it is a denial of the relationship to the object.

Analysts are enviably touched, contaminated, and seduced by these dynamics. As noted, the effects of PI are strong and can produce intense countertransference reactions.

Certain aspects of the intra-psychic and interpersonal communications between analyst and patient can continue beyond the hour or even past termination. Analysts speak among themselves of being hounded by a session and having it follow them into their personal lives. The analyst can unwittingly bring home clinical situations and even find the patient's material invading their dreams. In the moment-to-moment clinical situation, countertransference anxiety can be so great that the analyst is pushed to act out and rapidly return the patient's unbearable projections. This can occur in many ways. Some PI mechanisms produce intense reactions in both parties. Others produce more subtle effects within the analytic relationship. Pick writes:

The analyst, like the patient, desires to eliminate discomfort as well as to communicate and share experience; ordinary human reactions. In part, the patient seeks an enacting response, and in part, the analyst has an impulse to enact, and some of this will be expressed in the interpretation. This may range from an implicit indulgence, caressing the patient with words, to responses so hostile or distant or frozen that they seem to imply that the deprivation of the experience the patient yearns for is of no matter; a contention that a part-object mechanical experience is all that is necessary.

(Pick 1985: 158)

She is pointing out that both the analyst and patient are often drawn to some sort of acting out that can be very secretive and subtle, yet extremely gratifying. It removes the anxiety and threat both may be feeling.

Ideally, the analyst tries to understand any residual projective fragments that have been discarded, left behind, or lost by the patient through PI. An image that is helpful to me is the elementary school teacher who, after the school day is over, finds various notebooks, coats, and lunch-pails scattered about the school yard. The items have to be examined, recognized, and returned if the owner can be found. In a psychoanalytic process, we are always dealing with temporarily bequeathed psychic elements even after the patient leaves treatment.

The analyst's charge is to be a holding and transformative object. There are times the analyst must work through certain mental dynamics even after the patient has left the room. This is quite different than the accidental or temporary holding function that sometimes occurs between the first and the last therapy session when PI is not fully analyzed.

The analyst is often required to continue "meeting" with the patient within the context of PI. In other words, long after the patient is gone, the analyst can still be struggling through specific internal object relations.

I will now examine some of these problems with clinical material. I will present a case in which the hour ended and the analyst was left feeling alone, a case in which both patient and myself frequently felt used, persecuted, or controlled, and two cases where I began acting out the sadomasochistic, envious, and fearful elements of the patient's internal object relations.

Case study 1

I had seen Miss A for two years in psychoanalytic treatment and during that time she had positive feelings toward me that she never spoke to directly. She would never volunteer any transference feelings, but when I would comment on their absence she was very forthcoming. She told me she felt very safe, thought of me as always "on her side," and saw my office as a "special and wonderful haven." We understood this as a phantasy in which I was a person with whom she could do no wrong and always felt welcomed. Miss A would resist any exploration of this one-sided idealized transference. Therefore, I always felt suspicious of what else might be afoot.

One day she seemed unusually uncomfortable and anxious. After sputtering back and forth, she explained how her friend had said that given how I practiced, I must be a "Freudian." Miss A felt very insecure and worried. To her, a Freudian was one who is only interested in sex and money. She was not sure if she could trust me any more and was concerned that I was subjecting her to "questionable Freudian techniques." When I suggested we explore her sudden mistrust, try to understand how this had come about, and see what it meant, she assured me all was well and I had "no need to worry." This was said in a way that seemed ominous or mysterious.

After the hour, and during the next two days, I had certain difficulties. I felt she would turn on me and get rid of me. I felt as though the person I always knew and trusted was suddenly an adversary. Dr Jekyll was about to become Mrs Hyde. Examining these strong feelings, I started to understand how she had turned the tables on me. In her childhood, Miss A often was left to deal with her manic-depressive father who could dramatically shift from friendly "dear old Dad" to a selfish or frightening figure. While she had often spoken of this and its continuing manifestations in her adult life, it had not been a clear part of the transference up to now. She had turned passive into active by the use of PI. She projected the parts of her that were scared of being abused by a "Freudian" father object into her mental representation of me and then onto me interpersonally.[2] This was accomplished by the subtle teasing threat of "Oh, don't worry," much like the wolf had assured little Red Riding Hood to not worry. I then felt afraid of being rejected and attacked by her. Fortunately, I was able to understand this as a concordant countertransference where I identified with her vulnerable feelings and feared her as the nasty father object. I was able to regain my footing by the next hour. When I introduced these ideas, the roles we seemed to be playing out, her hidden wishes and fears, and her use of PI as a way of coping, we were able to explore them and gradually work through them.

Ogden (1979), synthesizing many ideas, including those of Bion (1959) and Rosenfeld (1952b), states:

> projective identification . . . is a psychological process that is simultaneously a type of defense, a means of communication, a primitive form of object relationship, and a pathway for psychological change. As a defense, projective identification serves to create a sense of psychological distance from unwanted (often frightening) aspects of the self; as a mode of communication, projective identification is a process by which feelings congruent with one's own are induced in another person, thereby creating a sense of being understood by or of being "at one with" the other person. As a type of object relationship, projective identification constitutes a way of being with and relating to a partially separate object, and finally, as a pathway for psychological change, projective identification is a process by which feelings like those that one is struggling with, are psychologically processed by another person and made available for re-internalization in an altered form. Each of these functions of projective identification evolves in the context of the infant's early attempts to perceive, organize, and manage his internal and external experience and to communicate with his environment.
>
> (Ogden 1979: 362)

With Miss A, one can see most of Ogden's ideas illustrated. Miss A used PI to defend herself from the fear of her internal father, to communicate her affective states to me, to relate to me in a way that paralleled early intrapsychic parental connections, and to encourage me to struggle with her internal states in a manner that might enable her to handle them better herself.

Case study 2

In this second case, I related in sadistic and controlling ways, triggered by the patient's PI mechanisms.

Mr J was a twenty-four-year-old man whom the courts sent to me. He had committed a series of petty crimes over the years and showed no remorse. He justified his actions as necessary and felt the court system "had it out for him." Mr J thought the judges, parole officers, and social workers all were unjustly picking on him. I saw him in once a week psychoanalytic psychotherapy for several years. He would become paranoid that I was using him and forcing him into therapy. At that point he would break off treatment until he returned to fulfill a court requirement.

If I asked him to commit to a regular weekly hour, Mr J felt I was controlling him. In turn, he controlled me by making us have a random, week by week schedule. I noticed that we had fallen into a routine where I asked him about the next appointment at the end of each hour. He would then deliberate about when he might be able to come, which ate into my time before the next patient. I started to feel controlled, like he was "just taking his sweet time." I was irritated and felt under his thumb. Technically, I felt that if I pointed out how he lingered at the end and his possible motivations, he would feel accused, get defensive, and retaliate; so the next time I inquired about scheduling at the beginning of our hour. I was painfully aware that I was turning the tables on him. As he tried to sort out when he could come in, Mr J became more and more irritated. He said I was manipulating him and stealing his money. He became paranoid and told me that he wasn't paying me to discuss paperwork. As he felt more trapped, he became verbally abusive. I started to feel intimidated.

At that point, I interpreted that he was scared I was controlling him and he was feeling like he would do something he would regret but felt unable to stop it. He said he did feel controlled and felt like he might make a commitment to see me that he would later regret. Mr J said he didn't like to make mistakes and is very careful to avoid making a wrong move. This moved us in the direction of discussing his overly critical superego. He felt lacking and weak much of the time. I showed him how, through PI, he discharged this punitive part of himself into his objects for relief. Then he quickly felt attacked and controlled by those now punitive objects. I told Mr J that he wanted me to be his helper, a person who could show him the way out of his anxieties and confusions, but in his mind I quickly changed into a bad person who would abandon and attack him. He relaxed enough for us to discuss his feelings and thoughts a bit more.

Fortunately, my acting out was momentary and I regained my footing enough to comment on his anxieties. This led to a shift in his normally defensive stance. Nevertheless, I found myself getting into countless little sadomasochistic cat and mouse games with this patient. We seemed to take one step toward exploring his mental conflicts and one step sideways into acting out his internal phantasies and fears.

Another example of this patient's use of PI occurred in an hour where he felt very persecuted and worthless. He spent the hour telling me how "the system" was against him. He claimed "they" were making countless accusations that made him appear to be a real criminal. I interpreted that he felt ashamed of himself and unable to know what to do about it. He calmed down for a bit. The rest of the hour he told me how his situation would be comparable to me being accused of having sex with minors and the humiliation I would feel at being falsely accused.

At the end of the hour, he walked out the door and said, "Now watch out for those minors!" I felt he was trying to use PI to discharge his shame into me to escape his anxiety. I told him, "You are trying to share your shame with me, so I know what you feel like." While his PI efforts were also defensive, I chose to interpret the communicative function.

Grotstein's (1986) contributions regarding PI specify the multiple aims, the simultaneously occurring states of self and object differentiation↔fusion, and the intrapsychic as well as interpersonal aspects of PI. Grotstein's idea of the ego discharging unwanted aspects of itself into an object is close to what my patient seemed to be doing with me in the transference. He tried to jettison the poisonous parts of his controlling internal objects by projecting them into me. He then identified with me through the more controlled, defeated, and enraged parts of himself that felt withheld from my emotional supplies. In regards to setting the schedule with Mr J, these roles were switched. My complementary countertransference turned into a concordant one. In other words, I started off feeling like I was being made out to be the persecutory father. This shifted to me feeling victimized, which made me want to turn the tables on him and victimize him back.

In a brief paper delivered in 1949, Paula Heimann stated:

> the analyst's counter-transference is not only part and parcel of the analytic relationship, but it is the patient's creation, it is

part of the patient's personality. The emotions roused in the analyst will be of value to his patient, if used as one more source of insight into the patient's unconscious conflicts and defenses; and when these are interpreted and worked through, the ensuing changes in the patient's ego include the strengthening of his reality sense so that he sees his analyst as a human being, not a god or demon, and the "human" relationship in the analytic situation follows without the analyst's having recourse to extra-analytic means.

(Heimann [1949] 1989: 77–78)

As Heimann notes, the analyst tries to continuously understand how the emotions the patient arouses in him or her can be of value to the treatment. In the case of my patient Miss A, I was successful in doing so. In the case of Mr J, I went back and forth between interpreting the PI process and throwing his struggles back at him to get relief from his unconscious and interpersonal pressures.

As Sandler (1976) has clarified, the analyst is always involved in some sort of acting out that is best understood as a specific measure of "role responsiveness." PI is the most basic mental mechanism which invites that type of dynamic. The analyst serves a containing and translating function in the PI process, whether the patient is still in treatment or not. Perhaps it is best to say that neither patient nor analyst is ever out of treatment.

Case study 3

Miss B told me, in the first hour, a tale about dating a man who could not commit to her and was "wishy washy." Miss B portrayed herself as solidly interested in him and clear about what she wanted: a commitment. When I introduced the idea of a regular appointment hour and the possibility of multiple weekly visits, she immediately felt it was something that she would find "overwhelming," "way too much," and something she "couldn't possibly commit to." We suddenly seemed to get into a debate and a tug of war. I tried to use logic and explained that I needed to see her regularly, and at least once a week so I might be able to help her. She responded by becoming more anxious and repeated that she couldn't commit to anything right now and that commitment just "wasn't her style." I was too thrown off by her abrupt switch in presenting herself to interpret her projection of her own fear of commitment into the date which she now felt with me. We left it that we would meet again, but clearly she was now in charge, with appointments happening "whenever" and "maybe once a week at the most." This was very much like the ongoing dynamic with Mr. J and his reluctance to commit to regular hours. However, the underlying phantasies were different. I felt that if I made interpretations that were specific about this fear of commitment, Miss B wouldn't have been able to take them in. I felt she would have taken them as a more concrete pressure to submit to me. In fact, later on this is what some of her fears turned out to be.

What I did say to Miss B was, "You are fearful of an involvement with me, which may be a clue to some of your difficulties. Let's take it up next time." As we ended, I noticed I had gone over by ten minutes. This felt like we had become too close on one level and not close enough on another. It alerted me to the blurring of boundaries so often produced with excessive or pathological PI mechanisms.

Looking back on the session, I believe I enacted the smothering, controlling object by telling her that I needed time to treat her. Pick (1985) writes:

> The contention that the analyst is not affected by these experiences is both false and would convey to the patient that his plight, pain and behavior are emotionally ignored by the analyst. [I am suggesting] that if we keep emotions out, we are in danger of keeping out the love which mitigates the hatred, allowing the so-called pursuit of truth to be governed by hatred. What appears as dispassionate may contain the murder of love and concern.
>
> (Pick 1985: 165)

I would add that not only would we be mitigating the love by ignoring the countertransference, but also denying the aggression, pain, and confusion we feel that has been projected into us. With Miss B, I felt the urge to pursue her and convince her of the importance of multiple visits. I was forcing her to commit and to submit to a relationship with me. This was an acting out on my part based on her projections of a greedy, needy, and forceful part of herself. She then sided with the part of herself that felt victimized, dominated, and manipulated. Only over the course of many months of treatment did the particulars of these feelings and phantasies come to light and a working-through process begin.

Case study 4

Miss M was a patient who entered treatment for help with job troubles. She felt she always worked extremely hard for others but never got recognized for her efforts. In fact, she felt like others took advantage of her generous nature and piled on more work because of it. After the first few hours of treatment, my impression was that she related to her objects, including myself, in a masochistic manner that was based on fear and tightly managed rage.

The patient's father had left the family when she was an infant, and her mother seemed to collect and discard boyfriends at will. She treated people as though they were expendable. Miss M told me she "got the message" early on to be good or risk her mother's total rejection.

After the patient's health insurance ran out, we began discussing what fee she could afford. She said she wanted to "simply know" what my fee was and if she couldn't pay it then she would stop attending. When I told her my fee was somewhat negotiable depending on her income and how often she attended, she became tense and silent. The more we tried to discuss the fee, the greater her anxiety grew. I asked her what she would like to pay, based on her current income. She was visibly sweating and sprang to her feet and demanded to know my fee so she could decide to remain in the room or leave for good if she couldn't afford it. I interpreted that she felt very worried about hurting me if she revealed her own thoughts and desires on the matter. I added that she worried she could cause trouble between us. She started to cry and said, "Yes. I also think you would get rid of me if I open my mouth!"

This was the beginning of a complex and rich therapeutic process. We gradually explored her fears of me being like mother and possibly rejecting her for what Miss M felt to be unacceptable aggressive needs and toxic thoughts. In the transference, she projected her easy-to-ruffle, rejecting-mother part of herself into me and she sided with the threatened-little-girl part of herself. In that early hour, I had experienced a complementary countertransference in which I began to act out some of the characteristics of her internal objects. I sensed that she was anxious about the fee setting, but I kept ploughing ahead with it in a somewhat sadistic and stubborn manner, almost forcing her to have an opinion. In these ways, I was pushing her into a place that felt dangerous and sure to lead to pain for somebody. Her phantasy of her own destructiveness, which would push me into being rejecting and attacking, was to become known later in the analysis. However, this PI and countertransference acting out helped us start to see her fear of me as a rejecting persecutor.

It was important to Miss M's sense of internal safety that she keep me matched with her phantasies. Even though this meant I was an attacking or non-understanding figure, it was better than facing the pain of not having a caring object. The sense of loss was overwhelming. Regarding patients who try and keep the analyst matched with their internal expectations, Feldman (1997) writes:

> the lack of this identity between internal and external reality may not only stir up envy, or doubts about the object's receptivity, but create an alarming space in which thought and new knowledge and understanding might take place, but which patients find intolerable.
>
> (Feldman 1997: 232)

Analysts struggle to understand the patient's projections while all the time feeling tempted and pushed to act out the patient's unconscious object relations. PI is a dynamic mental mechanism that naturally engages the analyst's countertransference. It is a dynamic in which the ego attempts to make use of the analyst as a translator, toxic dump, or special reservoir for the unwanted, confusing, or threatened parts of the self the ego is unable to cope with. I have been presenting case material to show the frequent and usually unavoidable acting out of countertransference feelings that hopefully lead, sooner than later, to a full enough understanding on the part of either analyst or patient that a mutative interpretation is made.

Feldman (1997) writes,

> the patient's use of projective identification exerts subtle and powerful pressure on the analyst to fulfill the patient's unconscious expectations that are embodied in these phantasies. This impingement upon the analyst's thinking, feelings and actions is not an incidental side-effect of the patient's projections, nor necessarily a manifestation of the analyst's own conflicts and

anxieties, but seems often to be an essential component in the effective use of projective identification by the patient.

(Feldman 1997: 228)

Therefore, a patient's PI efforts are most likely to bring about some type of impact and result if they affect the analyst. Often, if a patient feels the analyst ignores these efforts, they may double them or they may give up and try elsewhere, acting out in other relationships.

Feldman continues, "what is projected is not primarily a part of the patient, but a phantasy of an object relationship" (1997: 234). This is the reason the analyst is often tempted to act out. The PI mechanism brings the analyst in touch with core phantasies of a particular type of relationship that lives within the patient's mental structure. The urge for the analyst is to become an active participant and act out the according feelings and behaviors. In psychoanalytic treatment, first the analyst and later the patient strive to understand these intrapsychic projections and what the elements of that phantasy relationship are. Verbalization, exploration, and understanding then provide a vehicle to work through the various conflicts, fears, and pains associated with those phantasies.

Chapter 7

Projective identification, self-disclosure, and the patient's view of the object

The need for flexibility[1]

Jacobs (1998) writes:

> Our technique calls for restraint, neutrality, abstinence. But with some patients this leads to resistance. In such instances we may need a different approach to engage these patients. Some patients need more of us.
>
> (Jacobs 1998: 247)

Some patients seem to need a modified method of interpretation at particular junctures in the treatment. Others demand a flexible approach throughout the analysis. This is usually due to acute paranoid phantasies of being attacked, rejected, and abandoned.

Rosenfeld (1983) felt PI was used for more than just defensive purposes:

> one has to realize that projective identification is not just one single process but includes many different types of projective identification. There are also processes which are similar to projective identification but not identical with it and it now seems important to differentiate and understand these processes in greater detail.
>
> In a previous paper (1971a), I suggested first of all that it was important to differentiate between projective identification used for communication and projective identification used for defensive purposes such as ridding the self of unwanted parts of the self. I also described a third very important form of projective identification which is frequently observed in the transference relationship of the psychotic patient which seems to be based on a very early infantile type of object relationship. In this form

of projective identification one observes that the patient believes that he has forced himself omnipotently into the analyst and this results in a fusion or confusion with the analyst and anxieties relating to the loss of his self. Here the projection of omnipotent or deluded parts of the self into the analyst often predominates.

(Rosenfeld 1983: 263)

With some patients, making direct and specific interpretations of the transference and PI mechanisms is what helps ease their anxiety. This is the avenue I try first because it usually works. If the usual approach to dealing therapeutically and analytically with a patient doesn't seem to help, and I have explored the reasons why, I may try a modified contact.

Concerning the importance of working with the transference, Strachey (1934) writes:

instead of having to deal as best we may with conflicts of the remote past, which are concerned with dead circumstances and mummified personalities, and whose outcome is already determined, we find ourselves involved in an actual and immediate situation, in which we and the patient are the principal characters . . .

(Strachey 1934: 133)

Whether the analytic situation is "flexible" or "standard," it is hopefully an exploration of the transference/countertransference dynamics and the PI matrix, since this is where the patient's unconscious phantasies and anxieties manifest.

With more territorial individuals who see the world as divided into puppets and string pullers, a more cautious stance can prove helpful. First, I make comments about the PI mechanisms they use with external objects in their day-to-day life. Next, I interpret the interpersonal context of PI, between patient and therapist. I may stay at this level for a long time. In fact, it may be as far as some patients can go. Making genetic PI interpretations also seems helpful if this type of patient becomes anxious. It certainly is a retreat from the transference and an avoidance of the here-and-now relationship; but usually these are cases where nothing else works. Finally, after laying groundwork with interpretations of their PI efforts with external objects and of the interpersonal

context of the transference, I proceed to more standard interpretations of the intrapsychic nature of PI within the here-and-now
transference. This flexible approach is a way of warming up to the
mutative moment in which the interpretation directly refers to the
object of the patient's phantasy, the analyst.

Again, I only mention this warming-up approach to working
with PI as a method I have had to use as a deviation or modification to more usual interpretive techniques. A few very difficult
patients have benefited from it. I would stress the need for the
analyst's careful examination of their countertransference, to avoid
using this modified approach to act out the patient's PI phantasies.

Both patient and analyst need to free associate during the
session. The patient is encouraged to speak his mind in totality.
Then, the analyst must quietly examine the contents of his own
mind for information that applies to the situation and judge what
would be useful to use in some type of verbal intervention. I often
find my emotional response to a patient takes the form of a
conscious mental picture or story concerning some type of one- or
two-person conflict. I then find a way to put that countertransference image into words, if the analytic moment seems right. My
interpretation is formulated on the current relational and internal
interplay between analyst and patient. Strachey (1934) has summed
up the vital points in making interpretations. He writes:

> a mutative interpretation can only be applied to an id impulse
> which is actually in a state of cathexis . . . interpretations must
> always be directed to the 'point of urgency'. At any given
> moment some particular id impulse will be in activity; this is
> the impulse that is susceptible of mutative interpretation at
> that time, and no other one . . . but as Melanie Klein has
> pointed out, it is a most precious quality in an analyst to be
> able at any moment to pick out the point of urgency . . . a
> mutative interpretation must be specific: that is to say, detailed
> and concrete.
>
> (Strachey 1934: 149)

Some patients are so gripped by paranoid phantasies that they
hear most any interpretation as an attack, even when it is detailed
and concrete. Some have such sadistic superegos that they take any
interpretation as a cruel judgment. These patients are difficult to
maintain in treatment because interpretations that normally soothe

actually make things worse. The analyst is caught, with the patient, in a vicious cycle. What works best with some of these cases is to interpret that cycle.

However, interpreting the source and intent of the projection can push patients into being more defensive and regressed. Making an interpretation about other aspects of their PI phantasies can allow them to explore their thoughts and feelings without feeling as pressured to re-own their unwanted affects and thoughts. Knowing enough about the patient's phantasies and anxieties to position the interpretation where the patient will best receive it is important. Malcolm (1995) has done interesting work in this area. Some patients can take the information in if I say, "I am really stuck right now. I feel I can't say much without making it worse." This would be the use of self-disclosure in the service of the patient's ego. Essentially, I would be disclosing my feelings as the stuck and cornered aspect of their ego, which has become lodged within my psyche through PI.

The topic of self-disclosure has many proponents and many detractors. In recent years, there have been numerous discussions on the topic (Aron 1997; Chused 1997; Gerson 1996, 1997; Maroda 1997; Renik 1995; Burke 1992; Cooper 1998). *Psychoanalytic Inquiry* (1998) devoted an entire journal volume to the topic and the *Journal of Contemporary Psychoanalysis* (1995, Vol. 31) brought together several discussants on the topic. Many other papers, panels, and workshops have occurred in the last few years.

However, the issues are far from being resolved. Most of the literature available tends to be from analysts within the inter-subjective, interpersonal, or self-psychology schools. There is a marked absence of material from the Kleinian school on disclosure. I hope to fill some of this void with a few thoughts on the use or misuse of disclosure. Weigert (1954) writes:

> the unconscious of the analyst is a receiving organ. His countertransference, lifted into consciousness, becomes an important source of information in the analytic process. Any rigidity, any automatization of attitude or procedure can become a defense against intuitive insight and block the passage from the unconscious to the conscious processes of the analyst. It is therefore important that the spontaneity of the psycho-analyst not be muffled by the rigidity of his technique.
>
> (Weigert 1954: 703)

This captures the essence of being flexible and receptive to the patient and whatever they bring to the analytic relationship. Countertransference is often the best tool to detect PI within the transference. It is also the vehicle through which self-disclosure usually emerges. However, there is no particular reason to share one's own thoughts and feelings about matters outside of the immediate clinical situation.

I feel self-disclosure is rarely necessary, but when it is, it is for very specific technical reasons. Rather than a supportive gesture based on ideas of relational connection or intersubjective inter-action, self-disclosure is best used as a clinical tool of interpretation that specifically targets the patient's phantasies about their objects. The actual disclosure is a revealing of particular countertrans-ference thoughts and affects that have been generated by the patient's PI mechanisms. So self-disclosure and analytic flexibility, as I am defining it, are not shifts away from analytic treatment to supportive therapy. It is more of a therapeutic stretching of certain analytic postures to accommodate moments of extreme difficulty in the patient–analyst dyad. Therefore, this differs from Pine's (1984) ideas on using supportive techniques to supplement the standard interpretive approach.

In other words, clinical judgement may deem the best inter-pretation to be made in the moment to be a description of how the patient's projections affect the patient's object. This is also an exploration of the intricacies of the patient's defensive relation-ship to their object rather than a direct interpretation of the leading anxiety that pushes them to engage in their defensive maneuvers.

Clinical judgement helps the analyst match and balance inter-pretations to the patient's level of psychic urgency at any given moment. These interpretative decisions are made by evaluating the affect, physical gestures and sensations, and associations in both analyst and patient. Neutrality and abstinence are necessary and helpful procedures, yet there are times when they can be loosened. For example, some patients with paranoid character structure will debate over why coming in once a week isn't just as good as coming in twice a week. Similarly, they might argue that they can achieve the same degree of health from three times a week as they can from four times a week. With some of these patients, trying to explain the rationale behind our clinical recommendation would be an acting out by the therapist of "I will prove to you why you must be here," as well as an avoidance of the transference. This is usually in tune with their tug-of-war PI phantasy.

With other patients, giving them the "facts" can be helpful in paving the road to future interpretations. It can temporarily help them to trust the relationship enough to stay rather than flee. It also helps them feel like they have some power or say in a relationship they may feel to be dangerous or confrontational. Providing a matter of fact response can assist them to proceed with their material. At the same time, offering our clinical rationale when asked can be used as a coercive weapon to circumvent resistance. Therefore, clinical judgement is crucial. Again, flexible approaches are only helpful for select cases. Using flexible approaches, including self-disclosure, should be a carefully thought out detour from standard technique used for specialized reasons.

Few Kleinians choose to disclose their countertransference affects or phantasies to the patient in the form of PI interpretations. This is a very complicated theoretical and technical issue. I will try to bring some clarity to this matter by showing how I approach clinical material in which disclosure became part of the PI process and the transference–countertransference matrix.

Case study 1

One patient, Frances, was mired in obsessive phantasies about power, control, and justice. She used manic defenses to always be correct and better than her analyst. Any interpretations I made, she had already thought of. This was to prevent the breakdown of her omnipotence and to avoid the loss of her fragile, idealized object. We could have no differences. Part of her anxiety was about me keeping secrets. Frances felt I might have knowledge about her or her problems that I didn't share. This was unacceptable because it showed we were separate and different. It also made her feel inferior and humiliated.

During one period of her analysis, Frances became convinced that I had an opinion about her condition that I wasn't sharing. She demanded to know. Her insistence to have what she "had a right to know" escalated over the course of several sessions. It began to take on an obsessional and paranoid quality. She would not rest until I handed over "the secret." Frances felt I had a piece of her and she was ready to fight for it, to prevent a collapse of her integrity and feeling of power. After one rather grueling hour, with her becoming highly agitated and demanding, I felt cornered, controlled, and on the verge of being fired. In other words, I was sure she was about to quit her treatment unless I gave in and surrendered the goods.

Between these sessions, I found myself thinking and worrying about our relationship. It occurred to me that I was feeling as she often had growing up. She had felt bullied and controlled by an alcoholic father and a manipulative mother. Frances obsessively confessed all her shortcomings to her mother, since any aggressive or sexual feeling made her dangerous and sinful. By confessing to her mother, she regained her feeling of being better than her family. Omnipotence or loss and confrontation were her choices. Using my countertransference and my knowledge of her background steadied me.

When Frances arrived for the next hour, she refused to use the couch and demanded I tell her what I thought of her. She was anxious and agitated. She said she was on the verge of quitting. Frances was an obsessive neurotic, mostly organizing her mental life within the depressive position. However, as she easily regressed into paranoid-schizoid persecutory phantasies I felt it important to be very sure of what unconscious state she was in that day before making my interpretation. If she were mostly managing her inner world from the paranoid-schizoid perspective, I felt it would be unwise to make a transference interpretation about her thoughts and feelings toward me. This usually makes such a patient increasingly defensive and prone to a paranoid flight. In such a situation, I find it more clinically helpful to interpret the ego's vision of the object. This might include some self-disclosure. Therefore, I was ready to tell Francis that I was feeling confused and cornered, like things would go sour if I did not succumb to her demands. I was prepared to say that I was willing to share my thoughts with her about how she was doing. Nevertheless, I felt nervous about what she needed and how everything suddenly seemed to have so much weight, as if everything could rise or fall based on what I said.

When I began to tell Frances that I was willing to talk with her about her worries and to try and help her out with what she needed, she calmed down. She visibly regrouped and began to relate to me from much more of a depressive stance. I was less of a dominating dictator in her eyes. By acquiescing somewhat to her phantasy about our tug-of-war, she felt less gripped by such severe anxieties. When I saw that she had reintegrated somewhat, I decided to make more of a standard PI interpretation concerning the transference.

I said, "You want me to tell you what I think of you. You grew up with a father you wanted to be close to and get inside and understand who he was. You wanted to look up to him and be close to him. You craved to know how he felt about you. Instead, you had a father who was angry and drunk most of the time. You felt blocked from knowing him and from knowing if he cared about you. Then he killed himself and you felt you would never be able to get inside him and know him. Now, you are letting yourself be more vulnerable with me and are starting to want to know about me. You want to know how I feel about you, but you are worried I am blocking you as well. This makes you furious and sad and you want to try and push your way in. That conflict of wanting to be inside of me and feeling shut out is happening more and more lately. You are hoping I will see that and help you out." This was a more oedipal-based interpretation that directly addressed her urges and fears.

Frances listened intently and seemed to relax immediately. After a long silence she began associating to memories of her childhood and her desires to be close to her father. Frances also told me she wanted to find out more about me but felt unsure if I would be nice or if I would be mean and withhold things. Based on my assessment of her intrapsychic structure, her unconscious phantasies and anxieties, and my own countertransferences, I was able to make sense out of her PI mechanisms and offer an appropriate interpretation.

These deviations from regular technique only apply to some patients who are very defensive and paranoid. These are the patients who are unusually rigid, controlling, and scared of others.

One paranoid, psychotic patient was so anxious about not getting a handshake from me at the end of each hour that she alternated between shouting at me for being a cold, mean bastard and begging me for some sign of compassion and love. She was so locked into her phantasy of me as a teasing, distant father whom she needed desperately and immediately that asking her to discuss it was like pouring gasoline on a fire. We were at a stalemate. I shook her hand at the end of the hour. Not surprisingly, she complained that it was a miserable, cold gesture and she wanted a "real handshake." Overall, what did happen was that we became less stuck.

Gratification is nevertheless a tricky matter. Some patients will become insatiable and others will pose the question: "If you fed me that time, why not all the other times?" I think it is inaccurate automatically to assume a person with ego defects needs gratifying support. This woman could not and would not continue unless I gave in to her demand and her need. Some patients do indeed create an ego emptiness from excessive PI. It is an emptying of the self into the object. Also, through excessive and destructive PI and splitting, the ego can become fragmented and disintegrated. As with all patients, deficits, conflicts, demands, and needs are always found together, never apart. The way a patient can demand immediate satisfaction, pushing and manipulating the therapist into various levels of acting out, is always a danger and must be noticed, explored, and analyzed. However, it is a situation that can't always be avoided.

Another patient, whom I will present in great detail later on, came to me to stop smoking. His symptom – inability to stop smoking – was a fragile oral compromise that helped him from becoming floridly psychotic. When in the first meeting he asked me if I had ever smoked, I said yes and that I had quit. This type of clinical decision, to make a shift in my standard clinical technique, was based on an on-the-spot assessment of the patient's ability to maintain connection to a phantasy of a good object. This patient appeared on the verge of severe paranoid-schizoid fears and delusions. Sometimes, an interpretation will do. At other times a combination of self-disclosure and interpretation is needed.

Unfortunately, some patients are so inundated with persecutory phantasies about the torturous character of their world and their objects that this type of technical deviation only postpones the inevitable flight out of treatment. However, gratification via the therapist's self-disclosure can sometimes foster further analytic exploration and interpretive work. This disclosure can serve as a momentary buffer to the patient's annihilation anxiety, making it possible for some patients to proceed to the more standard or typical analytic work.

This change in typical technique would only be applicable with select patients who are overwhelmed by internal destructive forces and who take interpretation as attacks. These patients are not amenable to analysis at that clinical moment, thereby requiring a temporary parameter. In this sense, the parameter isn't "non-analytic." It is simply a necessary precursor to, or place-holder for, future analytic work. It prepares the soil for some patients to enter a more traditional analytic treatment.

With one borderline case, I chose to make a comment that was both gratifying, self-disclosing, and interpretive. The patient asked me why I hadn't called her when her father was dying. If I had simply been quiet, she would have reacted violently because her anxiety about being dependent on me was very high. Therefore I chose to say, "I thought of calling you, but felt it would be too intrusive or confusing. However, your wanting me to call you sounds like you would have liked me to. I think you want me to call you so I can take care of you and be like a loving father. At the same time, I think you wanted me to call because for you to call me feels like your being dependent, weak, and vulnerable and that scares you." My self-disclosure was in the form of an interpretation, and it was a comment that pointed out the PI aspects of her struggle with loss, dependency, and rejection.

I consider all these technical shifts away from standard or ideal analytic procedure to still be true to the basic analytic approach. The goal remains the same: the analysis of the transference and PI dynamics, unconscious phantasies, and the principal conflicts regarding destructive and loving forces.

The flexible approach can be a partial collaboration with the resistant side of the patient. This tradeoff is only helpful if absolutely necessary. One patient would always become concrete, paranoid and withdrawn with here-and-now interpretations. I found over time and with experimentation that it was better to make more reconstructive comments than here-and-now transference comments. These genetic reconstructions were helpful and often led to her making associations to more current anxieties, but I was also collaborating with her avoidance of the transference. My approach with her was a technical judgement based on her being very defensive, paranoid, and lacking certain symbolic functions. If I tried to explore these areas, she typically regressed quickly into a fight-or-flight reaction. When she told me that her male friend from college had visited and they ended up "sharing the same bed," I asked how that was. I thought it was clear that I was asking her how she felt about being in a sexual situation with a man she had only been friends with up to now. She replied, "Well, my ability to stretch out and use the whole area of the bed was compromised."

If I dug deeper, she rapidly decompensated into a markedly paranoid stance; therefore I felt unable to say or do much of anything. In this way, through PI, she controlled me as she felt controlled by her objects. She projected the controlled and helpless little girl part of her ego into me and dominated me with the cold, crazy, and cruel mother aspect of her ego. Although she related to me this way many times over the years, I was still amazed at how cold and distant we could be. She was still apt to react with fear and retreat when I made transference comments or when she thought I was doing something unfair and controlling.

The analytic standards of neutrality and abstinence are helpful therapeutic tools. However, the degree to which these tools are helpful in a treatment depends on the details of the patient's current phantasies and anxieties. In some portions of a treatment, the ratio of analytic standards to non-analytic interactions can vary widely. At certain times in an analysis, the treatment might be filled with extra-transference material, extra-transference interpretations, mutual acting out, and various interpersonal interactions. The analyst has to be aware of this shifting ratio and mindful of why it is occurring and when to intervene to change the balance. However, the clinical ingredients of day-to-day analytic therapy are always in flux.

Strachey (1934) felt that extra-transference interpretations were helpful in bring the focus back to the transference, that they act like an important vessel for the vital contents inside: the mutative transference interpretation. He writes:

> the fact that the mutative interpretation is the ultimate operative factor in the therapeutic action of psychoanalysis does not imply the exclusion of many other procedures (such as suggestion, reassurance, abreaction, etc.) as elements in the treatment of a particular patient.
>
> (Strachey 1934: 159)

I would add that the flexible approach to analytic treatment with certain patients is another factor to be found alongside the important mutative transference interpretation. In fact, for some patients the flexible approach makes the use and success of the mutative interpretation possible.

Many patients relate to the analyst by PI and splitting. Klein (1946) writes:

I have repeatedly found that advances in synthesis are brought about by interpretations of the specific causes for splitting. Such interpretations must deal in detail with the transference situation at that moment, including of course the connection with the past, and must contain a reference to the details of the anxiety situations which drive the ego to regress to schizoid mechanisms.

(Klein 1946: 21)

Certain patients are so internally disrupted by the excessive use of splitting and PI that a flexible approach to interpretation is useful.

Case study 2

Franz had seen me for seven years. Throughout this time he frequently pulled me into a sadomasochistic relationship where he first felt attacked by my interpretations and then would pull back and become oppositional. During these times, Franz felt I was picking on him and being cruel.

The time in his psychoanalytic treatment I wish to focus on involved his upcoming graduation from college. He was about to receive his degree in psychology and was very nervous about starting his career. His phantasies about not being liked in job interviews, not being able to compete with other new grads, and general worries about venturing out of the protection of college brought on intense anxiety. He felt trapped and began to see me as part of the group of people and places he was annoyed by. His fear turned to anger and contempt as he shifted to a manic defense. He split his objects into those that were accepting and wonderful and those that were rejecting and nasty. Franz projected his bad objects into me and his local job search. Within a few months, he was convinced that it was stupid to remain in the area when such fantastic career opportunities awaited him elsewhere. He imagined wonderful opportunities and friendship in distant locations. He devalued his therapy and any potential job offers he had in his home town. It came to a point where he was literally thinking of moving to a far-off city he had never been to solely on the idea that they might have entry-level psychology jobs. Franz seemed oblivious that he was about to sever his long-term relationships with his analyst, friends, girlfriend, and family.

I found myself echoing with the feelings of a bad object that had been discarded, deemed as unnecessary and worthless. These countertransference feelings were the result of his destructive PI process. These were phantasies of being unwanted and unaccepted in his new post-college life. At first I acted out these feelings by giving him parental advice on the advantages and disadvantages of moving so abruptly. This led to us being like a rebellious teenager/concerned parent pair. I was aware of this but also quite caught up in it. At one point in our stalemate, Franz pointed this dynamic out to me. I agreed with his observation and said, "I guess I am a bit thrown off course, confused. After working together for seven years with lots of ups and downs, you told me a few weeks ago that you will probably be gone in two months. I guess I really don't know how to proceed. What should we talk about? It feels so abrupt. It's unclear what to do. I am not sure what you want." This was a deliberate self-disclosure of the effects he was having on his object and a statement of what I felt he was probably unable to deal with directly, without projection. He had projected these unbearable feelings into me and I was now struggling with them.

Franz paused and thought about what I said. He replied, "I think I know what you mean. I've been feeling so overwhelmed by the idea of starting a career that I have not wanted to deal with anything. I am trying my best to ignore all my relationships and just think about escaping somewhere. When I start to think about going to interviews and having people not like me, reject me, I can't bear it." I said, "I think you have been so overwhelmed with that anxiety that you have wanted me to hold onto it for you. So then I look like I'm a lecturing parent. You're hoping I can cope a little better and help you out." In saying this, I was interpreting his projection of his own judgmental superego and his demanding oral urges that usually left him feeling either unsatisfied and angry or persecuted by the needs of others. The result of our work in this session was a decrease in his reliance on the manic defense and PI as well as more insight into his anxiety. My self-disclosure was the use of PI-induced countertransference to make an interpretation.

Through the process of splitting and PI, I had acted out portions of this patient's phantasies. I had begun to pick on Franz. I was an external vessel for his overwhelming self-doubts and fears of rejection. When I revealed my confusion to him, I was showing my own struggle with doubt, loss, and rejection. This helped him to have hope in his own ability to struggle with these troubles. On another level, I had interpreted the character of his object's struggle, an unbearable aspect of himself he had felt pressured to expel into me.

If the patient's phantasies are primarily about their objects (whether it be that the object is caring, persecutory, or easily hurt), selective self-disclosure can be helpful. If the patient is mostly focused on a phantasy about themselves, it is less helpful.

Self-disclosure is not a "reality check" for the patient, nor is it a supportive measure. It is an intervention that is not often necessary, but it can occasionally prove useful with some patients in some circumstances. In these moments it serves as a way to investigate the composition of transference and PI phantasies and to see if the analyst's experience is the same as the patient's. It is more of a clarification of the patient's phantasy.

Cautionary notes

Disclosures made outside the arena of interpretations are often countertransference acting out. Making a self-disclosure in the service of an interpretation can easily be acting out as well, disguised with the rationale that it was technically necessary. Therefore, one needs carefully to assess who will truly benefit from such a disclosure.

Self-disclosure should not be a licence for anything goes. Some therapists have taken to self-disclosing a wide variety of personal thoughts and feelings without too much scientific reasoning. It is hard to cite examples of what would be off limits, but such things as sharing one's dreams with the patient are hard to justify.

I would consider this type of interaction a wild use of counter-transference and a way of avoiding the digestion of the patient's PI processes which easily do evoke feelings, thoughts, and dreams.

Another form of self-disclosure that I feel would be counter-productive is the expression of affect as a way of showing the patient how they impact others or how affect should be expressed. This seems at best some type of educative, supportive counseling rather than analytic; at worst it is manipulation and suggestion.

I believe it is dangerous to think we can provide the mold of what is right and how to be. This is more of an attempt at re-parenting and making the patient into our image than an analytic exploration. Analysts who practice this way seem to be working mostly within the context of external reality and interpersonal interactions. They appear to have lost sight of the huge impact of phantasy in a person's life and how that quickly dissolves any simplistic one-to-one answers in a complex analytic situation. While some patients with gross cognitive impairments may need this type of direction, most patients don't. Unless the treatment is already limited by managed care, acute psychosis, or addiction, more directive and suggestive methods seem counterproductive.

Persecutory anxieties and a lack of symbolic ego function so grip some patients in the paranoid-schizoid position that they equate the analyst as the bad object without any as-if quality. These paranoid individuals rely on destructive splitting and excessive PI mechanisms to cope with their frightening internal experiences. Unfortunately, this generates a vicious cycle in which good objects are unavailable or destroyed and countless bad objects invade the ego.

These patients test the ordinary limits of analytic treatment. While staying within a Kleinian perspective in my technical approach, I use a certain analytic flexibility to help keep these patients in treatment long enough to begin addressing their fragile psychic states. Flexibility may include the select use of self-disclosure. This would be limited to information directly related to the transference and to PI dynamics operating in the moment. Hopefully, this flexibility will be a containing experience that gradually allows the treatment to move into more of a standard analytic situation. Analysts should proceed cautiously when applying this flexible approach or when using self-disclosure, for countertransference acting-out or collusion with the patient's PI mechanisms is a real threat. Self-disclosure, even when helpful, need not be a reason to stray from the time-tested emphasis on the analysis of transference, PI, and intrapsychic phantasy.

Chapter 8

The relationship between projective identification, symbolism, and loss within the paranoid-schizoid experience

In this chapter I use one in-depth case study to explore the destructive PI process that certain paranoid-schizoid patients engage in. These difficult-to-reach patients are caught in a pathological cycle of loss and intense object-related conflicts that push them to rely on excessive and aggressive forms of PI. This overuse of PI dynamics causes a fundamental problem in normal symbolic functions. PI is the cornerstone of healthy symbolism, which helps the developing ego deal with various anxieties and enables the potential for creativity through displacement and sublimation.

However, some patients are dealing with the loss of an internal maternal object who provides a containment–symbolization function. While this is often the result of actual maternal failure, or traumatic experiences between mother and child, this loss is kept alive with a destructive PI process. The ego defensively blocks acknowledgment of any symbolizing capacity in the maternal object out of fear of facing rejection and persecution by that object. Destruction of symbolization in the object provides an artificial respite from the threat of annihilation yet quickly brings on even greater levels of internal chaos and anxiety. This leads to a frantic search for the next, better symbol; but this new symbol quickly collapses under the same pathological object relations matrix.

Melanie Klein (1930) has described the infantile ego's struggle with its object-related aggression. The desire to destroy the breast, the vagina, and the penis (which stand for the whole objects of mother and father) generates great anxiety. The ego wishes to hold onto its good objects and therefore feels anxious about hurting them. As a result, the ego begins to equate its part-objects with other things, both internally and externally. Projected aggressive feelings again turn these objects into dangerous or damaged objects, promoting the ego to make new and different parallels. These new locations can be found in other relationships, certain pursuits, concrete objects, or particular ways of viewing the world. This is the formation of symbolic function, which shapes sublimation and creativity. The balance between plentiful good objects and the healthy use of splitting and PI fosters this positive growth. These normal aspects of development can be derailed by excessive internal pressures from bad objects, intensive and unmodulated ego aggression, or a stressful external environment.

Symbols only become completely formed psychic structures when the ego reaches the depressive position. At that point, symbols represent whole objects and an amalgam of love and hate felt toward those objects. Segal (1978) noted that these depressive symbols are part of a healthy integration of loss, fear, and disappointment.

Symbolization begins in the paranoid-schizoid position as elementary, unconscious phantasies with brittle constellations of positive and negative affect. Splitting is again the major mechanism that bolsters early symbolic organization. Therefore, when symbols emerge within the paranoid-schizoid position, the symbolizing maternal container is an idealized object.

The more fragile the bond between ego and object, the more that symbols threaten the ego. When destructive forms of PI and excessive oral aggression erode the splitting process, the ego begins to lose hold of its idealized objects. These objects then easily shift into persecutory objects. This creates a cycle in which the ego desperately tries to maintain all good visions of the world to ward off a sense of loss and attack. Manic and omnipotent styles of relating and narcissistic delusional states are common in building back the lost object and preventing attack.

The ego feels pressure to reestablish contact with an ideal object that provides acceptance and love without conditions. Symbols are a potential threat to this and therefore the ego must avoid or destroy them. All these internal struggles create terrible binds.

The symbolizing function of the idealized maternal object becomes feared as well as envied. Under normal circumstances, the early ego uses splitting to keep the ideal and the bad aspects of self and object apart. When PI destabilizes this splitting process, the ideal object is contaminated or destroyed. The ego experiences this as a loss of safety, a loss of power (achieved through identification), a loss of love, and a loss of a symbolizing function.

At that point, the ego has a terrible choice: to attach to an object that is a constant reminder of loss and persecution or be without a protecting maternal object that translates, modifies, and symbolizes otherwise disturbing inner conflicts. A symbol is inherently healing to the psychic system, restoring ties to the object and resolving unconscious relational conflicts. To these patients, however, their internal hostility is so great and the PI process so destructive, that symbols and the maternal symbolic function become overly infused with hostile and rejecting feelings. In other words, oral aggression, transported through PI, reduces symbols to potential threats to internal safety and stability.

These types of patients see the symbolizing function of the analyst as a threat and therefore retaliate or defend themselves. Insight, the analyst's containing and symbolizing activity, is experienced as something that catches the ego off guard. It reveals something that was previously unknown and therefore unpredictable and frightening. In response, the patient will try to keep the treatment very safe, predictable, and narrow. Everything must be already understood or known. New knowledge or change is dangerous.

The transference relationship is constructed through multiple projections and splitting mechanisms that manage the patient's anxiety and phantasies about the analyst's body and mind. The sum of this internal construct is a new symbol in the internal landscape. If the patient cannot effectively master the conflicted libidinal and aggressive aspects of this object relationship, then the ego attacks its own symbols, using denial, splitting, and PI. In trying to eliminate the anxiety, the ego tries to create a new, safer symbol through continued reliance on PI. Into this new symbol is projected the most toxic of these conflicted feelings, usually phantasies of loss and persecution. Since this process occurs in the paranoid-schizoid position, the new symbol is fragile and easily destroyed by excessive aggression, greed, or envy. So, sooner rather than later this new symbol loses its safety-enhancing and containing abilities and becomes as chaotic and threatening as the previous symbol. Unless this process is interrupted by the understanding, containing, and interpreting function of analysis, this self-defeating search for a new and better symbol as a respite from persecution and loss never ends.

The case of Sam the smoker

Sam had called me to see if I could help him stop smoking cigarettes. He was twenty-seven, living with a girlfriend he had been with for five years, and working for the Postal Service. Sam had smoked for the last eleven years and had tried to quit many times. He had tried various over-the-counter remedies but was never successful in stopping.

I told him I could help him to explore any possible psychological reason for smoking and any psychological issues that might be preventing him from stopping. Sam said he wanted to meet and discuss these matters further.

My impression, when talking to Sam on the phone, was of someone very anxious and scattered. He seemed somewhat immature for his age. There was a feeling of desperation in his voice, yet a concrete focus on cigarettes possibly to contain that free-floating anxiety.

Summary of three initial sessions

Sam came in and readily gave me a great deal of information about his family and his childhood experiences. While he didn't say this, my impression was that all the information was to show me the nature of his real problems beyond the smoking and to help me understand the kind of fear, confusion, and anxiety he experienced as a child and still felt as an adult. My countertransference feeling was that of being with someone who was not only extremely nervous but not fully in touch with reality as well.

Sam told me, "I almost killed my mother. When I was born, my mother almost died. She was in the hospital for months. My father took care of me for the first six months of my life." I was of course struck by his phrase, "I almost killed my mother." I made a mental note to watch for associations to guilt, annihilation anxiety, and fear of reprisal from the mix of reality and phantasy. I was also struck by how Sam was without his mother from the very beginning of his life and cared for by his father instead.

Sam continued, "I sucked my thumb and carried around a security blanket until I was eleven years old. I have always been afraid that my father will die. From as far back as I can recall, I worried about that. My parents never got along. My father is really obsessive and neurotic. My mother is just plain out weird and paranoid. She is suspicious of everything. They got divorced when I was six years old, but then they got back together. They split apart again a few years ago. I have never been able to sleep at night, since I was a little kid. These days, I lie awake until two or three in the morning every night, sometimes later. All I can think about is my father dying. Also, I can't stand my job so I think about that sometimes. I guess things haven't gone that well for me. When I graduated high school, I was supposed to give a speech in front of the whole school. Just before I went on stage, I started to feel really peculiar and dizzy. I shit my pants and started to cry. My father took me home and cleaned me up. I was out of it for days, staying in bed. Something like that happened a few years ago when I got into a motorcycle accident. Well, I came really close to getting hit on a motorcycle, but I wasn't actually hit or hurt. But, I couldn't speak to anyone for about a month. My girlfriend and my father took care of me and cooked me meals. I wasn't hurt physically, but I felt really strange."

Sam went on to tell me how everyone in his family pressures him to become famous and wealthy. He said he always feels uncomfortable and worried about what they think of him. This idea of disappointing the needs or demands of his family would come to color the transference later in the treatment.

I didn't necessarily take what Sam said about his history as fact or fiction. I simply respected it as his current psychological view, which was generating a particular set of internal phantasies, object relations, and interpersonal styles. So far, part of this inner landscape seemed to include the idea that he had almost killed his mother, the idea that his father could die at any time, the sense of needing to be special in the eyes of his family, and a great deal of general anxiety that often overwhelmed him.

Sam continued, "It started when I was a kid, but continues to this day. My mother always tells me stories about people getting killed, raped, or beaten up. Sometimes, it is a horrible story she has heard on the news or read in the paper. Other times, I think she just makes up something gruesome."

Suddenly, Sam changed his direction. He said, "I hope you don't feel burdened by me asking for a receipt when I pay my portion of the insurance benefit. I didn't even ask if it is OK to bring this hamburger in with me. It is lunch time but I should ask. I am sorry. I hope you are OK with all that. Anyway, where was I?"

I interpreted, "You were talking about your mother's stories of death and destruction. Maybe you are worried you are hurting me and destroying our time together." This comment was based on Sam's shift from talking about mother to apologizing about his "offenses." In other words, I wondered if Sam was using PI to deposit some of his anxieties into our relationship. Sam said, "I sure hope not. But, I do worry that I am dying. I have been to lots of specialists to get special tests to see if I have terminal cancer from smoking. Each one says I am in perfect health. But, I don't believe them. I think they are deliberately hiding something. I am sure I have something very wrong, maybe terminal cancer. Why won't they be honest with me? I think they are trying to screw with me. They just look at me like there is something mentally wrong with me, but I know the truth." I said, "Maybe you feel there is something emotionally wrong with your mother and you feel like she has given you terrible feelings and thoughts. She tells you about terrible things happening to other people and now you feel like there is something terribly wrong with you." "I don't know," Sam replied.

When he said, "I sure hope not," he took my question about his transference feelings and phantasies as a concrete statement concerning a current threat. He seemed to erase the as-if quality of it. In that respect, Sam appeared concrete and simplistic. However, he continued the complex, psychological theme of someone being in danger by switching the threat to cancer. Now, he was in danger of dying from cancer. Here, I think he was breaking off the intrapsychic connection to me when it was too overwhelming and creating a new relationship, via PI, with the cancer threat. I think the cancer threat became a symbol for the emotional threat he felt at that moment.

I met with Sam for the next eighteen months, twice a week. By that time, Sam was less confused and less anxious; and he was less disorganized in his thinking. However, his paranoid-schizoid functioning continued to dominate his perspective of the world.

A session during the fourth month of treatment

Initially, Sam would tell me a great deal about his smoking history, how much he smoked, and the many times he tried to stop. He seemed rushed and anxious as well as looking to me to somehow magically make it all better right away. There was a strange sense of us talking about smoking when something else much more intense floated in the background.

In this session, Sam mentioned in a casual, neutral manner that he often felt trapped and controlled at work and would go behind the Post Office building to smoke and pace about. He felt his boss both ignored him and made his job miserable by purposely giving him difficult tasks. Sam said, "He makes my life hell for some unknown reason."

Next, Sam told me he had taken LSD when he was nineteen. He worried that he had caused some sort of permanent damage to his brain and had feared for many years that he would lose control over his thoughts. Again, from the strange, vague, and anxious state Sam was in and from my countertransference feeling of being with someone who was not fully in touch with reality, I decided to introduce a more organizing and immediate focus to his communication. I interpreted his LSD worry as a fear of losing control over his feelings should he face certain thoughts about his life. This was a general sort of interpretation that directed Sam's worry away from the external fear of LSD to an internal psychological context. Also, I was trying to decode the more distant symbolic into the more present, object relational experience he was having.

Sam responded by discussing his ongoing fears of having LSD "flashbacks" and losing his mind. I still thought this was a disguised way for Sam to talk about a frightening experience of his mind falling apart. So, I said, "So you feel controlled and on the edge of losing control." Sam said, "Yes. I do. I feel lost in life. I have never had any direction. I just float around." Thus, my interpretation seemed to have shifted his fears from a concrete phobia to a richer emotional plane.

Now, Sam became angry, anxious, and tearful, yet in a detached and odd sort of way. He said, "My parents always wanted me to be a doctor. My father is a surgeon and my mother is a nurse." I said, "So, maybe that is part of your feeling controlled, by them wanting you to be just like them. Maybe cigarettes help you with the strong feelings you have about your parents." Here, I tried to tie his presenting complaint to his deeper emotions. I presented the idea that the cigarettes were a symbol for his conflicted feelings toward his parents. He needed his parent/cigarette, but felt worried about a toxic dependency.

Sam said, "No. Cigarettes have me hooked because of the nicotine. And, I just don't like the rules." So, he responded by shifting away from the emotional feelings he was having and focused on the concrete item I had brought up. But, he was able to still reference his feelings. Sam recalled important feelings about his childhood. He said, "When I was growing up, life was very, very strict. But, it wasn't like my mother and father had lots of rules. In fact, that was sort of the whole problem. My mother always broke all the rules. She snorted cocaine all the time and in front of everyone. When we went to this concert, I think I was like ten years old at the time, she started a fight with this big biker guy and got a black eye. A big fight broke out and everything. I was mortified. As a child and later as a teen, I was always completely shocked. I was always feeling embarrassed or mortified. She showed up drunk to the parent–teacher night one time. I couldn't look my teachers in the eye from that day on."

I said, "It must be frightening to have a mother who can't control herself or take proper care of you. It might have made you very anxious to have no rules growing up, but wanting mother to have rules for herself. As a result, it sounds like you have strong, mixed feelings about rules." Sam replied, "Yes, I am mixed. Well, yes. I think so."

After about seventeen months of analytic work, Sam was able to stop smoking. During those seventeen months, he frequently gave me updates on how much he was smoking and how he wanted to stop. However, most of our time was not spent discussing cigarettes. In fact, in the whole scope of the treatment, this was a very small part of our focus. Again, I think this is because the smoking topic was a safe way for Sam to enter into treatment and a safe way to maintain control when talking about his internal world became overwhelming. Also, we were able successfully to explore the feelings and phantasies that cigarettes held symbolically.

The last two months of treatment

Sam started off this session by saying, "I haven't smoked for two days! Now that I have stopped, I have been thinking of what cigarettes mean to me. I think smoking represents freedom for me. I feel totally free and unburdened when I have a smoke." I said, "Maybe you are talking about being free from your mind's worries and conflicts. Maybe you feel controlled inside so smoking gives you the feeling of being free from that control." Sam was able to take in my interpretation and begin to deepen the discussion.

Sam said, "Yes. That is the way things are. The world makes you do stupid things. They force you to have a 9–5 job, to pay bills, and do all sorts of other ridiculous bullshit. So, with smoking, I feel controlled by the habit but I feel a great freedom from the stupidity of the world at the same time." Instead of being able to say, "I feel as if I am being controlled by others," it was more a statement of fact.

In retrospect, perhaps Sam felt I was forcing my opinion on him. If I had asked him what he felt freed and unburdened from, he might have felt more in charge and less persecuted.

I wanted to deepen Sam's focus from the persecutory external world to his own inner turmoil. To work through this PI dynamic, I said, "Maybe you want a feeling of freedom from being controlled by your family." "Yes," Sam replied. "My mother manipulates everyone into her own way of thinking. She controls you and everything you think!" Noticing how he said "she controls YOU [analyst]," I replied, "So, you try to avoid feeling controlled at work, out in the world, and with mother. How do you try and avoid that feeling here?" Sam told me, "I don't. That is different and not important." I replied, "You have mentioned before that you worry how I see you." He said, "Well, yes. But, it is mostly something I feel about other things like my job. I used to feel that way in school: first elementary, then high school, and finally in college. Now, it is my job."

When I confronted Sam's external projections of persecution by bringing up the transference, he deflected it. But, he had been more able to address his fears of his mother's controlling ways. So, I went with that direction. I said, "I think your mother plays a big role in what you are talking about." I was shifting the focus to the genetic root, but still away from the projections into school and work. Sam replied, "Yes. She is always calling me, sometimes three or five times a day. She calls to either ask if I am looking into how to become more successful or to tell me a gruesome story about some murder or rape." I interpreted, "You must feel your mother is trying to push her mind into yours and control you with demands and threats." I used the word "threats" because it sounded like mother was essentially calling to say, "either become successful or something horrible will happen to you." Sam agreed with my comment and went on to elaborate how irritating and overwhelming it is to have his mother calling all the time.

At this point, I began to think of Sam's father. On the one hand, Sam's father seemed so supportive of Sam, a real ally. Based on Sam's experience of his father, as relayed to me, I thought of father as helping Sam when Sam had completely collapsed psychologically and as helping Sam to keep functioning day to day.

On the other hand, I pictured Sam's father as rather weak in light of mother's outrageous behavior, and possibly even colluding with that behavior. So, based on my countertransference reverie, I said, "Maybe you feel like your father. You both are unable to stand up to your mother and you feel you can't stand up to your company, or to life. Your father sounds like he never felt in charge of things. Maybe you aren't sure how to feel strong either." Sam replied, "One time when I was twelve years old, we all ended up in this crappy old bar in a lousy area of town. My mother wanted to stop in for a drink. Of course, she got rip-roaring drunk and she started dancing and stripping off her clothes. She had most of her clothes off and my father finally stepped in. It was the first time I remember when he ever set a limit with her. My mother is weird about stuff like that. At home, she does everything in the nude. She cooks, cleans, and watches television in the nude. Ever since I remember, I had to beg her to get dressed whenever friends came over."

I wanted to focus on how this may have shaped Sam's relationship with his own self and his own ability to deal with aggressive and other strong feelings. So, I said, "These kinds of things may have left you feeling like you can't manage your own life and left you feeling you can't have a say in the world around you, whether it is with me, your job, or other people." Sam replied, "That is interesting. That might be. I want a say. I don't know."

In this next session, Sam began by reporting on his smoking. He was still not smoking, but had thought about how much it had been a part of his life. He told me he felt frustrated by how much of "a slave" he had been to the habit. I was thinking about Sam's internal world and how he felt trapped with maternal objects that had their own freedom at his cost. I said, "Maybe you envy how free and easy other people have it." Sam replied, "I find myself lying awake at night worried about the teacher at my meditation class. I feel he is always looking at me strangely, like he is judging me or laughing at me. And, I don't like being in the class sometimes because the other students look at me weirdly too. The teacher says I am too spacey and sensitive. He told me I say things that don't make any sense and he asks me if there is something wrong with me. Other people have said that before. It bothers me. I don't understand what their problem is!"

Now, this is an example of how I say something and Sam replies with what seems on the surface to be a very unrelated and disorganized thought. Indeed, his replies are often paranoid and at times psychotic. However, I noticed that many of these seemingly odd replies were merely Sam's associations and defensively veiled references to either the transference or expansions and elaborations of my interpretations of PI. This is not a process unique to Sam's psychology but one common to more disturbed patients. It is something one must listen for and be able to translate.

Dynamically, I think the object relationship that Sam is in, at that moment, becomes overwhelming, due to a PI cycle of aggression, greed, and persecutory guilt. My interpretation may focus his conflicted feelings on that object relationship to the point of it becoming a threat to him, his object, or both. So, using even more projective mechanisms, he relies on symbolism to create a new, safe object relationship. Technically, we are still having the same discussion, but the props on the stage have changed.

Therefore, when Sam jumped from my general comment about feeling envious of other's freedom to the specific focus on his meditation class, he was becoming more detailed about a situation where he felt trapped and judged, without freedom. He was explaining his feeling of others having more sense and clarity than he could hold in his own mind. His reference to feeling judged by the meditation teacher was a reference to his worries about me and how I felt about him. If one follows the speech and associations of a disturbed patient in this analytic fashion, the patient is much more understandable and therefore potentially more reachable. This primitive symbolic function, fueled by PI, is the underlying communication to be translated.

I told Sam, "What others are calling 'spacey and weird' might be them noticing how anxious or worried you are, preoccupied with your thoughts and feelings." Sam replied, "I never feel nervous unless I am here or at night, lying in bed." I asked, "What are you afraid of at night?" I choose to ask this first as I wasn't sure if he was referring to his fears of father dying or something else. I already knew coming to see me made Sam anxious of being judged. Sam replied, "Well, I am sure there are maggots in the mattress, or some kind of filthy bug. And, sometimes, I get afraid they can come out and bite me or give me a rash or something. I have checked the bed in the daytime but I think they are only there at night. I have asked my girlfriend about it and she says to not think about it. But, I am sure they are there. I have sprayed the mattress with different sprays but the bugs must be resistant to it. I feel like they are crawling all over me sometimes."

I asked, "So, when was the last time they came out?" I was thinking that this delusion of maggots was based on his unwanted feelings coming out and him not being able to cope with them. In terms of symbolic function, I wondered if the bugs represented a conflicted relationship with an object and that symbol had now become persecutory and overwhelming rather than the symbol being an effective way to cope with an internal struggle.

Symbols are containers for intrapsychic struggles. However, in the paranoid-schizoid position, these contained struggles and conflicts easily become one-sided and overwhelming when colored by excessive reliance on PI, leading to the desperate construction of another symbol. Since the core phantasy and feelings aren't effectively dealt with, the new symbol quickly becomes pathological as well.

Responding to my question about when the bugs last appeared, Sam said, "On Monday." I said, "That is the day you said was really tough. You had a run in with your boss and later that day your mother called you and wanted to see you. I wonder if at night you feel all alone with your feelings, like nasty bugs you can't control. Maybe you had a lot of feelings about your mother that night, feelings you have a hard time coping with. The bugs are your feelings that you can't deal with. I think that if you can understand those feelings better, the bugs might not be a problem." Sam said, "I think I see what you mean. But, I don't want anything bad to come out." I said, "Let's see why those feelings are so bad, so frightening. You must get anxious here with me for the same reason. You think bad feelings will come out like nasty bugs. But, I think we can deal with them." Sam said, "I don't want anything bad to come out. But, I am not nervous. In fact, I feel great. I am really happy most of the time. Life is good and I am happy."

Clearly, Sam's anxiety about his bad bug-like feelings was overwhelming and he had to pretend to be happy instead of overwhelmed. Through interpretation, I attempted to address the primitive symbolic nature of the invasive mother bugs and Sam's fear of his own feelings becoming unleashed and crawling all over without control. Sam's anxiety about facing these feelings and conflicts drove him to solidify his feelings of being "bugged" by his mother into literal maggots that he needed to spray. The mental became concrete, safe and inaccessible.

In the next session, Sam told me he was thinking ahead and noticed his insurance benefits would run out in several weeks. I told him it was actually in place for a longer period of time and he might even be eligible for more after that. But, I asked if perhaps he had other thoughts about staying in treatment. Sam answered, "Well, when it runs out, I am sure that will be enough. I need to apply what I learn to my everyday life. I feel stagnant being here, just thinking about stuff. I need to live and get on with my life. It is time for me to be a part of the world instead of dwelling on everything. I need to rely on myself."

I said, "I wonder if you have mixed feelings about being here. You want to count on me, but probably worry about what that means and what the consequences might be." Sam replied, "I had this dream. I hope you don't take it personally. I don't want to hurt your feelings. So, don't take it personally. Well, let's see. I was in your waiting room. There were all these women. Out on the street were all these men. I didn't know anyone out on the street, but I think I knew most of the women in the waiting room even though I was sitting by myself. I was sitting out there, really worried about going in to see you. Your office was like a big bank vault, but then, after a while, it turned into a little, dirty, jail cell. When I walked into it to see you, my mother was there instead of you. And, that was the end of the dream. Weird! I don't know if I like being here any more. I feel pretty trapped in this therapy."

I felt this dream clearly contained Sam's phantasy and feelings about me, his mother, and his father. I thought his important yet distant father was out in the street. He knew the women (mother) in the waiting room, yet described himself as quite isolated and distant from them, on his own. I clearly went from a "safe" bank vault to a persecutory jail cell and mother replaced me as Sam's analyst. And, in asking me to not take it personally, Sam tried to take the emotional and symbolic meaning out of it, erasing the persecutory, the needy, and aggressive elements from the relationship.

I interpreted, "You are hoping for the safety of me and the bank vault, but you worry that I will turn into a controlling prison cell and be like mother." Sam said he felt guilty talking about his mother in a negative way. I replied, "Maybe when you have negative feelings to express they feel like dirty bugs and you worry I will be angry and change from being safe to trapping you. You are often very cautious with me, maybe that is why." Sam said, "I am that way with everyone. I don't want anyone to take things wrong. I don't want anyone to get the wrong message." I said, "It sounds like our relationship is like a minefield, it could turn sour." Sam said, "Yes. It feels that way." In saying it "feels" that way, I was encouraged that Sam could momentarily hold a reflective stance rather than embrace the regressive, concrete, and persecutory.

I thought Sam was telling me about the fears that kept him from getting too close and kept him from feeling safe enough to express some of his conflicts and negative feelings. So, I interpreted, "I think part of you wants my help and safety, but then you think you will turn me into something dangerous with your negative feelings. That leaves you feeling trapped and controlled. So, you are not sure if it is a good idea to rely on me or not. Then, you try and be independent because if seems safer." Here, I was focusing more on the persecutory phantasies of what Sam called guilt. Also, I was interpreting his fear of his aggression mutating the object into a retaliatory foe. To use his object as a container or a symbol was a threat, as he felt the object-container would collapse and retaliate. I think that when the basic object relationship feels so fragile and threatening, there is little hope or strength in the ego to use symbolism to create a new object. So, with the more disturbed patient such as Sam, they are either trapped with a symbol that is persecutory and abandoning or they desperately run from one pathological symbol to the next. Externally, this is what we call acting out, as this internal flight frequently takes on behavioral manifestations.

Replying to my transference comment, Sam said, "I think you are right. I think I need to move out of Marin County and leave this whole area. It is time to get moving and make my life happen. It is time to put it all together and take off." I said, "If you feel it is dangerous to rely on me and express your feelings, you probably do feel like it's better to skip town before you get trapped in my jail. But, let's see if we can solve some of those feelings next time." Here, I took up Sam's concrete stance and tried to place us back in a relational and psychological context.

At his next session, Sam spent the first ten minutes telling me how tired and exhausted he was. He explained it in a vague way, hinting that he was very stressed, not sleeping well, and worried all the time about work. When I tried to find out more details about how he felt and what exactly was going on, he said, "There is no need to discuss it, it is not a problem, really." At this point, I think Sam felt our relationship was too fragile, threatening, or untrustworthy. So, he seemed to cut off the internal connection with me.

Next, Sam told me how his manager at work appeared to be on the edge of either a mental breakdown or a heart attack. The manager appeared exhausted and tense to Sam. Sam felt this was brought on by the manager being overworked. Sam said, "I am thinking of going to the president of the company and suggesting that we all make some kind of intervention to save him. What do you think I should do? I am worried my manager would be upset if I did that, but it looks like a matter of life or death." After turning away from his contact with me and my questions, Sam projected our relationship into his manager. Thus, he created a new symbol through PI. However, the unresolved phantasies remained. Therefore, his manager appeared tired, exhausted, and stressed. Also, it seemed plausible that Sam was projecting a combination of himself as a frightened child and his out-of-control mother onto the manager and hoping someone, like his father or me, would intervene and make things bearable.

I interpreted, "You often worry about your father, your boss, and my feelings as well. Maybe, you are overwhelmed by that and want my help. But you are worried that it is not OK to make a fuss over yourself and need help." Sam answered, "I feel awful. I don't know how much longer I can take it. I am worried all the time about so many things." Here, I think Sam heard my interpretation as permission to let me in on how he really felt. So, he was temporarily able to reveal how upset and fragmented he was.

However, now he needed to project these feelings due to his fears of retaliation; he wanted to create a more distant, safe symbol to experience these feelings in. Sam said, "My meditation teacher gave me some special coaching the other day. He was very encouraging and spent extra time with me. That felt wrong, very bad. I feel like I am a terrible burden to him. It isn't right. I have been very troubled about it."

Thinking of both the transference, the PI dynamics, and its genetic roots, I interpreted, "Maybe you worry about hurting me and other men, like your father, by depending on us too much and wanting us to intervene and help. You worry that relying on me will make me feel burdened and then resentful and judgmental." Here, I was linking his vision of being destructive to the object to his fear of the object's retaliation. This, I think, is the fundamental problem that creates pathological symbolic functioning in the paranoid-schizoid position and is caused by excessive, destructive PI functions. Sam replied, "Well, that is why it is wrong and dangerous!" He was agreeing with me, but as if it was a fact. Rather than being able or willing to reflect on this frightening way of seeing our relationship, he kept it as a concrete fact.

In this next session, Sam began by telling me about work. He felt very stressed and said he felt his boss treated him unfairly. Sam told me, "Why does he make me do so much? I feel guilty leaving early to come here, but I can't take the overload. He is too much. I am overwhelmed." As Sam went on about work, I understood what he was saying to mean that he was feeling persecuted by his own sense of guilt over abandoning his boss. This was a different man than the manager Sam had worried about, but I think he felt he had abandoned both of them and was now in danger of their revenge. In this PI phantasy, both Sam, his manager, and his boss were all equally heartless. This led me to say, "You are very strict with yourself, very rule bound about time and other things. This must make you feel very pressured from the inside and from the outside." I choose to interpret the feelings and the dynamic process that was held within the symbolic work story, in order to better focus on his immediate anxiety.

Sam replied, "I called my father and asked him about it. He said I should relax and I shouldn't take it all so intensely. He said I am doing OK." At first, I was taken by surprise at this. Then it made sense. I pictured father trying to help Sam with Sam's feelings about his mother's crazy behavior. It seemed that Sam still felt conflicted by whether the rules were being followed correctly and if everyone was trustworthy and predictable, or if everyone was unsafe, irresponsible and out of control. He applied this to himself as well as others.

Next, Sam said he had woken up at four o'clock in the morning the previous day and went into work to try and catch up on things. He said he had woken up in a panic about all the work he was behind on. Now he was exhausted. I interpreted that he was unsure if he was out of control like mother or not, so he had to put in extra to be sure he was responsible and in control. He wanted to keep the peace with his boss. What I didn't add was that I thought his boss represented Sam's angry demand for care and rules, angry at the Sam/mother for not being a good caretaker. It seemed to work better to titrate my interpretations in this way because when I said the whole concept all together, Sam tended to become scattered. Replying to my comment, Sam said, "That feels right. I think you see how it works." Here, Sam was able to stay with my comment and not turn to a new symbolic object through anxious overuse of PI – but not for very long.

Now I tried to add the genetic piece. I said, "The way your mother broke the rules and the way you felt about it must leave you unsure about how to deal with things now." Sam began to sniff loudly and clear his throat over and over again. He looked like an animal with something caught in its throat, desperately struggling to maintain its breath. This was a reaction that had occurred other times throughout the treatment, always when I raised some difficult topic. Once he stopped, I pointed out the connection between what I had just said about his mother and his intense physical reaction. In other words, I tried to bring attention to the shift from mental to somatic and the change from mental persecution to physical suffocation. I also pointed out how he might feel I am choking him with painful memories. Sam told me he simply "had a history of doing that, maybe allergies or something." He took the psychological meaning out of it, as it was too dangerous and painful to hold in his mind as a symbolic, relational concept. Instead it was merely an action without meaning. This concrete approach to something that probably has psychological significance is part of what Bion (1959) has termed an attack on linking. It is a deliberate unconscious effort to undo the tie between thought, emotion, and meaning. However, it is a different process than the PI strategy used to create symbols to hold/hide the phantasies and feelings about a conflicted object relationship.

I told Sam I thought his choking might be an anxiety reaction to what I had said. Sam replied, "In grade school, the teacher would get mad at me for doing that, but I couldn't help myself." I asked Sam what he was thinking and feeling as he snorted and choked. He said, "I heard my parents have a skunk in their basement. They can't find it and it is tearing up some stuff they have stored down there. And now the whole house smells like a skunk." What I noticed was that Sam had indeed answered my question, but in a symbolic manner, shifting his direct feelings into a loose association away from my question but with the affect remaining intact. Interpreting this, I said, "You seem gleeful about their suffering. You are answering me and letting me know you are angry with your parents and want some revenge. You have suffered and now they suffer." So, after his attack on linking, his thought process became concrete and simplistic. However, the affective bond to the object was intact, but now projected into a new symbol, the skunk problem.

Sam replied, "They can't call in an animal control officer to help because my mother is growing pot in the basement with special lights!" I said, "I think you are angry with her for always breaking the rules and making herself the priority instead of you, so you are happy to see her suffer with the skunks." Sam said, "They sent me to a strict Catholic school while they went to transvestite parties and sex-swapping meetings. It doesn't seem fair." Here, Sam was being much more direct with his feelings. He felt his parents' neglect and contrary actions were unfair and he told me so. With my understanding and containment, via interpretation of his PI and his problems with symbolism, Sam went from thought derailment and defensive symbol formation back to the core phantasy and immediate relational focus.

Sam began by telling me he was worried about his insurance benefits running out and him being unable to continue treatment. He said he had been "feeling crazy." I said, "Maybe part of that tension is about not being able to continue our work together." Here, I tried to extend the "feeling crazy" into something more relational and with meaning rather than separate and without context. Part of the analyst's function is to take in the projected and split-off elements of paranoid-schizoid phantasies and translate them into more whole-object, depressive elements with psychological meaning. This is the container function of words and interpretations that Segal (1978) described, as well as part of the overall container–contained relationship of analytic work that Bion (1957) has described.

Sam now switched to talking about his daily eating habits. He said, "I like to have everything predictable. I don't know why. I eat the same thing every day. I have to. I can't stop even if I wanted to. In the morning, I always have a glass of milk, one black coffee, and a banana. For lunch, I have a hamburger without fries. And, I always drink a six-pack of bottled water every day. For dinner, I have some sort of pasta every night. I have been doing this for at least a year without a change. Before that, it was different items, but I had them every day too. If I go out to a party or something, I will eat differently, but otherwise that is it."

I replied, "You were talking about feeling crazy and out of control and worried about the predictable relationship we have built. Now, you are making yourself feel balanced and secure by talking about your predictable foods that you can count on. You have rules for what you eat and those rules give you a feeling of security." Here, I was pointing out Sam's way of gaining control after he started feeling anxious. I was also interpreting his use of symbolism in an effort to go from one collapsing object relationship to one that felt more reliable. It is noteworthy that the initial reason for Sam entering treatment was another oral compulsion, smoking. At this point in the treatment, his concern about smoking and his actual dependence on cigarettes has lessened. By now, Sam has become much more engaged with me in a more psychologically investigative manner. He is more willing to look at how his mind functions and how he perceives his objects. However, he is still prone to avoiding links between feelings, thought, and phantasy as well as having troubles with symbolism. While he certainly demonstrated a massive use of defenses, particularly PI, and the loose associations characteristic of the more disturbed patient, we were making more and more sense out of what he experiences and the nature of how his internal world is constructed.

Sam told me he felt "off balance and irritated" when he doesn't follow his strict dietary requirements. I took what he said and added it to my thoughts about a pattern Sam had built into the analytic relationship. For months, he had brought two bottled waters to his sessions, which were typically around his lunch hour. He gave me one and we both had a water during the session. I felt this, like most actions, served multiple purposes. I thought it was both defensive as well as geared toward attachment. It was a guarded and controlled effort to keep us safely organized with predictable parameters, yet bring us close at the same time. So, I interpreted, "I can see how you might start to feel off balance and anxious without all the food rules. I think bringing waters in for us is like that too. It is a way for you to feel safe and organized with me, but it also is a way to build up our relationship. You are being cautiously friendly. So, there is a lot of meaning to your food rules and to our waters. Without them, you start to feel nervous, alone, and threatened."

Sam responded, "It was a tradition in my family to have apple juice at breakfast. Everyone had it every day. Even on vacations, we would all go to the restaurant and order apple juice." This response to my interpretation was enlightening. It appeared Sam was evading my transference comment by turning to something outside our relationship. However, he was actually deepening the direction of my comment by both seeing us as family and addressing the genetic root of his actions with me. Also, I think the direct focus on our relationship created too much anxiety. Uncertain if I would remain safe or turn into the mother–jail cell, Sam created a safer symbol to put us into, the family apple juice. Due to the dependency on PI, the paranoid-schizoid patient is often mentally running from one symbol to another, just before the last one collapses. Gently interpreting the anxiety and phantasies in the current moment, in the current symbol, in the transference, and in the extra-transference situations can help the patient deal with what are often intense fears of abandonment and persecution. In this way, the analysis of PI helps the patient rebuild, fortify, or trust the current symbols they are using without having frantically to search out new ones which are equally unreliable. Again, these symbols are often the core object relational phantasies about the mother or the analyst that are then projected elsewhere.

With these ideas in the background, I said, "You are telling me about the apple juice, but I think there is something more about it. Just like the water brings us together, you are remembering how your family came together with apple juice. It is a nice memory, but maybe hard to have when so many other things pulled your family apart." Sam responded with startling clarity, "Maybe my mother treated me like just one more glass of apple juice, instead of what the apple juice meant. Yesterday, my father said he is proud of my efforts at work." I said, "He is someone you feel safe with and trust, but I wonder if you feel secure about that relationship." This comment was based on my sense that father was a figure who switched back and forth from dependable to undependable or even betraying. Sam responded, "Yes. But, I don't feel OK without him in my life."

Now, I chose to bring the focus back to the transference and said, "Maybe you aren't sure if I think of you as just a water-break or if I realize there is something very important going on here." Sam said, "Well, I like what we talk about. I don't know. Well, I will have to think about it."

At the start of this session, Sam told me he had thought about my ideas regarding attachment to me with the water. He said he disagreed. He said it was just as easy to get two waters at the store as it was to get one, so it really didn't mean anything. Then, Sam told me how invasive his mother was even in his adulthood. He related a story of his mother coming to his workplace and barging in on a meeting he was having. Loudly, she invited him to lunch. Embarrassed in front of his coworkers and feeling cornered, he agreed. They went to lunch and mother proceeded to get drunk and cause a scene. Sam said this is typical of how she manages to spoil his life at work and away from work on an ongoing basis.

Thinking some of his comments were a reaction to my last interpretations, I asked Sam if my comments felt invasive. He replied, "No. I just worry about the topics. I worry that you will want me to discuss things that feel bad. Sometimes, I feel you are attacking me and saying there is something terribly wrong with me or with my personality. So, I think of ways to defend myself and avoid the topics altogether. I kind of know logically that you aren't doing that, at least on purpose, but I feel that way nevertheless." I felt Sam was probably projecting an abusive mother object and his own guilt-ridden critical self into me. I also felt hopeful that he was being reflective and "knowing logically" that I wasn't attacking him. So, I said, "I wonder if you hear me that way because you are very strict and critical of yourself. If you are harsh with yourself, you will expect me to be too."

Sam replied, "Maybe. But, my job isn't a matter of me being scared of getting criticized or controlled. It is real. All jobs suck, at any company. It is just some giant conglomerate making sure it sucks all the life and money out of everyone and everything. It is always bad. Working is bad. Just having any job is wrong. At least, all the jobs I have ever had have been like that."

So, this session seemed to be stuck in situations that were supposed to have no meaning. Sam felt his mother was bothering him and that was all there was to it. Jobs were bad and that was that. In retrospect, I think I could have been less pushy with my interpretations and questions. I think Sam may have felt overwhelmed or threatened by how clearly he dealt with his feelings toward his objects in the last session. In this session, he took a more cautious approach. In retrospect, Sam was probably feeling anxious and conflicted about ending the treatment. Those feelings and ideas became clear in the next session.

Sam began by timidly stating, "Please don't take it badly, but I am going to stop coming. I have met my goal. I haven't smoked in over a month. That is longer than ever before. I got help, but I don't need it any more. A big part of this is that I simply can't afford it without the insurance benefits, which have run out. But, I also feel I have achieved my goal."

I had anticipated this since Sam had made comments about stopping before and I knew his insurance was up. Thinking of his fears and phantasies, I said, "I wonder if staying is difficult because we are exploring your feelings. You have mentioned how you dread the 'bad topics.' Also, you might feel I am being pushy with my questions."

Sam replied, "No. I don't feel I have any problems now. I have worked on my issues and have met my goals. So, I am ready to leave. But, I feel bad that you are going to take it personally. It is just time for me to stop, but if you take that wrong I will feel bad. Also, some of the things you want are not what I want or think. Society is wrong about the value of work and lots of other stuff. It is not important to have a job. I don't want to work at all. You want me to stay at my job and you think there is something seriously wrong with me mentally. I am just a normal guy who doesn't think I should have to work. What is wrong with that?"

Listening to Sam, I thought he was projecting his own loss, anxiety, and persecution into me. It was just too overwhelming for him to acknowledge his emptiness, his confusion, and his fear. So, I said, "You see me as being on the other side, on the enemy's side. Maybe what you see in me, feeling bad and saying what you should do, is what you are struggling with on the inside. It would be frightening to feel trapped at work and frightening to feel like something isn't right with the way you think." Sam replied, "I don't deserve to be here. I don't want to be here. I don't need to be here." I interpreted each of these three statements by saying, "You want to be with me but feel anxious that I will be like mother, that I will trap you, and be invasive. So, you feel like running to safety."

Sam was partly able to respond to this level of interpretation. He said, "Trapped, yes. I feel trapped by everything and everyone. But, it is definitely not psychological. It is sociological and cultural." I said, "Maybe you are not sure if you can trust me or rely on us working as a team." Sam's affect shifted from more paranoid to more sad and anxious. He said, "I feel so bad, so trapped. I don't feel well. My head is spinning and I feel like things are not going well." He went on, obviously feeling overwhelmed with fear and anxiety about both our relationship and my reaction to his termination.

I said, "I want you to think it over, but if you feel you must stop because of money or from how overwhelmed you feel, I will understand." I offered this reassurance because I thought Sam had become trapped by his internal objects and imagined I would retaliate violently if he didn't stay in treatment. I thought this was a recreation of him feeling mother had to have everything her way, or else. Sam responded, "I could come back later, maybe." This was said as both a timid question and a statement. I replied, "I would welcome you back." Sam looked surprised and said, "You would?" I said, "You must fear that I will be upset with your leaving and I will not want to see you again. Maybe you feel if I don't get my way and control you like mother does, I will be angry and want revenge." Sam said, "Yes, sort of. I just hope you don't take it personally and get mad or freak out!"

Sam began, "I feel very guilty. I feel bad. I am afraid I am disappointing you. It is really been bothering me." I interpreted his combined fear of hurting me and being vulnerable to my angry attack, a typical result of excessive PI within the paranoid-schizoid position. I said, "You are feeling scared that stopping will change our relationship for the worse. You imagine me getting hurt and angry and not liking you any more." Sam responded, "I am normal. I have no problems. You think I have problems. I have successfully quit smoking. My father, my girlfriend, and all my friends tell me I have really changed since coming here. They say I am way more centered and relaxed. They advise me to keep going because they see the results. But they don't understand." I replied, "They don't understand how trapped and worried you feel." Sam said, "I am not ready to discuss things." After a period of silence, I said, "When we discuss our relationship and your feelings and fears about it, you get very overwhelmed." Sam said, "I am sorry. I just don't want to do it. Sorry, but that is it."

Actually, Sam continued discussing it in a roundabout way. He said the day the insurance benefit ran out was his "glorious day of freedom." To that, I interpreted, "you see me as both a helper and a slave master." Sam remained in his persecutory state and responded, "I am normal. I have normal problems. It is society that has all the problems. The world is sick."

Here, Sam was using splitting and PI to put his problems into the world, seeing himself as all OK and normal, and then rail against the bad outside world. This way he didn't have to face his frightening internal world. Sam said, "I feel finished and I want to genuinely thank you for a positive learning experience." He was able to thank me for learning at the end of treatment, but to admit he was learning as we went along and let me in on what he was learning was too threatening. This was illustrated two weeks later in a letter I received, a format safer than face-to-face. Sam wrote, "Dear Dr. Waska: Thank you very much for helping me quit smoking and examine aspects of my life that I couldn't have looked at without your help. I really appreciate your concern for my well-being. I will always think fondly and gratefully when I reflect on my conversations with you. Thank you again. Sincerely, Sam."

Melanie Klein explored symbol formation in 1930. Segal began writing about it in 1957. Both felt symbolism was achieved by the ego's displacement of aggressive feeling toward the mother's body. Displacement of these anxieties formed a trail of symbols. The symbol is the creation of PI processes and part of normal development and healthy ego functioning. Segal (1957) states:

> the symbol is needed to displace aggression from the original object, and in that way to lessen the guilt and the fear of loss . . . The symbols are also created in the internal world as a means of restoring, re-creating, recapturing and owning again the original object.
>
> (Segal 1957: 42)

I would add that in the paranoid-schizoid position there are early precursors to symbolization that are primitive attempts to deal with the loss of the idealized object and the fear of attack from the bad object(s). Segal seemed to be exploring this when she stated:

> Symbol formation is an activity of the ego attempting to deal with the anxieties stirred by its relations to the object. That is primarily the fear of bad objects and the fear of the loss or inaccessibility of good objects . . . Symbol formation starts very early, probably as early as object relations, but changes its character and functions with the changes in the character of the ego and object relations.
>
> (Segal 1957: 40–41)

Segal pointed out the link between PI and symbolism in 1974:

> projective identification also provides the basis of the earliest
> form of symbol-formation. By projecting parts of itself into the
> object and identifying parts of the object with parts of the self,
> the ego forms its first most primitive symbols.
>
> (Segal 1974: 36)

Envy, greed, and hate can be so strong that the ego viciously
attacks the symbolization process and the ideal object that serves
that function. The ego tries to reduce the symbol down to its most
crude form, a concrete, singular element that the ego can disprove
and destroy.

In the paranoid-schizoid experience, symbols are not steady or
dependable because they represent a full spectrum of different parts
of the same object. This is too risky. These are patients who need
things and people to be a fixed way, always predictable and always
good. In the paranoid-schizoid position, the ego has not fully
achieved whole-object relating, ambivalence, and integration of
affect. Symbols, due to their inherently ambivalent character,
potentially trigger the phantasy of losing an idealized object and
facing an attacking bad object. Particularly in the case of more
disturbed patients, where they have experienced external trauma
(early and/or current) and a history of chronic disruption of the
mother/child bond, this phantasy of loss and persecution prevails.
So, rather than transform or creatively sublimate the ego's conflicted feelings about the mother and her body, symbols can amplify
the dangers of object relations in those patients consumed by oral
aggression, fearful of loss, and on the watch for persecutory objects.

When the paranoid-schizoid ego is still struggling with part
objects, unmanageable levels of aggression, and fragile love feelings,
sublimation and smooth transition into more mature depressive
coping strategies is unavailable. Healthy symbolization is impaired.
Specifically, two problems often occur. Rather than moving on to
create new symbols when the old ones become too full of conflict,
the ego becomes stuck in a vicious cycle with only one symbol and
overloads it via PI or destroys it through envious attacks. Thus, the
ego feels it is trapped within a persecutory struggle with bad objects
or it feels abandoned and empty, with hopelessness leading to
annihilation anxiety. On the other hand, the paranoid-schizoid ego
can frantically project its conflicts and create a string of new, but

equally unreliable symbols. Since the ego uses the same excessive PI process containing unresolved aggressive and libidinal states, these new symbols quickly crumble and the ego is again left in a chaotic and precarious position.

Sam was a man who used symbolism as a defense against primitive phantasies of primary loss and persecution. Intrapsychically, he functioned in the paranoid-schizoid position and relied on excessive PI strategies to defend himself from his dangerous internal objects. Thus, his use of symbolism was prone to dysfunction and decay because of excessive aggression, greed, and his manic use of PI. For Sam, symbolism provided only temporary respite, not genuine relief or integration of conflicting feelings and urges.

Sam equated his mother's selfish acting out and sadism as her withholding her soothing containment and therefore preventing mutual symbol-building experiences. He felt she was deliberately ignoring his need for containment and protection by choosing to act out without self-containment. She acted out in destructive ways that prevented and perverted symbol formation with Sam. I think Sam perceived his mother to be privately and selfishly making symbols in her own mind, with the things and people she chose. In other words, he felt excluded from her secret relationship with the world. Thus, he mentally attacked her and symbolic function in general. But, when he tore down one maternal symbol, he felt extremely anxious and had to construct another. This led to a vicious cycle of betraying, bizarre, malfunctioning symbols.

When I explored his mother's rule-breaking and self-serving behaviors and focused on how this made Sam fearful and alone, Sam felt my interpretations forced him to face the painful reality of this lifelong trauma. He frequently reacted by breaking off the object relationship most current in his mind and rapidly shifting to a new, but highly volatile symbol. In other words, he projected his intense feelings and part-object phantasies into a new location, creating a new situation as a defensive maneuver. However, that new symbol rarely sustained these aggressive, greedy, envious, and persecutory phantasies for very long. So, his PI maneuvers continuously destroyed symbols and he was forced to find new ones. This left Sam confused, scattered, and unattached to any particular object for very long.

Another way of stating this is that Sam's inability to use symbolism in a healthy, productive manner was generally due to the vicissitudes of the paranoid-schizoid position and a pathological PI cycle. More specific to his individual psychology, Sam constantly generated malfunctioning symbols because of his own aggression, envy, and greed toward his parents. These uncontained, intense phantasies about his primary objects created such a fear of loss, abandonment, and retaliation that he felt each symbol provided little safety or predictability. He demanded much from each symbol but never trusted them to provide. Also, the actual historical and current experiences of chaos and emotional abuse with his mother left him unsure where to put his trust at in any given moment.

The analytic relationship, through the patient's PI attempts at entering the analyst's body and mind, becomes the primary symbol for the patient. This was the case for Sam. As Segal (1978) clarifies, symbolism grows out of the infant's projective attacks on mother's body and mind. When the infant feels this relational symbolism results in damage, loss, or retaliation, symbols become unreliable, empty, or distorted. In order to shift successfully into the depressive position, the paranoid-schizoid ego must find a way to manage, mitigate, and master these derailments.

With Sam, this meant facing the aggressive feelings he had and working through his intense phantasies, based on actual experiences of loss and persecution. This working through was partly successful in the work we did, dealing with the fearful, fragile symbols he created. Like many other cases with such troubled patients, some work was accomplished and much was left unfinished. But I think Sam left treatment with less anxiety about loss and persecution and less reliance on pathological symbol formation and excessive PI mechanisms. He dealt more realistically with his mother and he achieved a better clarity regarding the numerous conflicts he normally projected and denied.

Chapter 9

Hate, projective identification, and the analyst's struggle[1]

When PI is a forceful evacuation, in phantasy and interpersonally, of certain libidinal and aggressive states, the ego can reinternalize an injured object, causing depression and schizoid terror, or reinternalize a now hostile and dangerous object, causing persecutory delusions. While PI can foster ego maturity and integration and represent a means of communication in healthy whole-object relations, I will be using one clinical case to focus on the ways PI can be more of a bullying way of relating.

Envy and aggression are considered constitutional by Melanie Klein (1957), based on her understanding of Freud's theory of an innate death instinct. In his paper "Instincts and their Vicissitudes" Freud stated: "hate . . . is older than love. It derives from the narcissistic ego's primordial repudiation of the external world and its outpouring stimuli" ([1915] 1959: 82).

Both Freud and Melanie Klein influenced W. R. Fairbairn's work. He constructed a revised theory of the unconscious. In working with his patients,

> he [Fairbairn] discovered [that] traumatic experiences in infancy . . . caused them to feel unloved for themselves "as persons." When innate strivings for interaction, especially those based on incorporative wishes, were not lovingly responded to, these infants came to feel that their love was bad or worthless. Deprivation had not only intensified their oral needs but had also imparted an aggressive quality to them, and frustration due to the mother's lack of love had made such patients experience their own love as demanding and aggressive . . . he [Fairbairn] conceptualized . . . aggression as a reaction to frustration or deprivation . . .
>
> (Moore and Fine 1990: 71)

These three lines of thought (Klein, Freud, Fairbairn) illustrate the complexity of constitutional, relational, and environmentally induced aggression in mental functioning. These factors are so overwhelming for some patients that near-impossible levels of defense are generated to cope with their persecutory anxieties and depressive reactions. These are often patients who are in the paranoid-schizoid position, who use incorporation, splitting, projection, and PI as primary methods of organizing the world. If the exploration of transference and resistance cannot be conducted due to excessive aggression in the relationship, an analytic process becomes highly problematic.

This chapter deals with the treatment of a patient who was hostile. The treatment abruptly ended due to the analyst's and patient's inability fully to understand and manage the hostility. By the end of the treatment, however, this patient made some reflections on her way of relating. Her aggression and my reaction to it prevented a closeness in our relationship, but the concept of PI helped us better understand some of the ways we didn't get along.

Each patient has a different set of internal self- and object-representations (Kernberg 1976) which come into play with the analyst's own mindscape. The PI "task" is the unconscious and conscious effort the analyst makes to understand the nature of the patient's projections and how that patient re-identifies with those projected phantasies.

Case study

M was an obese and oddly dressed middle-aged woman who was ambivalent about her marriage and entered into a twice-a-week treatment. She felt her life was a "major disappointment." She wanted to find out why she couldn't be happy in her marriage and why she couldn't find a meaningful job. The psychoanalytic psychotherapy lasted one year. She said she had been "the least favorite child" in her family. Her parents told her she was "stupid and dumb" and "useless and unneeded." While both parents would beat her, her father more actively abused her and her mother neglected her. Starting when she was ten, she abused drugs and alcohol. At twenty, she married a submissive, yet volatile man and proceeded to have two children by him. I say "by him" because she felt these children "just happened to her." She felt her children controlled and burdened her and she parented like a domineering and demanding drill sergeant in retaliation.

M felt a lack of love, respect, or happiness in her twenty-year marriage. She had been dismissed often from jobs because of what the employers saw as a pattern of lazy entitlement. All these feelings of grandiosity, harshness, and loneliness represented childhood introjects of family experiences colored by her own projections. Countertransference can be broadly defined as the analyst's total reaction to the patient. This would include the analyst's personal transference, interpersonal reactions to the patient's personality, and all intrapsychic responses to the patient's projection of internal objects through the dynamic of PI. My countertransference was dislike and dread. The intensity of these reactions helped me to discover my PI task and gradually understand the meaning of a dream I had.

I disliked M immediately, which was a startling feeling to have. She had an irritating demeanor that I later understood as the interpersonal component of PI. She would stomp around instead of walk, routinely slam my door, and collapse with a crash onto my couch. I would find all my waiting room magazines strewn about and my furniture rearranged. I asked her to stop this and invited her to talk about what it meant. When I suggested that she was irritated or angry she would say, "Damn right!" M appeared fat, dumpy, awkward, uncoordinated, and a physical wreck. She was also arrogant and flamboyant in how she walked, talked, dressed, and related. These were all triggers that brought me into a sado-masochistic PI process, in which we traded disdain and fear back and forth. The intensity of my thoughts and affect were the clues that I was involved in a situation that included dimensions beyond my usual countertransference. Ogden (1982) has described this process as one in which

> the projector fantasies ridding himself of an aspect of himself and putting that aspect into another person in a controlling way. Secondly, via the interpersonal interaction, the projector exerts pressure on the recipient of the projection to experience feelings that are congruent with the projection. Finally, the recipient psychologically processes the projection and makes a modified version available for re-internalization by the projector . . . one's projective fantasies impinge upon real external objects in a sequence of externalization and internalization.

> (Ogden 1982: 371)

During treatment with M, she seemed entitled, moody, and chaotic. She would change the radio station in my waiting room to a rock/pop station, turn up the volume, and dance around the waiting room. She seemed surprised when I asked her to stop. In a parallel yet exaggerated manner, she was hostile and cynical when I was two or three minutes late to one session and asked me to explain my "sloppy style." There were frequent power struggles as to the fee arrangement and scheduling and a sense in her presentation that she, more than anyone else, deserved a lower fee because of how difficult her life was. When I made comments about her seeming to be unhappy with me, M would tell me about her lack of respect for others and deep feelings of insult at the idea of having to work for anything in life. She would say, "I want to be totally taken care of, I want to receive but not have to give back."

When I proposed that her aggressive stance was a way to try to master her childhood feelings of worthlessness and powerlessness in relationship to her parents, her marriage, and myself, she then associated to phantasies of wielding supreme control over others and, consequently, her fears of being abandoned and rejected. These moments of insight and exploration would quickly erode back into her more outright hostile stance, where she identified with the aggressor and placed me in the role of the rejected and abandoned one.

M's unique style of relating left me with specific counter-transference feelings. I felt I was with a robot-like imposter or with a cold and ominous "presence." This left me fearful and mistrusting. She seemed manic, yet internally dead. Many words flowed but were empty echoes. I frequently felt like the unwitting sidewalk stroller who sees the lost wallet on a string and follows it behind the bushes only to get mugged.

An example of PI involved feelings she portrayed interpersonally when paying her bill. She would literally throw her check down on my table with a look of "Here, take my last dime!" I had the phantasy of her checks being covered with the blood and spittle of her hard work and slavery to some horrible millstone. This phantasy helped me understand the intense feelings of rage, entitlement, and personal insult that M lived with.

M left me frustrated and wanting more. Fairbairn's idea of the "exciting object" was useful in understanding her transference. Grotstein (1993) unfolded this notion by saying:

this word [exciting object] may actually be an apt one to describe a mother's or father's actual behavior toward the child. In other words, the term may refer to a seductive or overstimulating parent whose excitations the infant must painfully internalize to control . . . the exciting object is so only because it is the inescapable Janus-face of the rejecting object. It is important to realize that Fairbairn has described an unconscious demonology, as it were, in which there is a system of "no exit", . . . there is a closed system . . .

(Grotstein 1993: 434)

M projected her unfed and confused child parts into me and related to me as a just out-of-reach, rude, and provocative parent.

For Fairbairn, aggression is always a secondary by-product of relational frustration. Grotstein (1993: 436) goes on to point out that, "hate constitutes, first and foremost, an object-relationship and cannot be considered separate from it." Klein, following Freud's discoveries, saw aggression as an innate, constitutional component of the mind, on a par with infantile sexuality. Although the ideas of Freud, Fairbairn, Klein, and Grotstein don't necessarily match theoretically, I find them quite compatible clinically. Patients present such multiple layers of complex intrapsychic object constellations that there is plenty of room and necessity for an inclusive way of thinking.

My supervisor at the time I saw M thought that M was so fearful of being penetrated by my interpretations, and that her defensive rage was so strong, that she was not analyzable. I partially agreed but had to be careful not to cling to that thought as a way of disposing of this difficult case. Indeed, this was perhaps a clue to the PI process in which she was the bad seed in my family of patients, much like she had perceived herself to be the bad seed in her own family of origin. This element of the PI process had now entered the relationship between my supervisor and me.

Throughout treatment, M told me she wished to terminate. She finally told me in a cold and dictatorial manner when she would stop. When I invited her to explore this "threat," she told me that her husband did not want to pay for her treatment any more so "there was nothing to discuss." M agreed that she could easily find a part-time job to pay for her treatment. However, she did not want to ever have to work again and said that she would only return to therapy if her husband gave her more money in the future. Her "giving me notice" was the interpersonal aspect of an intrapsychic PI repetition process in which she abandoned me much in the way I believe she had felt chronically rejected. It was about this time that I had a countertransference dream, no doubt fueled by the hostile and defensive nature of her transference and PI.

I have had dreams about patients before, but never in this manner. M often left me frustrated, confused, and guilty. The dream revealed a deeper facet. The night following a regularly difficult session with M, I dreamed of a murder. In the dream, I attended a large rock-music concert (perhaps the radio station she had tuned to) and began wandering through the crowd. I was looking for someone. There was a fat, nondescript, "hippie" woman that I lured into a nearby cottage (M was a former "flower child" and was obese). In a back room I murdered her by slitting her throat (perhaps to save myself from her regular accusations). After disposing of the bloody evidence, I left the cottage and proceeded to blend in with the crowd. While I was fearful of being caught, I did not feel guilty. Upon waking, I felt shock, guilt, and anxiety. Only after close examination did I begin to understand what had occurred.

In the four weeks between this dream and M's termination, we felt there was a shift in our relationship. She said, "It feels safer and more comfortable to come to therapy." Patients are well aware of the changes in the analytic relationship and of the analyst's psychology. I hated her less. It seemed I had killed the source of the hate.

Through PI, M put her self-loathing, her hatred toward various internal objects, and her fears of those objects' retaliation onto (interpersonally) and into (intrapsychically) me. This resulted in an atmosphere of hostility and fear between us. These feelings overcame me, just as she had always felt overwhelmed. There was a modest, temporary transformation in these primitive self- and object-representations due to my unconscious struggles to master them. It was my task to detoxify and translate these internal states into something more usable for both of us. I think my dream allowed me to modify her poisonous projections a bit, so I was not as affected by them. As a result, I started to act in a more accepting way and was less standoffish to her. This interpersonal shift allowed her momentarily to introject a safer version of her internal world. Again, this was only temporary and still was vastly over-shadowed by her grim, persecutory internal world.

Most of M's internal process had been kept private. In a parallel way I fought an important battle in the distant reaches of my dream world. It was in the unconscious phantasies of sleep that I was finally able partially to master this diabolic force. In fact, I sought it out and actively did away with it, feeling the murder was a "necessary evil."

In the first part of the PI process, I was given an opponent. The second part of my task was doing battle with that opponent in a way that was somehow different than how the patient had managed before. Once I put an end to this internal threat, I was a new intrapsychic and interpersonal object. She then had a modified object to internalize. The internal demon was dead and our interpersonal relationship momentarily felt more safe, mutual, and satisfying. While the difference in my interpersonal stance allowed her to introject a more benign object, I failed to make interpretations about the internal aspects of our relationship and her anxieties about it.

I interpreted to M that our more friendly interpersonal atmosphere was the result of her feeling less threatened and less enraged. She agreed. In the task of working through PI, the patient relates a specific unfinished psychic agenda. Then the analyst must understand, modify, and interpret the patient's projections in a way that allows the patient to identify with them in a new light. Next, the patient identifies through both interpersonal and intrapsychic channels, the same channels the original projections emerged from. I failed to carry through with the interpretive aspect of the task. In the long run, she had a different interpersonal experience which may have temporarily offset her inner fears, but it did not address them directly.

During the last session, M told me that she had discovered the consequences of her behavior and the difference between thought and feeling. While this rather global and grandiose statement may have been a symbolic gift to me in thanks for my efforts to survive in the treatment and an attempt to gratify her own narcissistic needs that she projected upon me, I believe there was more to it. The consequences of her behavior had been the termination of our relationship and she was only able to hint at this mildly. The comment about the difference between thought and affect showed me a bit more about her inner world. She felt constantly threatened by an engulfing, smothering, and controlling object. M's ability to begin exploring the difference between thought and affect was a sign of a momentary shift from the more regressed paranoid-schizoid state into more of a depressive position, if only temporarily. She momentarily saw me as a not-so-threatening partner with whom she could allow previously warded off thoughts and feelings, without being subject to persecution.

All this helped me to understand why reaching her had been so hard. I had been frustrated that she could not or would not reveal more of herself in our relationship and instead seemed to hide in a hostile shell. I now realize that the treatment represented a psychological step that both of us took, separately yet together. We both struggled with a differentiation process, attempting to escape from the grasp of hate and secondary hostility. The secondary aggression was a reaction to the suffocating fusion she felt. By projecting these elements into my psychic landscape, the patient asked me to do what she was unable to do. I was to neutralize the overwhelming affect and sort out some sense of safety. It was my task as her analyst to be an auxiliary-ego function through a PI process. I was unable to provide ample containment for her projections but I did find a way to use the aggression against itself, in a dream state prompted by her decision to terminate.

Once I had regained my psychic balance, the therapeutic relationship momentarily shifted. In a complete analytic treatment, this would need to occur over and over again with the critically important addition of direct interpretations. M did not resolve her fundamental conflicts or achieve any structural cure, yet the first step toward structural change was taken. Our shared internal object relations loosened. This was a case in which aggression was the main currency between analyst and patient and led to a specific task for the analyst within the interpersonal and intrapsychic process of PI.

The PI task encompasses the analyst's understanding of the patient's internal cast of phantasy characters, their complex and ever-changing dynamics, and the subsequent translations of these elements via interpretations. This usually entails a detoxification and modification of the projected materials before a translation can occur. Regarding this particular case, once I could detoxify some of her projections, I felt my psychic balance was restored and a minor shift in both of our worlds began. Specifically, the nature of the aggressive forces was modified. This temporary shift occurred as the result of many factors, but PI played a major role.

Due to limitations within the psychoanalytic treatment and my avoidance of the transference and interpretive stance, I believe there was more of a pathological PI process than would have otherwise occurred. This of course speaks to the importance of the analysis of both transference and countertransference. M was able to bring rage, envy, and grandiosity to bear in a manner that quickly created an intense PI experience within the analytic relationship. While the case of M was an aborted treatment, there was a momentary interpersonal shift in the patient and in the analyst/patient relationship.

Our patients try to engage us in different conflicts at many levels of structural integration. We must be able to identify the nature of what is being presented and the interactions the patient seems to be inviting us into. Hostility and hatred are often the conflicts brought to our consulting rooms, and PI is frequently the mode of transportation. If properly understood, PI can also be the primary vehicle for the working-through process.

Chapter 10

The role of projective identification in pathological greed

PI is the vehicle for many different phantasies, defenses, and methods of relating to the object. One aspect of the patient's character structure that can be strongly mobilized through PI is greed. This greed can be a normal, healthy need and desire or it can be pathological in nature. There is a group of borderline and psychotic patients experiencing life in the confines of the paranoid-schizoid position who bring greed into the transference as their primary way of relating. Through PI, their greedy hunger for idealized objects and idealized versions of themselves becomes alive and dominates the treatment setting.

A distinction between the different clinical presentations of greed is useful. Some patients are overtly hunting the object down in order to take all they can from it. Other patients are very conflicted about their greedy phantasies and will make it their mission to protect, indulge, and side with the object as a way to counteract their destructive urges. Using case material, I will explore the varied manifestations of greed and PI and their combined impact on the patient's psychic equilibrium.

Melanie Klein and many of her followers have explored the idea of envy and noted how certain patients come destructively to envy the analyst's thoughts, ideas, abilities, and interpretations. This can lead to an impasse or negative therapeutic reaction, designed to defeat the analyst. I think that greed is at times the core conflict in these standoffs and at other times the greed serves as a defense against envy.

In a panel discussion on envy, Frankiel *et al.* (2001) highlighted the use of devaluation and fusion as two of the many ways the ego can avoid awareness of differences between self and object. At the same time, envy of these differences leads to aggressive, counter-therapeutic acting out. In some of these cases, the ego uses greed to take over and cannibalize the goodness of the object. The ego steals what it feels it is lacking. Envy seeks to destroy the nature of difference and greed seeks to take it over. Depending on the nature of the psychic crisis, one, the other, or both will be used. Some patients seem to feel, "if I can't steal it, then I will destroy it." In these cases, envy would be the defense against failed greed.

In the same panel discussion, Spillius (in Frankiel *et al.* 2001) also emphasized the use of spoiling and devaluation to prevent awareness of differences. She feels envy is encountered in most patients to some degree when they realize their dependence and then react against it. Again, I think greed comes into the clinical picture when the envious neutralizing of the good object and its differences fail. The ego tries to absorb the object and all of its envied goodness as its own when destroying it doesn't work.

While it is hard to isolate greed from envy, there are certain types of patients in whom greed seems to be the primary way of relating to the world. Depending on the nature of phantasy dynamics and the excessive reliance on PI, greed can be oriented toward the object or toward the self.

Also, some patients are more outwardly greedy and aggressive, demanding whatever the object has that the ego feels without. In extreme cases, the ego feels the object owes it everything and must pay up. This resentful view of life is in line with Spillius's view of envy and grievance. I think the goal of envy is mostly the pleasure of making the object pay up once and for all. In contrast, greed is the demanding for constant payment. The bill is never fully paid. The ego wants to feel completely satiated and to be fed on demand from then on. In this way, greed is a more insidious problem. Envy can be appeased by one angry blow to the object; greed is an ongoing, desperate and aggressive hunger that can never be fully met.

The main driving force behind this endless demand is a pathological PI cycle. Idealized and then broken, failing or destroyed objects are circulated back and forth through the mechanism of PI, followed by gratified and then collapsed, ravenous, or persecuted aspects of the ego.

Case study 1

Simon was a patient who had grown up feeling no access to his parents' love. He felt continuously victimized. He had six other siblings and was molested by one of his brothers for a number of years. He felt his parents didn't want to be bothered by him. Simon came for help with depression. While many sad and unfortunate things had happened to Simon, I noted that he seemed to make a point of presenting himself as the passive victim of life. He had lost his wife of fifteen years in an auto crash two years prior to seeing me. Simon had remarried, but was now recently divorced. He felt extremely angry, bitter, and depressed about these painful events but was ashamed and insulted to have me notice. He wanted his wife back and if he couldn't have that he wanted a new girlfriend right away. His demanding cry of "How come I can't have one instantly!?" was a thin shell for his underlying feelings of humiliation, greed, and loss. Very quickly, it became clear that he could not tolerate being dependent and would not admit to being affected by anyone or anything. Indeed, he told me that would mean he was admitting or confessing to something quite intolerable. Here, he was expressing envy and narcissistic superiority, probably both protecting him from and intensifying a deep sense of loss and persecution.

Most of his life, Simon was considerably overweight. It was clear early on in the treatment that eating and constant thinking about food was a place where his greed for idealized objects was acted out. He ignored his doctor's orders to diet and his friends' advice to eat differently. Simon told me, "I know intellectually I should eat less, but I don't care. I want all I can get and I don't care about the consequences." I interpreted this as an external symptom of his internal greed and his feelings of not being able to get what he so desperately wants. I interpreted that food was the one object he could control and literally have as much as he wanted when he wanted. It would not disappoint him, betray him, or abandon him. So, I was showing him, through my interpretations, a PI cycle in which he put the idealized object of his psychological hunger into food and then displayed no mercy. His angry, greedy need was externalized via his constant overeating, thinking about food, and not caring about the consequences of overeating.

After a few months in treatment, Simon told me he was thinking about stopping and would continue for a few weeks and then say goodbye. He felt there was no point in coming to see me if there was no crisis in his life. It was true that the initial feelings of despair and thoughts of suicide were now gone. Now, we were beginning to explore how he related to the world and his internal relationships. This was a threat to his inner equilibrium. Simon felt very clear about stopping treatment and didn't seem to want to discuss it. Nevertheless, I tried to engage him in exploring it.

I interpreted that he wanted continuous emotional feeding from his objects and felt they were never able to give him what he needed so badly, so he turned to food. I said I thought he, on some level, realized how much he wanted from me and others and that this frightened him. So he tried to protect both of us from that greed by rationing himself. He will only use me if he is in crisis, but otherwise is trying to hold off. In other words, Simon wanted to gobble up his objects but was scared of the consequences. Again, this was part of an ongoing PI cycle that left him chronically angry, greedy, emotionally hungry, and psychologically lost without stability. Simon responded to my interpretation by saying, "I do feel like I want so much from others that I could use them up and cause a disaster, a problem of some sort. But, I can't help myself. I need more than most people have. Is that my fault?"

When Melanie Klein stated that greed never cares about consequences, I think she was emphasizing the ego's lack of empathy for the object. Clinically, I find many patients like Simon do care, unconsciously and consciously, but it is for their own safety rather than the object's. Therefore, when Simon said he felt guilty about wanting too much from his relationships, he was actually more frightened of how the object would retaliate. So, as a compromise, he starved himself from eating up all of his internal objects and took out that greedy aggression and lingering loss on food.

Even though he was obviously in great pain over the recent divorce and the prospect of starting a new job, Simon claimed indifference. As I mentioned, he presented himself as the victim of life, so he felt more persecuted than sad about losing his wife and his second marriage. He felt it had been taken away or stolen. I believe this was a projection of his greed, in which he wished to take and steal from his objects. Unable to maintain this defensive denial and indifference for long, Simon began to manifest a manic defense. Excessive or pathological cycles of PI tend to bring on more and more anxiety until the ego feels overwhelmed and in need

weak and pathetic. R learned later in life that his mother had cheated on his father several times.

Being an only child, R felt caught in the middle of his parents' fighting and tried to act as referee. R remembers feeling like his parents' drinking and fighting took up all the space and prevented him from getting much attention or love.

In analysis, R recalled his childhood as being a time of anger, fear, and worry. He was often angry that his parents' fighting and drinking destroyed any chance of peaceful and playful contact with them. At the same time, R felt that his relationship with them was tenuous. To voice his opinion would create additional friction in the home. It felt dangerous. R said, "It would have been the last straw. My parents would have turned on me." He felt it was better to go along with things the way they were than to try and change them or mention his feelings about them.

I met with R twice a week for six years, using the analytic couch. Diagnostically, he showed borderline features and was troubled by anxiety, panic, and depressive episodes. He exhibited a combination of paranoid-schizoid and depressive traits, fluctuating between being more organized at times and less functional at other times.

R used a mixture of defenses, but relied heavily on denial, PI, rationalization, and manic independence. This manic defense would break down at times to reveal a hopeless, dependent side of his personality. He felt despairing about any change or improvement. Over the course of his analysis, R related to me in various different ways, sometimes more primitive and paranoid, sometimes manic and grandiose, and sometimes quite integrated and self-aware.

R is a patient who functions with a certain type of psychological organization highlighted by certain phantasies and feelings. Specifically, I will focus on the way greed and PI shaped R's internal experiences. He and many similar patients seem to have great needs and desires for emotional feeding from their objects, but deny and deface that hunger for a variety of reasons. Therefore a conflict between greed, aggression, and the imagined consequences of unleashing that hunger define the person's character.

PI becomes the vehicle for this endless cycle that, without a working through and resolution, remains a self-destructive and increasingly chaotic way of experiencing the world.

One theme in R's treatment was his constant yearning for acknowledgment, interest, and attention. Simultaneously, R feared the consequences of this greed and emotional desire. During the first year, he asked me how I would prefer to be addressed. He explained that he didn't know what to call me as I had never told him what I prefer. I pointed out how he obviously had something in mind but was deferring to me. I wondered out loud if his desire to be closer to me by using my name brought on anxiety. R said he was uncomfortable calling me something without me telling him what I felt most comfortable with. I interpreted he was being very careful not to disclose what his desire was and to keep himself safe by waiting for me to give him instructions. I added that he must feel frustrated and caught by his conflict between wanting to build a personal connection and not wanting to offend me. R said, "Yes, but I don't feel I have the right to just start calling you something without your OK. My last therapist told me what to call him and told me that we should feel like friends. Why haven't you told me that? Why can't you tell me what you want?" I responded by telling R he was welcome to call me whatever he wanted, but that his dilemma showed us how he wanted more in our relationship but feared the consequences of barging into it without permission. Therefore he put his want into me and asked what I wanted. R's curiosity, affection, and wish for more were all tainted by greed, aggression, and persecutory phantasies. This made his feelings more predatory and filled him with phantasies of dread and suspicion (Rodrique 1955). Over the course of the next two visits we explored these phantasies about how expanding our relationship and expressing his growing trust in me was colored by a sense of greed, which caused thoughts about violating boundaries and bringing on negative results.

I think this difficult situation for R was the result of R's phantasies about the effects of his greed on his objects. He feared he was too greedy and that this hunger for more of the object would make the object angry. This was part of his PI phantasy of taking too much from the object, leaving the object depleted and enraged. R tried to deal with this phantasy by using even more PI strategies, a common manic approach the ego uses when faced with this type of persecution phantasy (Klein 1955). R attempted to put his desire into me by asking me, repeatedly, to make the choice on what he should call me. This was a way to make me the one in control, and R could be passive and safe, but secretly obtain the closeness he wanted without having to claim ownership and without risking the imagined consequences. I interpreted this to R and he responded,

"I think I do that a lot. It is easier to have people tell me what I want or what they want. Then, I am off the hook. It is way riskier to show what I want. Then, I have to act on it and it may not turn out the way I hoped. I want to respect you, I don't want to be selfish or rude." I said, "So something that feels good, a move toward expanding our relationship, could turn sour." R said, "Sure. If you are not careful." Noting the ambiguous "you," I said, "You are warning both of us to be careful. We should tread lightly."

Patients like R are struggling with pathological levels of greed that are self-destructive and self-perpetuating because of their reliance on PI. The greedy ego demands more than the object can produce and this creates frustration, anger, and deprivation, which in turn generates more greed. Many of these patients have experienced childhoods in which there was significant external deprivation and emotional neglect. In addition, these patients' developing egos have not internalized a sense of relief, forgiveness, reparation, or love that can manage or mitigate these greedy phantasies. As a child, R certainly did not experience any ongoing external love or understanding that could help him make sense of, deal with, or work through the traumatic family environment he grew up in.

Segal (1955) has clarified several important points in regard to Melanie Klein's concept of the depressive position. She states:

> the infant at that stage [the depressive position] is still under the sway of uncontrollable greedy and sadistic impulses. In phantasy his loved object is continually attacked in greed and hatred, is destroyed, torn into pieces and fragments; and not only is the external object so attacked but also the internal one, and then the whole internal world feels destroyed and shattered as well. Bits of the destroyed object may turn into persecutors . . .
>
> (Segal 1955: 386)

Segal continues to state how in normal and successful development, the infant receives the ongoing experiences of love from the environment. This reassures the ego about the safety and trustworthiness of the object. This feeling of confidence is internalized and identified with. In this way, the infant builds a sense of being able to repair, soothe, and restore its objects. This leads to less reliance on manic defenses and other systems of internal anxiety reduction such as PI.

However, Segal emphasizes that this positive psychological growth can be derailed. She states, "if there is little belief in the capacity to restore, the good object outside and inside is felt to be irretrievably lost and destroyed, the destroyed fragments turn into persecutors, and the internal situation is felt to be hopeless" (1955: 387). I think this was the case with R.

Specifically, I believe greed is often the psychological element that tips the scales from a meager and fragile sense of whole objects that can be healed and restored to a hopeless sense of persecution and abandonment. Fueled by excessive dependence on PI, this frightening phantasy leads to defensive attempts to escape the consequences of an angry object that cannot be soothed. One such strategy is to shield the object from one's greed as a way to protect the ego, not the object, from the vengeful, attacking object. Wanting more from the object but hiding that hunger out of self-protection is part of what R did in his struggle with what to call me. This same theme surfaced in other ways.

R began to show me the less passive side of his cautious, careful approach. It became clear that his worried, frightened approach was side by side a more greedy and demanding feeling of wanting his object to be an ideal and constant caretaker.

R resented his parents for many things. R told me he was never given lavish birthday parties. R had an idealized version of how parents should acknowledge their children, and birthday parties were an example of this. R felt he should have been given surprise parties, with all his friends present. Each person should have given him a nice card, had something thoughtful to say, and brought a gift. A nice cake and colorful candles were necessary. The list went on. Some of what R wished for seemed appropriate, but the way he talked about it felt entitled and grandiose. I felt like I was listening to a greedy, spoiled child who felt cheated.

Unfortunately, R carried this desire for a perfect birthday into adulthood, as a vehicle to express his greed and frustrated wishes for an ideal object. It also hid the painful loss he felt at not having an adoring or interested object. He wanted all his adult friends to remember when his birthday was and to give him a surprise party with nice cards, a cake, and gifts. Since this never happened in the perfect way he envisioned, R felt unimportant and abandoned. He resented his friends for not providing what seemed to R like an ordinary request.

However, his friends had no reason to know about this wish other than R having casually mentioned how he likes his birthday. R told me he felt guilty "unleashing" this yearning hunger for attention. He said, "In a way, I feel greedy and selfish. I don't want to demand a surprise party. Plus, it wouldn't be a surprise if I had to ask for it. And, I feel guilty and selfish reminding everyone all the time about how important it is for me."

I interpreted R's PI cycle of greed. I said that he wanted all of us to just know his needs automatically and provide for them, but he felt greedy so he kept it all inside. I suggested that keeping these greedy wishes inside made him angry and even more hungry for attention. He was keeping score of who loved him and who didn't, who cared and who didn't. R replied, "I feel very greedy and selfish about all this. The same goes for people calling me to go out on the weekend. I don't want to have to call them all the time. Why can't they just call me? But, I feel weak, dependent, and pathetic to have to tell people I want a party or that I want to have them call me. I am a nice friend, so why can't they give me the things I need?" Here, R was revealing the struggle between greed, shame, and his conflict over depending on the object. The fragile state of vulnerability and loss was right under the surface, side by side with this greedy need. It seemed that if he depended on the object, it might let him down. It might not be ideal unless he demanded it to be so.

Technically, I approached this greedy narcissism and fear of dependence by consistently interpreting the simultaneous phantasy of fear and greed. Due to his particularly aggressive use of PI, R swung back and forth between wanting to eat up all of the object and fear of being devoured by the object's rage or greed.

So I clarified, explored, and confronted R's constant hunger for more of his object. I emphasized the primitive guilt and fear he felt regarding rejection, loss, and attack or persecutory punishment. In other words, his fear of punishment was not so much a neurotic fear of making someone angry, him getting punished, and then things getting better. It was more absolutist in that he would be permanently rejected, devalued, and emotionally attacked. I conceptualized R's struggle as more to do with phantasies of annihilation as a result of deprivation. In many cases, including R's, greed is not so much a defense against primitive and persecutory loss as a pathological state of mind that goes hand in hand with primitive, persecutory phantasies of loss. I think this combination of PI, greed, and loss creates some of the worst ego fragmentation and makes for very difficult treatments.

I routinely interpreted the way that R's greed created the phantasy of an angry, rejecting, and withholding object. True to form, the greedy patient wants more than the analyst, friend, or lover can offer at any given moment. So while R would momentarily take in my interpretations and seem to profit from them, he would quickly want more. When he said, "I see that. Yes, I can understand that now. So, what do I do about it?" Tell me how to change it", he was discarding and devaluing his gain, our union and our work. He was demanding something new, better, and bigger. This left R hungry, dissatisfied, and disconnected from our relationship and the analytic caring I was providing. Therefore, he created a sense of deprivation and emptiness within the transference, a PI of his own inner void.

R's method of dating women threw light on his internal struggles with greed, loss, and persecution. He was extremely desperate to find someone, almost anyone, to be with. For years, he had been a member of three different dating services, as well as being part of two internet dating companies. At some points, he was literally going out on dates with new women every day of the week. R said, "I have to stay busy. I need to be with people and at least feeling like I am on the road to maybe finding someone. Otherwise, I feel so alone and hopeless." He was able to maintain several relationships over the years that lasted almost a year each. However, he said there wasn't a feeling of genuine love on his part in any of them. They merely made him feel better temporarily. As soon as one of these longer-term relationships felt rocky, R returned to his nonstop dating activities. Indeed, he often was still secretly dating several women even when he was in a committed relationship. He said this was "just in case" things didn't work out with the girlfriend.

I interpreted this as a combination of greed, fear, and persecution. Fueled by forceful, aggressive PI mechanisms, R wanted more than the relationship gave. He panicked that he was not being fed, felt starved, and felt like the object was deliberately depriving him. So he sought out a new, better, and safer source of nourishment. I interpreted to R, "You must begin to feel very desperate and in pieces, so you look for someone to heal that emptiness. Somebody to pick up the pieces and make it all feel better." Here, I was speaking to the internal chaos created by greed and the constant destruction and subsequent search for the ideal object. R reacted by feeling judged. He said, "When you say that, I feel like you are putting me down and saying it is a sick way to be. Now I don't want to be here because you are saying I shouldn't date until I do it in a healthy way." I replied, "You feel I am taking away the very thing you need for survival. I think you are more comfortable turning my observation into a judgement or a commandment because it is less painful than looking together at how hungry you get for contact with someone. Looking at those feelings and that hunger probably feels overwhelming." R said, "Yes. I would rather be judged any old day." Here, I was interpreting the way R used paranoid, persecutory phantasies to guard against the more frightening experiences of being deprived by a cruel and rejecting object. R's greed, when unfulfilled, led to intrapsychic fragmentation and panic.

Another example of R's struggle with greed, PI, and their internal and interpersonal consequences had to do with his reaction to not receiving what he wanted right away. Whatever the situation, if there was not immediate gratification, R had an intense reaction. He was filled with abandonment insecurity, narcissistic devaluation, and greedy demand. Specifically, R would date someone and seem to hit it off. Almost immediately, he would greedily try to capture the love and security he craved. He would say to the woman, "So, now we are girlfriend and boyfriend – right?" after only a few dates. R would expect daily phone calls and exclusivity right away. He would want an instant guarantee.

The new woman would see R as a new friend to date casually along with other men she might meet. When R found out she was dating other men, he felt she had cheated on him and betrayed him. This led to sorrow, rejection, and hopelessness. If the woman didn't feel any sparks and decided to not date R after the first couple of dates, R also felt terrible loss, rejection, and despair. This despair was from his phantasy of being deliberately scorned and thrown aside.

These intense feelings of abandonment and betrayal were the result of his projection of greed and the PI cycle of hunger–greed–persecution–loss. Thorner (1955) has noted how projection of greed leaves the ego feeling empty and alone. In addition, the phantasy of betrayal and attack from external objects is the result of projecting greedy phantasies into the environment. Finally,

Thorner points out how denial of greed leads to anxiety, help-lessness, emptiness, and depersonalization. This anxious–empty–depersonalization state occurred for R when he denied his greedy urges for an instant, idealized relationship. He reported feeling like a robot, going from one woman to the next. R said, "I meet them, I feel nothing. I turn away and I go to the next one. It feels like an assembly line. If I am not immediately energized by them, I lose interest and go elsewhere."

Interestingly, one of the complaints R had come into treatment with was the idea that he suffered from a learning disability. All through his school years, he felt it very difficult to concentrate. Unless he was immediately excited about the material and felt it was something he wanted to study, he couldn't pay attention for any length of time and forgot much of what was taught. Then R felt pressured and forced by the teacher to do his homework. This led to anger and anxiety. In my interpretations, I linked this lack of connection to new knowledge to the feelings of greed, denial, and the consequences of PI. In other words, he put his greedy expec-tations and hunger into the material and found it less than ideal, so he turned away from it. Then, he identified with the inferior object and felt pressured and persecuted by the greedy teacher to be perfect and perform well. His troubled relationship with school material was now repeated in his troubled attempts at intimacy.

Pathological levels of greed and PI create vicious cycles of chaotic object relations. Greed is felt to enrage and destroy one's precious object, which the ego needs for survival. Persecutory guilt, loss of a catastrophic nature, and inner fragmentation follow. This chaos pushes the ego to become even more desperately greedy, looking for the idealized object and seeking to save and protect that object. This effort to help or resurrect the object is ultimately an effort to save the self, because without the object the ego feels unable to function.

For many patients, including R, this desperation is a repetition of a child's desperate attempt to keep an emotionally sick or out-of-control parent/couple healthy so that they can maintain their duty as parents. The child needs their parenting, so he makes sure they are able to do it. This terrible dilemma in a child's early development is compounded by the child's phantasies, projections, and reintrojections of those situations. The internal/external mix of that PI process is what we as analysts deal with in the form of transference and extra-transference material.

Under the influence of excessive PI, the greedy ego experiences the object as extremely fragile and easily torn apart. So, in an effort to maintain a brittle alliance, the ego must find ways of protecting the object from the ego's greedy, destructive urges. In talking to R about this internal chaos, I told him, "You must feel like you have to protect me and others from what you feel and think – like we are fragile and you want too much."

When I made these types of interpretations to R, he said, "That really hits the mark. I do feel like I better keep those ideas to myself or I will cause trouble." I said, "What kind of trouble?" R replied, "I think people will leave me, not want me, and even hate me. Some kind of nasty conflict and then it is all over and I am alone. So, if that is how it works, why should I ever hope for more or try to change. What is the use? Why would I want to put myself in the cross-hairs? It is horrible now, but it could get worse. If I don't tolerate it, I will have nothing." I said, "So, if you let out what feels like greedy, selfish wishes for more – more love, more closeness, more communication – you feel you will destroy the crumbs you are lucky to have." R said, "It is sad and pathetic, but you have sized it up pretty well."

Several years into his analysis, R was working through some of these phantasies and conflicts. He told me how he could remember the exact day when he stopped showing his feelings to his parents, specifically to his mother. R said, "I can still see that day. I was really upset and felt like everything focused on my mother and her horrible moods. I felt so alone, but I knew there was no room for my feelings and that I might make things worse if I tried to speak up. I decided I would never again let my mother know what I felt. I would always keep it to myself." I said, "Maybe, you hoped she would need to know how you were, that she would want to know, even beg you to tell her. But, you would deny her." Here, I was speaking to what I imagined was his sadistic withholding, wanting to put some of his deprivation into his mother. R said, "Absolutely – sweet revenge." I said, "You wanted her to feel as hungry and deprived as you did." R replied, "Yes, I did. I had to live with it, now she had to as well."

Then I interpreted that R was continuing to use this strategy with me and others. I pointed out how he would often tell me only the basic facts of a story and tilt these facts to make it sound like he had been wronged or shorted in some way. I said, "I think you relate in that way so I end up being the voice of your anger and your hunger. It seems like if I take the bait I would end up saying something like, 'That is really awful of them. They were mean to you. You deserve so much more.' But, you never actually express those feelings to me directly. Maybe that is because you are afraid of my reaction to seeing how needy, hurt, angry, or hungry you are. Also, by not telling me, you get to withhold from me like you did with your mother."

Here, I was interpreting both the greedy desires for the object, the fear of reprisal, and the sadistic aggression. Also, I was commenting on the interpersonal aspects or interpersonal results of PI manifested within the transference. R said, "There is no time for me. Other people seem to need it all and if I try and grab a piece I could lose it all for good. So, I think I relate in special ways to keep others alive and happy. That way, I don't lose the connection." I said, "So, you try and not disturb our fragile relationship by these special strategies. But that must leave you feeling alone, angry, and even more in need since you are having to manage us instead of just enjoying being together." R replied, "It is like a constant, dull ache. But, I think I try and get rid of any anger or selfishness. I neutralize it to keep the peace."

Here, R was illustrating the greedy and needy ego's compromise. "To keep the peace" (avoiding persecution, attack, or conflict) and "to maintain the connection" (avoiding abandonment and primitive states of loss), the ego must find a way to deny, project, or neutralize its basic aggression and greed. This generates more isolation, anxiety, and greed, with even more manipulation and defense to follow.

R didn't want to bother the object and risk this attack and loss. So he tried to censor his greed, secretly expressing his need via logic, denial, and passive–aggressive moves. These strategies ultimately failed to provide him with the fulfillment he sought, so he was still left feeling abandoned and ignored, often in a persecutory way. This sense of persecution was both internal and external. Sometimes, he projected it and felt bitterly misunderstood and was angry that he had to deal with such emotional burdens all by himself. He resented others for having it so easy while he suffered and kept in his grief, hunger, and anger.

This masochistic, martyr approach alternated with a dread that if his need for comfort and his hunger for more nourishment from the object were exposed, he would be attacked and left. An example of this occurred when R came in and told me he "could barely face me." He said, "I was going to cancel this session, and I even am thinking of stopping coming all together. I feel so defective and damaged. I am so pitiful and worthless. Since we met last time, so many problems have happened. I found out I have a suspicious growth on my neck. I need to get tested. Larry, my best friend, got in a horrible car crash over the weekend and is in the hospital. He is pretty bad off. And a bunch of other things. I am so tired of complaining and bringing in my crap to you. I am sure that you are so sick and tired of being assaulted with my craziness that you have reached your limit." I said, "So if you cancel our time together it protects me from your attack. I will be spared." R replied, "Yes. That is right. And, it saves me from you being pissed off and getting rid of me." I said, "So in order to save both of us and to prevent me from being furious and throwing you out, you have to find a way of sanitizing your feelings and thoughts. You have to be carefree and problem free in order for this relationship to work and to be safe." R said, "Yes. And, because I don't feel I have the right to have problems, I feel I should ignore them. I guess I feel you don't think I have the right to complain either and if I do you will get angry real quick." So, R had to find ways of not bothering his objects. That would be risking alienation or annihilation. He associated wanting help or compassion from me with being so greedy and selfish that I would be outraged.

Melanie Klein (1935) has noted the difference between the depressive position and the paranoid character. The depressive is full of guilt, sadness, and anxiety about his damaged object. The goal for the depressive ego is to unify and repair the object. For the paranoid patient, the object is shattered by the ego's aggressive greed and becomes a multitude of attacking objects.

I think that greed not only contributes to the persecutory phantasies, as Klein has pointed out, but that greed combined with excessive and aggressive PI prevents the phantasy of a forgiving and understanding object that can tolerate imperfection in the ego. This was the issue with R when he couldn't imagine that I could understand his problems, let alone tolerate him having them in the first place. So, his guilt at burdening me with all his troubles was really a frightening phantasy of being attacked and abandoned for burdening me. To prevent this loss and attack, he had to find a way of protecting me. However, this was really a self-protection.

Therefore, with patients like R, a constant reworking of greed and aggressive PI defenses is critical to re-establish a sense of love, forgiveness, and contentment between the ego and its objects. This working through is best done in the venue of the transference, but extra-transference work is equally valuable. The sense of trust and caring within the analytic relationship is therefore vital to explore whenever possible.

Part of this exploration involves the acceptance of a particular mutuality that parallels a parent–child/teacher–student relationship. In other words, the analyst is in the role of teacher, in so far as facilitating the patient's insight and self-growth, via interpretation of transference, unconscious phantasies, and associated defenses. However, the main focus is the patient's own self-striving and desire for internal expansion. This is the truly supportive nature of psychoanalytic treatment.

A major goal of psychoanalytic treatment is to help the patient develop a creative and insightful relationship with himself and the various internal aspects of his mind and its objects (Rather 2001). Greed creates a turning away from this desire for self-growth and PI can make this gap wider and wider. There is a fundamental difference between wanting more of the object and from the object versus seeing the object as part of a self-directed journey for self-improvement. The greedy ego wants idealized, continuous feeding from the object. To have to do anything to achieve that goal feels like a spoiling, a betrayal, or a persecution to the greedy ego. "If I have to work for it, it's not worth it," is the feeling.

During one period of the analysis, R demonstrated this pattern of denying and destroying the collaborative potential of the analytic relationship, instead favoring a unidimensional experience of satiation. He claimed to be emotionally and intellectually empty and asked me to instruct him on the proper ways of feeling, thinking, and relating. R wanted me to tell him specific things to say to friends and coworkers and how exactly to relate to potential girlfriends. He said he lacked the knowledge and saw my role as educator and mentor. R said, "My parents were so busy drinking, fighting, and being consumed with their own petty issues that I was really left on my own. I had lots of freedom to do anything I wanted. But, that meant I had to figure everything out on my own. That wasn't fair or right. As a child, I didn't know what the hell was right to do! I wanted somebody to tell me how to solve problems and manage life. I never got that. I still don't have it. I am hoping you will give that to me, help me know what to do. That isn't too much to ask, is it?" Here, R was claiming he suffered from a basic deficit of external and internal parenting and that he needed and expected me to provide that.

Bion (1959, 1962, [1962] 1977) has noted the importance of the infant/mother couple serving as a container in which intolerable, shapeless anxieties can be gradually tolerated and understood. I think R felt constantly deprived of this parental function. In other words, R was denied the critically needed, healthy experience of normal PI within the infant/parent matrix. This sense of loss and the experience of neglect produced an acute sense of greed and rage. R was demanding me to produce what he felt was his right. He believed he was owed extra. Now, I think R also felt his objects (parents, friends, potential mates, and analyst) were all quite weak. The greedier R felt, the weaker his objects looked. Due to his split-off, projected feelings of dependency, need, and insecurity, his objects looked fragile. Therefore, R tried to control and hide his destructive greed. He did this by appearing empty and in need of mentoring, while in fact he was much more able to think for himself than he let on. Through ongoing PI dynamics, he projected his greedy need to control his objects into me, causing him to relate in specific sadomasochistic ways. R would tell me, "Please, just tell me what to do, what to think, how to be. Tell me who I am or who I should be. I need you to tell me what to say and how to be." I was placed in the role of puppet master, greedily pulling his strings if I so pleased. I could have him be my empty vessel, to shape and fill as I pleased. This was a test. Would I use R for my gratification, commanding him to fill my needs?

I worked with this PI and greed in several ways. From a genetic standpoint, I interpreted R's chronic hunger for his parents' interest and love and his wish for their encouragement of his creative spirit. I suggested that he grew so hungry for and angrily demanding of this parental gift of self-soothing and creative curiosity that he now erased his own intellect and insight in rebellion. Instead, he played dumb and demanded I fulfill his parent's failed function.

R's initial reaction to my interpretations was to avoid them on an emotional level. Instead of digesting them, he deflected them by making them distant, impersonal, and intellectual. In a sterile, arm's-length tone, he told me he had heard that people might have such reactions to being raised by alcoholics. I interpreted this defensive move as his refusal to take in my analytic food. I was offering him analytic nourishment, but in a way that required him to collaborate, to think, and to feel. He had to feed himself some of the time with me and he resented that. Ultimately, this collaboration put him in touch with a profound grief and loss. In other words, it moved R toward the painful depressive position, which he normally resisted with regressive paranoid defenses and marked PI maneuvers.

Rather (2001) has used some of Melanie Klein's concepts to develop ideas about the patient's reactions to the process of analysis. Rather's ideas help make R's way of relating to me more understandable. Well-constructed interpretations provide support, insight, and soothing experiences of being tolerated and understood. They also invite the patient to turn inward and become his own container and integrator. In R's mind, to turn to himself for help and understanding was an all-too-familiar place, a cruel and lonely place he remembered from childhood. To R, and patients like him, to participate in the analytic journey is to, in phantasy, invite pain and to suffer emotional collapse. R felt he would be exposed to the persecutory loss he felt in childhood. To prevent this internal decay, the greedy ego demands the object serve as the all-providing, constant flow of knowledge and care. So, greed is a defensive pose, an act of revenge, and an aggressive and offensive move to take over the object.

Greed is also part of the pathological PI process of taking over the object. As such, excessive PI and the aggressive nature of greed tend to decrease or destroy the ego's ability to use symbol formation. R wanted simple, concrete, and literal answers as to what to say and do. He wanted me to provide instant and magical phrases to utter to his boss or girlfriend to fix a problem or bring R happiness. R didn't want to look beyond the immediate problem, he just wanted me to fix it.

R was pushed back and forth by his greed and these PI dynamics. He shifted between demanding the object give to him and fearing the effects of those greedy demands on the object. The splitting and isolation of feeling from phantasy was maintained by a vicious cycle of greed and projection. Fear of permanently destroying the object, terror of being abandoned to one's own internal chaos, and the threat of deadly retribution combined into a state of chronic and intense anxiety. Depression frequently follows these patients as well, since they feel this alienation and annihilation are imminent and unstoppable.

The greedy ego, trapped by these states of anxiety, uses PI to discharge affect, defend itself, and attack the object. Communication is also a motivation in normal PI, but the greedy ego does not usually see the object as a potential or reliable helper with whom communication is worthwhile or safe.

As the result of excessive reliance on PI and the intrapsychic effects of greed, patients like R see the object as aggressive and predatory, only staved off by the ego's constant efforts to be nice, pleasing, and accommodating. Patients feel they don't want to cause this threatening object any discomfort. This is motivated by a combination of depressive guilt and concern as well as paranoid fears of being attacked and discarded. This is a vision of a greedy, aggressive object that will attack if not constantly placated.

The case of R shows the multiple effects of greed upon the ego and its object relations. While some patients struggling with greedy phantasies relate in a highly predatory and openly demanding manner, others are more conflicted about these wishes. These more conflicted patients try to hide their greed and find different ways to express it. Masochistic disguise and borderline oscillation between offensive and defensive displays of greed highlight these patients. The conflict both Simon and, in particular, R had with their greedy phantasies had to do with paranoid fears of retribution. They felt their greed would be met with outrage and attack. This was a phantasy of both permanent loss of the object as well as persecution and annihilation. In treating such patients, the analyst must be willing to follow the patient as they go back and forth through these phantasies and associated defenses and to analyze the PI forces that maintain these pathological cycles. Interpretation of the imagined effects upon the analyst, as well as the imagined reprisal, is important.

Chapter 11

Interpretation as shaped by projective identification[1]

Older articles by authors such as Heimann (1956) and Racker (1961) take on the concept of PI in ways that are the cornerstone of many contemporary arguments. Kernberg (1987, 1988) has offered his unique blend of ego-psychology and Kleinian theory in understanding this phenomenon. Grotstein (1986, 1994) and Ogden (1982, 1984) provide valuable insight from an American viewpoint, while Grinberg (1962) has presented ideas from a South American perspective. Spillius (1992), Joseph (1993), and Schafer (1994) describe the current British Kleinian outlook on PI.

Numerous authors have identified areas of theoretical and clinical significance from the PI concept. Some of these findings help the clinician in clarifying how, when, and why to make an interpretation. In other words, matters of psychoanalytic technique, including the question of how to best introduce an interpretation and from what vantage point, are partly a matter of understanding the intricacies of PI.

As illustrated in the last several chapters, PI is regularly encountered in the analysis of paranoid-schizoid patients, as well as higher-functioning patients in the depressive position. Schafer (1997) elaborates the similarities and differences:

> In the paranoid-schizoid position the focus is very much on aggression or self and other directed destructiveness, much of it in the form of envy and fear of envy, and on grandiosity, while in the depressive position the focus is on love, understanding, concern, reparation, desire, and various other forms of regard for the object as well as on destructiveness and guilt. The paranoid-schizoid position is also characterized by typical defenses such as splitting and projective identification; the

depressive position, by regression (to the paranoid-schizoid position), flight to a manic position featuring denial and idealization of self and other, or bondage to a reparative position relative to the imagined damaged objects. Mature functioning rests on one's having attained an advanced phase of the depressive position in which object love and sublimatory activity are relatively stable; however, regressive pulls are never absent.

(Schafer 1997: 4)

PI, as a pivotal aspect of the transference, shapes and defines the nature of the analyst's interpretations. By paying close attention to the different clinical manifestations of PI, the clinician is in a better position to make useful interpretations. For example, if PI is used for communication purposes, the matching interpretation might be quite different from that if the PI mechanism was used for defensive purposes.

If the patient's phantasy is to prevent separation, one interpretation might be helpful. If PI is used to get rid of bad parts of the self, another might be more helpful. Segal (1990) writes:

[H]ere is an example of the difference between interpreting only projection and interpreting projective identification. A student reported a case in which his woman patient, preceding a holiday break, was describing how her children bickered and were jealous of one another in relation to her. The student interpreted that the children represented herself, jealous about him in relation to the holiday break, an interpretation she accepted without being much moved. He did not interpret that she felt that she had put a jealous and angry part of herself into the children, and that that part of her was changing and controlling them. The second interpretation, for which there was plenty of material in preceding and subsequent sessions, was of very great importance, in that it could be shown to the patient how, by subtle manipulations, she was in fact forcing the children to carry those parts of herself.

(Segal 1990: 12)

Segal makes it beautifully clear that PI involves action and ongoing internal movement between subject and object. This is not a static process.

The interface of intrapsychic and interpersonal

PI is an intrapsychic event in which aspects of the ego interact with aspects of the internal *and* external object. Evidence of this interaction and the specific nature of its dynamics become clearer through close examination of clinical data. This data includes the patient's free associations, the analyst's countertransference, the interpersonal dynamics between analyst and patient, acting out in or out of the clinical situation by either analyst or patient, and symptom formation. Once the analyst becomes aware of the PI mechanism, he or she may decide to make an interpretation. This interpretation will be shaped by the specific nature of the PI process and exactly how he came to be aware of it. In other words, while PI is a complicated matter that is difficult to understand immediately and fully, it presents many guideposts for the clinician. Certainly, there is usually a combination of PI situations occurring at any given moment, but the analyst can tease out certain portions of them at any given clinical moment.

Noting the way certain patients rely on splitting mechanisms to project their transference feelings into the past or current external world, Melanie Klein (1952c) stated:

> reports of patients about their daily life, relations, and activities not only give an insight into the functioning of the ego, but also reveal – if we explore the unconscious content – the defenses against the anxieties stirred up in the transference situation . . . he tries to split the relations to him [the analyst], keeping him either as a good or as a bad figure: he deflects some of the feelings and attitudes experienced toward the analyst on to other people in his current life, and this is part of 'acting out'.
>
> (Klein 1952c: 55–56)

Hinshelwood (1991) writes:

> The practice of Kleinian psychoanalysis has become an understanding of the transference as an expression of unconscious phantasy, active right here and now in the moment of analysis. The transference is, however, moulded upon the infantile

mechanisms with which the patient managed his experiences long ago.

(Hinshelwood 1991: 465)

Very much in line with Klein's idea of the patient's acting out is the acting out of the patient's PI phantasies by either patient or analyst.

Case study 1

Miss A was not able to make her usual appointment times due to a medical procedure. This meant we would not meet for a week. After she told me, she went on to another topic as if nothing of importance had happened. When I commented on this, she said there was nothing to make of it and moved on to another topic. After getting lost in other directions for most of the session, our time was up. I found myself asking her if she wanted to come in at other times during the week so as to not miss the whole week. She said no and we ended.

Miss A was a patient who for years had denied any differences between us and denied any dependence or attachment to the analysis, let alone to me. This was the result of her destructive narcissism and her primitive fears of loss and persecution. In our sessions, she put her affect into me and was left cold and uninterested. I, temporarily under the sway of those feelings, felt compelled to see if there was a way for us to meet. Internally, she attacked the value of our time together and projected it into me. I became the one who cared. As a result, I became involved in the patient's acting out.

During the next session, we explored the meanings of these PI maneuvers. She was able to discuss her feelings of disappointment, excitement, loss, and victory over not meeting. This was difficult for Miss A, as she usually kept her feelings hidden. She liked to feel independent and able to do everything in her own mind without my help. Normally, she fought against sharing her feelings and thoughts with me. Fairly often we would end up in some type of power struggle and only later see how she was trying to hoard her thoughts and defend them against me, someone who tried to "steal" them.

This particular example of processing PI is of almost textbook clarity. In reality, most PI situations emerge piecemeal and over time. Often, the analyst is put off balance and acts out with the patient to some degree over a long period of time before realizing what might be happening.

Sometimes, PI maneuvers become obvious through the interpersonal aspects of the analyst–patient relationship. By observing, reflecting, and commenting on the interpersonal behavior a patient exhibits, or the interpersonal pattern both parties are drawn into, the analyst can begin to explore more internal and intrapsychic motivations. In other words, the interpersonal realm often acts a vehicle for the unconscious PI mechanism.

Case study 2

Mr B, a new patient, brought out countertransference feeling very quickly, triggered by interpersonal PI dynamics. In the first two sessions, he banged on my door five minutes before his time, even though there is an "in-session" sign posted. He asked me to get him a drink of water. When he told me some of his problems, he followed up with, "Now that you know that, what are we going to do about it?" I was left feeling controlled, put down, and used. Some of this leaked out in how I told him to not knock on my door. I felt I was being a bit reactionary and stern.

Slowly, I brought Mr B's attention to his way of relating to me and asked him to be curious about it. Bit by bit, we were able to understand his feelings of being ashamed, controlled, and powerless in having to see me. Instead of having to wait for me and be anxious and thirsty, he turned it around and felt in charge. Later, it came out that he felt the same way in his marriage and career and used the same type of defenses. He projected his feelings of vulnerability, weakness, and dependence into the object and proceeded to take charge and dominate. He wanted revenge for his feelings of inferiority. By starting with our interpersonal contact, we were able to explore his unconscious feelings and fears and understand how he used PI to cope with a precarious internal state.

What patients tell us, their stories about day-to-day life and their associations to uncovered phantasies, can elicit countertransference feelings in the analyst. These feelings can provide clues to PI mechanisms alive in the transference and in the patient's internal object world. The analyst must be constantly reflective about how they are feeling, what urges occur, and in what context they feel pushed to act or speak. Various thoughts, feelings, and phantasies emerge in the analyst as the patient pushes in one direction or another with their words and actions.

Case study 3

The patient, Q, had been in psychoanalytic psychotherapy for two years. Q was a 25-year-old gay male, originally entering treatment for severe depression. During a recent hour, he told me about an incident when he was roller skating. He had been skating for over a year for exercise and now was on an unfamiliar course. He had been doing fine and having fun until he went around a turn and came to a sharp decline and picked up speed. Out of control, he began waving his arms about and started to scream. He crashed through some bushes, skidded across the ground, lost his shin pads, and rolled into a large pile of dirt. He then went into great detail about how he skinned his knees and got dirt in his mouth, ears, and nose. The whole telling of the story took on quite a histrionic tone. My countertransference feeling at that point was "he is acting like a very pitiful, flamboyant, and stereotypical homosexual."

Q told me the story in such a way as to not only portray himself as the weakest, least masculine, and most ridiculous skater possible but also in a way that provoked me to feel critical. I asked him if he was aware of how he was telling the story and he said that he probably looked like an "uncoordinated fag" in his roller skates and that he felt very ashamed. After some investigation, we both came to understand much about this transaction. This particular hour contained elements that had surfaced in the transference before, yet there was a unique moment of clarity in this hour due to the understanding of his projective identification.

In this particular hour and other following hours, I came to see how he deposited various internal aspects of himself into me for safe keeping, as well as different types of aggressive and libidinal gratification.

Q's mother was sadomasochistic and hypochondriacal. She used misery as a way to chain Q to her side. He complied with this early on by identifying with her. Through cooking, cleaning, and sewing he was able to be with her and please her by providing her a narcissistic extension. They shared in countless tales of woe about the family and the world at large. This symbiotic relationship led to Q fearing his father's rage regarding his less then manly behavior and his failure to be a "traditional son." Intrapsychically, he wished to be close to his mother by providing her with fuel for her sadomasochistic needs.

This intrapsychic phantasy was projected onto the external object of the analyst. He told me about the skating disaster as a way to be close and provide me with tales of woe. By his dramatic use of words, tone, and gesture, I was affected by this phantasy and covertly invited to play a particular role. The boundary between his self- and object-representations was, on the one hand, blurred by the mutual symbiotic state of woe he wished to have with me and, on the other hand, there was a differentiation created by my disapproval toward him. While I didn't show it outright, it emerged in the form of my confrontation and invitation to explore his way of relating to me. If I had acted on my displeasure, as his father had always done by calling him names and belittling him, the pathological differentiation process would have been even more marked.

The aim of his PI communication was multi-determined. He wished to recreate the masochistic union with his mother and to relate to me as a son who embarrassed his father so much that he received rage as a token of love. He also wished to demonstrate his phallic power to me via the skating but was careful to show it in a less than favorable light "just in case" I found the power as untenable as his mother did.

Q provides an example of how each patient's use of PI is unique. The complexity of mental functioning is certainly found in the dynamic of PI. By trying to understand the exact nature of his use of this mechanism I was better able to offer interpretations that would fit with his experience.

Summary

Melanie Klein proposed the term "projective identification" in 1946. She described an intrapsychic phenomenon by which certain parts of the ego were put into parts of the object, for defensive and protective reasons. Since then, Kleinians have elaborated on her concept and made it a cornerstone of Kleinian theory and technique.

From my clinical experience, I am of the view that PI is the most basic and unique form of human communication. This includes a dialectical process within both interpersonal and intrapsychic forums. Early situations between mother and infant are paralleled in the clinical hour between analyst and patient, the difference being the chronological and developmental passage of time, and the evolution of the original phantasy material.

The PI situation is the essence of much of the analytic relationship and can either create a fluid unfolding between patient and analyst leading to structural change or can lead to the limitation and subsequent eradication of the analytic relationship. PI encompasses and defines the entire transference state and is often the chief resistance. Therefore, unless PI is understood and analyzed as a fundamental element in the relationship, an interminable state of enactment and confusion can take over and at times terminate the analytic journey. By the mutual exploration of PI situations, the relationship can be freed from potential limitations and constrictions and the analysis can naturally proceed.

Each patient, regardless of diagnosis, engages the analyst in a specific manner, interpersonally and intrapsychically. This pattern of relating (the transference) is guided by the patient's unique set of internal object relations and their particular way of dealing with anxiety. PI is, therefore, a defensive mechanism that colors each transference/countertransference situation in a one-of-a-kind way. The analyst studies the various behavioral, relational, and psychological clues from the patient, from himself, and from the dynamic between both parties. In these ways, the analyst slowly understands the communicative nature or special function of each patient's PI efforts.

PI is often the leading mental mechanism patients employ within the transference setting. Therefore, the interpretation of PI is essential and figures prominently in any discussion of technique. Melanie Klein offered fairly specific theoretical concepts on how the mind functions and how anxieties shape internal dynamics. Her method of treatment and her theory of mental processes provide the clinician with a clear map of how to proceed. This set of guidelines is flexible enough to be applied in a way that takes into account the complexity and uniqueness of each patient–analyst pair.

Melanie Klein placed emphasis on the exploration of paranoid and depressive anxieties, the internal and external world, and the various manifestations of the life and death instincts.

In my clinical work, I apply a psychoanalytic technique designed to meet Klein's criteria. In making use of Kleinian theory, I place an emphasis on the patient's phantasy life, their depressive and paranoid anxieties that seem most current in the analytic hour, the patient's defensive posture, and the place of splitting and PI in their internal and interpersonal life. I also focus on issues of separation, loss, envy, and the desire for knowledge and power.

My case material shows how my particular Kleinian style is a mix of many of the PI approaches used by others, made unique by my own personality, flexibility, and emphasis on countertransference, as well as by my focus on issues of loss, greed, symbolism, and the unconscious dynamics of positive and negative phantasies. External and internal combine with interpersonal and intrapsychic to create the one-of-a-kind analytic environment found with each patient.

Love, hate, and the environment are the three ever-present ingredients in every PI dynamic and every transference situation. Therefore, these three elements and how they are technically handled will always shape the nature of the treatment. While there is a body of literature which demonstrates what Kleinian analysts actually do and say in regard to PI, the data is sparse. I have provided my own case material to supplement and sharpen this neglected area.

With all patients, I work at understanding the nature of the patient's phantasies and how PI is being used as a vehicle for them. This includes interpreting PI as a defense, a creative, loving, or adaptive act, a communication, a method of reparation, or an aggressive act. The individual struggles with ways of managing the destructive and loving forces within themselves, defined by either paranoid-schizoid or depressive anxieties. The outcomes of these struggles are the uniquely individual phantasies and patterns of defense that we encounter in the clinical situation. PI is a bedrock layer of these coping mechanisms. Therefore, the careful analysis of PI and its associated dynamics (such as splitting, introjection, and manic postures) is crucial to each analytic treatment. This exploration often uncovers the cyclical intertwining of PI, greed, loss, and the breakdown of symbolic function.

In moment-to-moment analytic work, the analyst may need to take different stances in regard to dealing therapeutically with repetitious PI mechanisms. Sometimes, clinical judgement requires that I contain the projection and interpret silently to myself. Most often, I contain the projections for some period, attempt to translate them to myself, and then interpret them. This sequence is only possible by noticing my countertransference and the patient's verbal and nonverbal associations to the moment-to-moment interaction in our relationship. If possible, I interpret both the anxiety and the defenses against it as they relate to the transference. "What is the patient wanting from me?" and "how is the patient showing me that?" are some of the questions I try to explore, first with myself and second with the patient. Given the confusing, rapid, and multiple layers of unconscious interaction taking place many times over in each clinical visit, these are all ideals we never obtain. However, they are helpful guidelines to strive for and form a useful map to follow in the course of an analytic encounter.

Listening closely to a patient's level of depressive or paranoid tension provides a gauge of how and when they may need an interpretation to help work through their current mental problems. In any given hour, a patient brings up so much material, connected to so many layers of different wishes and fears, that the analyst has to sort out what they will and will not address in that particular moment. The patient's multiple phantasies have common threads, but some are too disguised, unconscious, or defended to bring attention to in the moment.

Timing and evaluation of affect can be more important in determining when to interpret than the idea of simply locating and interpreting a resistance. The former is more matched with the immediate interpersonal, intrapsychic matrix of what is happening in the treatment situation. The latter is more the idea of pushing aside a block to the "truth," in line with Freud's original topographic model of resistance analysis.

This more gentle and paced approach results in interpretations that take longer to get to, but are usually more accurate. I believe this is in line with Strachey's (1937) recommendation to interpret the transference as it occurs, so it is current and alive. He writes:

> the prime essential of a transference interpretation in my view is that the feeling or impulse interpreted should not merely be concerned with the analyst but that it should be in activity at the moment at which it is interpreted . . . it will only be possible to understand the results of those procedures . . . if we pay sufficient attention to the mechanisms of introjection and projection.
>
> (Strachey 1937: 141)

PI influences both patient and analyst to the point that regular acting out by both parties is unavoidable. Rather than trying to deny or prevent such excursions, it seems more helpful to anticipate them and understand their intrapsychic function. Accordingly, the analyst's interpretations of the patient's PI mechanisms can provide a working through for both patient and analyst. In other words, interpretations are made for the benefit of both parties.

Many factors go into deciding how to interpret PI. Carefully examining how the patient is using the analyst, and how the patient is asking the analyst to use him or her, provides the analyst with clues that shape the interpretative process. I try and notice what roles the patient's phantasies and actions put us in. By this, I mean both mental images and actual interpersonal roles that become alive through PI acting out. I ask myself questions like who is giving or taking what from whom, who is controlling what, what is omitted, and what type of conflicts are being set up? I imagine the patient as creating a play, with us as the principal characters. He will introduce external characters who will offer disguise and diversion from the principal players. This internal dialogue is helpful in balancing and restabilizing myself during regressive PI moments and gives me direction in how to interpret the emerging clinical material.

At times, a patient may be so paranoid or confused by excessive splittings and PI that interpretation provides a way of preventing further disintegration of the ego rather than resolving them. With these types of patients, it is important that the interpretation be given within the current context of their paranoid delusions. An interpretation that focuses on or subtly forces reality testing will often escalate their anxieties and push them to erect even greater defenses. Therefore, it is better to immerse oneself into the patient's phantasy, especially the PI aspect of the phantasy, and interpret the anxieties within that phantasy. This process of just "sitting with it and in it" may take days, weeks, or sometimes months. Only later may the patient be able to tolerate stepping back and taking more of a big-picture look at themselves.

During periods of closeness to and awareness of the patient's unconscious phantasy material, the analyst can experience difficulties. Technically, the analyst always tries to avoid a premature interpretation of the patient's projection. Instead, he or she attempts to contain the projections of unwanted hostility or overwhelming desire. This can trigger intense countertransference feelings, manifesting in wanting to clarify details and confront the patient with reality. The analyst can act out by lecturing and educating the patient, out of frustration. This is really an aggressive act of spitting back the unwanted mental garbage the patient has put into the analyst. At these times, it is often better to contain this emotional garbage until both analyst and patient are more balanced. When the analyst is feeling less reactive and not as overwhelmed with persecutory or depressive anxieties, then these intrapsychic and interpersonal dynamics can be discussed. Containing the patient's mental discharges is a situation of psychic timing. When and how to reintroduce the patient's projections is the essence of the interpretive art.

When can both parties handle the open struggle of dealing with raw, painful, hateful, and scary feelings and thoughts without becoming overwhelmed? The analyst regularly poses this question to himself to determine when and how to intervene.

A patient's phantasies, anxieties, and defenses are often related to issues with separation, loss, or attachment. These conflicts may remain at a more primitive, raw level or be disguised by either defensive or healthy maturation, showing up as the urge to compete and a fear of defeat. Control and power are complex conflicts that originate from more basic issues of autonomy and intimacy. The ego often employs PI to cope with both levels of psychic struggle.

As mentioned before, greed and issues of symbolic formation are often interwoven with excessive PI cycles. All these difficult manifestations of PI are constantly in play within the therapeutic relationship. The analyst is brought into the patient's world via PI and it is through the analysis of PI that the patient's world can begin to change and become more integrated.

I have used clinical material from my own practice, as well as reports from the analytic work of other Kleinians, to show what actually takes place clinically with the phenomenon of PI. Moment-to-moment verbatim case material provides a rare clarity and honesty that is often lost or dimmed in discussions of theory. While some Kleinians seem to favor singular approaches to the interpretation of PI, I think my case material reveals what is more often the case. There are certain key elements that I and other Kleinians take up in our interpretive stance to PI, but these are usually used in combination.

The Kleinian theoretical examination of PI, starting with Melanie Klein's discovery of the concept, has had a wide and helpful effect on the analytic community. The greatest benefit has been the gradual growth in understanding just how exactly to interpret PI in ways that best match the patient's anxieties and phantasies, so as to give greatest relief and provide the optimum chance for change and integration.

Notes

4 Projective identification: some clinical and diagnostic considerations

1 Originally published in the *Journal of the American Academy of Psychoanalysis* as *Projective Identification: Some Clinical Considerations*, 1998, 25(3): 439–454. © American Academy of Psychoanalysis, reprinted with permission.

2 The developing and never static nature of the self exists in part as the combination of the sum total of psychological and biological needs and functions of the human organism. This includes aspects within somatic states, core affects, libidinal wishes, and fears and urges of a prey/predatory nature. These are united with all of the varied integrative, dynamic, and perceptual aspects of the ego, such as internal self- and object-representations, and the ability to generate complex compromise formations. These organizing functions of the human organism (in addition to the subjective experience of oneself as a person and a body, the experience of being both passive and active, and the sense of being both an individual "one" and of being part of a whole) are all fundamentally shaped, organized, and translated by unconscious phantasy to produce what is understood as the self. This end product of phantasy formation remains the central fulcrum from which all future experiences revolve in some manner or form.

Phantasy remains, from the birth of the organism, the foremost and fundamental organizing, binding, and translating energy of the psychic system. In this context, it must be remembered that phantasy states allow for the inner aspects of self- and object-representations to move and shift in order to defend, battle, and/or adapt to the inner motions of the often opposing and conflictual elements of other constellations of self- and object-representations. Phantasy allows for inner movement, mutation, and transformation within the matrix of self and object representational systems and provides the fuel for this internal motion. In other words, the introjected relationship between the infant and the mother does not remain static, it continues on with a life of its own, constantly being reissued, reshaped, and recreated by both internal and external reality.

5 Intrapsychic outcome in projective identification

1 Previously published in the *Bulletin of the Menninger Clinic*, 1998, 62(3): 366–377. © *Bulletin of the Menninger Clinic*.

6 Projective identification, countertransference, and the struggle for understanding over acting out

1 Previously published in the *Journal of Psychotherapy Practice and Research*, 1999, 8(2): 155–161.
2 I think it is helpful to use the distinction of "into" for the intrapsychic aspect of PI and "onto" for the interpersonal manifestation of the process.

7 Projective identification, self-disclosure and the patient's view of the object: the need for flexibility

1 Previously published in the *Journal of Psychotherapy Practice and Research*, 1999, 8(3): 225–233.

9 Hate, projective identification, and the analyst's struggle

1 Previously published as 'Hate, Projective Identification, and the Therapist's Struggle', in the *Journal of Psychotherapy Practice and Research*, 1999, 9(1): 33–38.

11 Interpretation as shaped by projective identification

1 Previously published in the *Journal of Contemporary Psychotherapy*, 2001, 31(4): 279–285.

Bibliography

Adler, G. (1988) Selfobject Function of Projective Identification, *Bulletin of the Menninger Clinic*, 52: 473–491.

Aron, L. (1997) Self-Disclosure and the Interactive Matrix, *Psychoanalytic Dialogues*, 7: 315–318.

Bion, W. (1957) Differentiation of the Psychotic from More Psychotic Personalities, *International Journal of Psychoanalysis*, 38: 266–275.

Bion, W. (1959) Attacks on Linking, *International Journal of Psychoanalysis*, 30: 308–315.

Bion, W. (1962) The Psychoanalytic Study of Thinking: II. A Theory of Thinking, *International Journal of Psychoanalysis*, 43: 306–310.

Bion, W. ([1962] 1977) Learning from Experience, in *Seven Servants*, Jason Aronson, New York.

Bion, W., Rosenfeld, H., and Segal, H. (1961) Melanie Klein, *International Journal of Psychoanalysis*, 42: 4–8.

Burch, B. (1989) Mourning and Failure to Mourn – An Object Relations View, *Contemporary Psychoanalysis*, 25: 608–623.

Burke, W. (1992) Countertransference Disclosure and the Asymmetry/ Mutuality Dilemma, *Psychoanalytic Dialogues*, 2: 241–271.

Caper, R. (1997) Psychic Reality and the Interpretation of Transference, *Psychoanalytic Quarterly*, 66: 18–33.

Chused, J. (1997) Patient's Perception of Analyst's Self-Disclosure, *Psychoanalytic Dialogues*, 7: 243–256.

Cooper, S. (1998) Countertransference Disclosure and Technique's Conceptualization, *Psychoanalytic Quarterly*, 67: 128–156.

Cycon, R. (1994) Sadomasochism in the Transference/Countertransference as a Defense Against Psychic Pain, *Psychoanalytic Inquiry*, 14(3): 441–445.

De Racker, G. (1961) On the Formulation of the Interpretation, *International Journal of Psychoanalysis*, 42: 49–54.

Fairbairn, R. (1952) *Psychoanalytic Studies of the Personality*, Routledge, New York.

Feldman, M. (1994) Projective Identification in Phantasy and Enactment, *Psychoanalytic Inquiry*, 14(3): 423–440.

Feldman, M. (1997) Projective Identification: The Analyst's Involvement, *International Journal of Psychoanalysis*, 78: 227–241.

Frankiel R., Harris, A., and Spillius, E. Bott (2001) To Have and Have Not: Clinical Uses of Envy, *Journal of the American Psychoanalytic Association*, 49(4): 1391–1404.

Freud, S. ([1915] 1959) Instincts and their Vicissitudes, *Collected Papers of S. Freud*, Volume IV, Basic Books, New York.

Gerson, S. (1996) Self-Disclosure, Personal Proclivity or Principle of Technique?, *Psychoanalytic Dialogues*, 6: 671–675.

Gerson, S. (1997) Analyst's Use of the Self, Self-Disclosure, Enhanced Integration, *Psychoanalytic Psychology*, 14: 365–382.

Grinberg, L. (1962) On a Specific Aspect of Countertransference Due to the Patient's Projective Identification, *International Journal of Psychoanalysis*, 43: 436–440.

Grotstein, J. (1986) *Splitting and Projective Identification*, Jason Aronson, New York.

Grotstein, J. (1993) A Reappraisal of Fairbairn, *Bulletin of the Menninger Clinic*, 57(4): 421–450.

Grotstein, J. (1994) Projective Identification Reappraised – Part 1: Projective Identification, Introjective Identification, the Transference/Countertransference Neurosis/Psychosis, and their Consummate Expression in the Crucifixion, the Pieta, and "Therapeutic Exorcism," *Contemporary Psychoanalysis*, 30: 708–746.

Hamilton, N. (1986) Positive Projective Identification, *International Journal of Psychoanalysis*, 67: 489–496.

Hamilton, N. (1990) The Containing Function and the Analyst's Projective Identification, *International Journal of Psychoanalysis*, 71: 445–454.

Heimann, P. ([1949] 1989) On Countertransference, in M. Tonnesmann (ed.), *About Children and Children-No-Longer, Collected Papers 1942–80*, Routledge, London.

Heimann, P. (1956) Dynamics of Transference Interpretations, *International Journal of Psychoanalysis*, 37: 303–310.

Hinshelwood, R. (1991) *A Dictionary of Kleinian Thought*, Free Association Books, London.

Jacobs, T. (1998) Comment, in O. Renik, The Analyst's Subjectivity and the Analyst's Objectivity, *Journal of Clinical Psychoanalysis*, 7(2): 237–252.

Joseph, B. (1978) Different Types of Anxiety and Their Handling in the Analytic Situation, *International Journal of Psychoanalysis*, 59: 223–228.

Joseph, B. (1987) Projective Identification: Clinical Aspects, in J. Sandler (ed.), *Projection, Identification, Projective Identification*, International Universities Press, Madison, CT, 65–76.

Joseph, B. (1993) *Psychic Equilibrium and Psychic Change: Selected Papers of Betty Joseph*, Edited by M. Feldman and E. Bott Spillius, Routledge, New York.

Kernberg, O. (1965) Notes on Countertransference, *Journal of the American Psychoanalytic Association*, 13: 38–56.

Kernberg, O. (1976) *Borderline Conditions and Pathological Narcissism*, Jason Aronson, Northvale, NY.

Kernberg, O. (1987) Projection and Projective Identification: Developmental and Clinical Aspects, in J. Sandler (ed.) *Projection, Identification, Projective Identification*, International Universities Press, Madison, CT, 93–115.

Kernberg, O. (1988) Object Relations Theory in Clinical Practice, *Psychoanalytic Quarterly*, 57: 481–504.

Kernberg, O. (1989) *Borderline Conditions and Pathological Narcissism*, Jason Aronson, New York.

Kernberg, O., Selzer, M., Koenigsberg, M. and Carr, A. (1989) *Psychodynamic Psychotherapy of Borderline Patients*, Basic Books, New York.

Klein, M. (1926) The Psychological Principles of Early Analysis, *The Writings of Melanie Klein* Volume 1, Free Press, New York.

Klein, M. (1930) The Importance of Symbol-Formation in the Development of the Ego, *International Journal of Psychoanalysis*, 11: 24–39.

Klein, M. (1935) A Contribution to the Psychogenesis of Manic-Depressive States, in M. Klein, *Love, Guilt and Reparation*, Free Press, New York, 262–289.

Klein, M. (1946) Notes on Some Schizoid Mechanisms, *The Writings of Melanie Klein*, Volume III, Free Press, New York.

Klein, M. (1950) On the Criteria For the Termination of a Psychoanalysis, in M. Klein, *Envy and Gratitude and Other Works, 1946–1963*, Hogarth Press, London.

Klein, M. (1952a) Some Theoretical Conclusions Regarding the Emotional Life of the Infant, *The Writings of Melanie Klein*, Volume III, Free Press, New York.

Klein, M. (1952b) On Observing the Behavior of Young Infants, *The Writings of Melanie Klein*, Volume III, Free Press, New York.

Klein, M. (1952c) The Origins of Transference, *The Writings of Melanie Klein*, Volume III, Free Press, New York.

Klein, M. (1952d) The Mutual Influences in the Development of Ego and Id, *The Writings of Melanie Klein*, Volume III, Free Press, New York.

Klein, M. (1955) On Identification, *The Writings of Melanie Klein*, Volume III, Free Press, New York.

Klein, M. (1957) Envy and Gratitude, *The Writings of Melanie Klein*, Volume III, Free Press, New York.

Klein, M. (1963) On the Sense of Loneliness, in M. Klein, *Envy and Gratitude and Other Works 1946–1963*, Hogarth Press, London.

Klein, M. (1981) Autistic Phenomenon in Neurotic Patients, in James M. Grotstein (ed.) *Do I Dare Disturb the Universe?*, Karnac, London.

Malcolm, R. (1980) Expiation as a Defense, *International Journal of Psychoanalytic Psychotherapy*, 8: 549–570.

Malcolm, R. (1986) Interpretation: The Past in the Present, *International Journal of Psychoanalysis*, 13: 433–443.

Malcolm, R. (1987) Melanie Klein: Achievements and Problems (Reflections on Klein's Conception of Object Relationship), in Robert Langs (ed.), *The Yearbook of Psychoanalysis and Psychotherapy*, Volume 2, Gardner Press, Inc, New York and London.

Malcolm, R. (1995) The Three 'W's': What, Where and When: the Rationale of Interpretation, *International Journal of Psychoanalysis*, 76: 447–456.

Malin, A. and Grotstein, J. (1966) Projective Identification in the Therapeutic Process, *International Journal of Psychoanalysis*, 47: 26–31.

Maroda, K. (1997) On the Reluctance to Sanction Self-Disclosure, *Psychoanalytic Dialogues*, 7: 323–326.

Mason, A. (1987) A Kleinian Perspective, *Psychoanalytic Inquiry*, 7: 189–197.

Meltzer, D. (1990) The Relation of Anal Masturbation to Projective Identification, in Elizabeth Bott Spillius (ed.) *Melanie Klein Today. Volume 1: Mainly Theory*, Routledge, London, 102–116.

Moore, B. and Fine, B. (1990) *Psychoanalytic Terms and Concepts*, The American Psychoanalytic Association, Yale University, New Haven, CT.

Ogden, T. (1979) On Projective Identification, *International Journal of Pschoanalysis*, 60: 357–373.

Ogden, T. (1982) *Projective Identification and Psychotherapeutic Technique*, Jason Aronson, New York.

Ogden, T. (1984) Instinct, Phantasy, and Psychological Deep Structure – A Reinterpretation of Aspects of the Work of Melanie Klein, *Contemporary Psychoanalysis*, 20: 500–525.

Ogden, T. (1989) *The Primitive Edge of Experience*, Jason Aronson, Northvale, NJ, 47–82.

Ogden, T. (1990) *The Matrix of the Mind*, Jason Aronson, Northvale, NJ.

O'Shaughnessy, E. (1983) Words and Working Through, *International Journal of Psychoanalysis*, 64: 281–289.

O'Shaughnessy, E. (1990) Can a Liar be Psychoanalyzed?, *International Journal of Psychoanalysis*, 71: 187–195.

Pantone, P. (1994) Projective Identification: Affective Aspects, *Contemporary Psychoanalysis*, 30: 604–618.

Pick, I. (1985) Working Through in the Countertransference, *International Journal of Psychoanalysis*, 66: 157–166.

Pine, F. (1984) The Interpretive Moment, *Bulletin of the Menninger Clinic*, 48(1): 54–71.

Prado, M. de A. (1980) Neurotic and Psychotic Transference and Projective Identification, *International Journal of Psychoanalysis*, 7: 157–164.

Psychoanalytic Inquiry (1998) Volume 18.

Quinodoz, D. (1994) Interpretations in Projection, *International Journal of Psychoanalysis*, 75: 755–761.

Racker, H. (1968) *Transference and Countertransference*, International Universities Press, Madison, CT.

Rather, L. (2001) Collaborating with the Unconscious Other, *International Journal of Psychoanalysis*, 82(3): 515–531.

Renik, O. (1995) The Ideal of Anonymous Analyst and the Problem of Self-Disclosure, *Psychoanalytic Quarterly*, 64: 466–495.

Rodrique, E. (1955) The Analysis of a Three Year Old Mute Schizophrenic, in *New Directions in Psychoanalysis*, Basic Books, New York.

Rosenfeld, D. (1992) *The Psychotic Aspects of the Personality*, Brunner/Mazel, Inc., New York.

Rosenfeld, H. (1952a) Notes on the Pyscho-Analysis of the Super-Ego Conflict of an Acute Schizophrenic Patient, *International Journal of Psychoanalysis*, 33: 111–131.

Rosenfeld, H. (1952b) Transference-Phenomena and Transference-Analysis in an Acute Catatonic Schizophrenic Patient, *International Journal of Psychoanalysis*, 33: 457–464.

Rosenfeld, H. (1954) Considerations Regarding the Pyscho-Analytic Approach to Acute and Chronic Schizophrenia, *International Journal of Psychoanalysis*, 35: 135–140.

Rosenfeld, H. (1958) Contribution to the Discussion on Variations in Classical Technique, *International Journal of Psychoanalysis*, 39: 238–239.

Rosenfeld, H. (1983) Primitive Object Relations and Mechanisms, *International Journal of Psychoanalysis*, 64: 261–267.

Rosenfeld, H. (1990) Contributions to the Psychopathology of Psychotic States: the Importance of Projective Identification in the Ego Structure and the Object Relations of the Psychotic Patient, in Elizabeth Bott Spillius (ed.), *Melanie Klein Today* Volume 1: *Mainly Theory*, Routledge, London, 117–137.

Sandler, J. (1976) Countertransference and Role Responsiveness, *International Review of Psychoanalysis*, 3: 43–47.

Sandler, J. (ed.) (1986) *Projection, Identification, Projective Identification*, International Universities Press, Madison, CT.

Schafer, R. (1994) The Contemporary Kleinians of London, *Psychoanalytic Quarterly*, 63: 409–432.

Schafer, R. (1997) *The Contemporary Kleinians of London*, International Universities Press, Madison, CT.

Segal, H. (1955) A Psychoanalytical Approach to Aesthetics, in *New Directions in Psychoanalysis*, Basic Books, New York, 384–405.

Segal, H. (1957) Notes on Symbol Formation, *International Journal of Psychoanalysis*, 38: 39–45.

Segal, H. (1974) *Introduction to the Work of Melanie Klein*, Basic Books, New York.

Segal, H. (1975) Introduction to the Romanian edition of *The Writings of Melanie Klein*, Free Press, New York; posted on website: www.chat.ru/~vatlin/klein_biography_eng.htm-46k

Segal, H. (1977) Countertransference, *International Journal of Psychoanalytic Psychotherapy*, 6: 31–37.

Segal, H. (1978) On Symbolism, *International Journal of Psychoanalysis*, 59: 315–319.

Segal, H. (1990) *The Work of Hanna Segal: A Kleinian Approach to Clinical Practice*, Jason Aronson, Northvale, NJ.

Segal, H. (1993a) On the Clinical Usefulness of the Concept of Death Instinct, *International Journal of Psychoanalysis*, 74: 55–61.

Segal, H. (1993b) An Interview with Hanna Segal, by V. Hunter, *Psychoanalytic Review*, 80: 1–28.

Segal, H. (1997) *Psychoanalysis, Literature, and War: Papers 1972–1995*, Edited by John Steiner, Routledge, London.

Spillius, E. Bott (1983) Some Developments from the Work of Melanie Klein, *International Journal of Psychoanalysis*, 64: 321–332.

Spillius, E. Bott (1988) *Melanie Klein Today*, Volume 2: *Mainly Practice*, Routledge, New York.

Spillius, E. Bott (1992) Clinical Experiences of Projective Identification, in Robin Anderson (ed.), *Clinical Lectures on Klein and Bion*, Routledge, London.

Spillius, E. Bott (1994) Developments in Kleinian Thought: Overview and Personal View, *Psychoanalytic Inquiry*, 14(3): 324–364.

Stein, R. (1990) A New Look at the Theory of Melanie Klein, *International Journal of Psychoanalysis*, 71: 499.

Steiner, J. (1993) *Psychic Retreats*, Routledge, London.

Strachey, J. (1934) The Nature of Therapeutic Action of Psychoanalysis, *International Journal of Psychoanalysis*, 15: 127–159.

Tausk, V. ([1919] 1948) On the Origin of the "Influencing Machine," in R. Fleiss (ed.), *Schizophrenia, The Psychoanalytic Reader*, International Universities Press, New York.

Thorner, H. (1955) Three Defenses Against Inner Persecution, in *New Directions in Psychoanalysis*, Basic Books, New York.

Torras De Bea, E. (1989) Projective Identification and Differentiation, *International Journal of Psychoanalysis*, 70: 265–274.

Waska, R. (1998a) Projective Identification: Some Clinical Considerations, *Journal of the American Academy of Psychoanalysis*, 25(3): 439–454.

Waska, R. (1998b) Intrapsychic Outcome in Projective Identification, *Bulletin of the Menninger Clinic*, 62(3): 366–377.

Waska, R. (1999a) Projective Identification, Countertransference, and the Struggle for Understanding over Acting Out, *Journal of Psychotherapy Practice and Research*, 8(2): 155–161.

Waska, R. (1999b) Projective Identification, Self-Disclosure, and the Patient's View of the Object: The Need for Flexibility, *Journal of Psychotherapy Practice and Research*, 8(3): 233–255.

Waska, R. (1999c) Hate, Projective Identification, and the Therapist's Struggle, *Journal of Psychotherapy Practice and Research*, 9(1): 33–38.

Waska, R. (2001) Interpretation as Shaped by Projective Identification, *Journal of Contemporary Psychotherapy*, 31(4): 279–285.

Waska, R. (2002) *Primitive Experiences of Loss*, Karnac, London.

Waska, R. (2003) Fragmented Attachments: the Paranoid-Schizoid Experience of Loss and Persecution, *Bulletin of the Menninger Clinic*, 67(1): 50–64.

Weigert, E. (1954) The Importance of Flexibility in Psychoanalytic Technique, *Journal of the American Psychoanalytic Association*, 2(4): 702–710.

Index

abandonment 14, 50, 66, 67, 76, 85, 86, 116, 144, 146, 161, 163, 179, 183; ego 155; eternal 100; fear of 150, 157; hopeless sense of 176
absence 30
abstinence 120, 126
abuse 50, 62; drugs and alcohol 159; emotional 157; verbal 109, 172
acceptance 132, 184
accusations 87, 110, 163
acquaintances 11
acting out 16, 46, 54, 70, 72, 86, 124, 128, 190; aggressive, counter-therapeutic 168; countertransference 75; mutual 14, 29, 31, 39, 90; selfish 156; struggle for understanding over 104–15
actions 114; thoughtful 97; words and 35
Adler, G. 94
affection 174
affects 11, 12, 40, 69, 76, 84, 88, 89, 90, 93; evaluating 120; expressing 129; integration of 155; intensity of 160; multiple 16, 33; negative 132; phantasy and 20–5; positive 132; split-off 48; thought and 164; transformation of 74; unconscious 25; unwanted 119
aggression 7, 84, 122, 140, 141, 154, 157, 165; competitive 81; constitutional 158, 159, 162;

denying 112; environmentally induced 159; excessive 156, 159; fear of own 18; greedy 170; object-related 131; oral 132, 133; primary and secondary 82; relational 34; sadistic 182; sexual 34; unmanageable levels of 155
agitation 122, 172
agreement: mutual 87; unconscious, global 16
alcohol(ics) 81–2, 122, 159, 172, 185
alienation 51, 183, 186
allusion 23
aloneness 82, 84, 106, 179, 181
ambiguity 175
ambivalence 90, 96, 155, 159
analytic relationship 5, 6, 7, 17, 26, 42, 86, 120, 153, 157; analyst "staying in role" 31; chief limitation to exploration and enhancement of 78; close 92; collaborative potential 184; dialogue 72; evolving 35; excessive aggression in 159; expanding 174, 175; fragile 182; history of 91; importance of what PI can do to 61; interpersonal shift in 166; limited 88–9, 93; long-term 90; making it work 183; multiple meaning of PI within 104; pattern built into 149; sterile 67; totality of 105; trust and caring 184; understanding of